Indigenous Legal Traditions

Legal Dimensions Series

This series stems from an annual legal and sociolegal research initiative sponsored by the Canadian Association of Law Teachers, the Canadian Law and Society Association, the Council of Canadian Law Deans, and the Law Commission of Canada. Volumes in this series examine various issues of law reform from a multidisciplinary perspective. The series seeks to advance our knowledge about law and society through the analysis of fundamental aspects of law. The essays in this volume were selected by representatives from each partner association: Debra Parkes (Canadian Law and Society Association), Philip Girard (Canadian Association of Law Teachers), Harvey Secter (Council of Canadian Law Deans), and Dennis Cooley and Nathalie Des Rosiers (Law Commission of Canada).

1 *Personal Relationships of Dependence and Interdependence in Law*
2 *New Perspectives on the Public-Private Divide*
3 *What Is a Crime? Defining Criminal Conduct in Contemporary Society*
4 *Law and Risk*
5 *Law and Citizenship*
6 *Indigenous Legal Traditions*

LAW COMMISSION OF CANADA
COMMISSION DU DROIT DU CANADA

Edited by the Law Commission of Canada

Indigenous Legal Traditions

UBCPress · Vancouver · Toronto

15 14 13 12 11 10 09 08 07   5 4 3 2 1

Printed in Canada on acid-free paper

Library and Archives Canada Cataloguing in Publication

Indigenous legal traditions / edited by the Law Commission of Canada.

Includes bibliographical references and index.
ISBN 978-0-7748-1370-9

1. Native peoples – Legal status, laws, etc. – Canada. 2. Native peoples – Canada – Social life and customs. 3. Native peoples – Canada – Government relations. 4. Customary law – Canada. I. Law Commission of Canada.

KE7735.I54 2007	342.7108'72	C2007-903206-0
KF8220.I54 2007		

Canadä

UBC Press gratefully acknowledges the financial support for our publishing program of the Government of Canada through the Book Publishing Industry Development Program (BPIDP), and of the Canada Council for the Arts, and the British Columbia Arts Council.

UBC Press
The University of British Columbia
2029 West Mall
Vancouver, BC V6T 1Z2
604-822-5959 / Fax: 604-822-6083
www.ubcpress.ca

This volume is dedicated to Perry Shawana,

who died shortly after completing his draft of the essay that appears in this book. Perry was greatly admired by all who knew him and will be sadly missed.

Contents

Preface / ix

Introduction: Which Way Out of Colonialism? / 3
Andrée Lajoie

1 "Getting to a Better Place": Qwi:qwelstóm, the Stó:lō, and
Self-Determination / 12
Ted Palys and Wenona Victor

2 An Apology Feast in Hazelton: Indian Residential Schools, Reconciliation,
and Making Space for Indigenous Legal Traditions / 40
Paulette Regan

3 Reconciliation without Respect? Section 35 and Indigenous
Legal Orders / 77
Minnawaanagogiizhigook (Dawnis Kennedy)

4 Legal Processes, Pluralism in Canadian Jurisprudence, and
the Governance of Carrier Medicine Knowledge / 114
Perry Shawana

5 Territoriality, Personality, and the Promotion of Aboriginal Legal
Traditions in Canada / 136
Ghislain Otis

Contributors / 169

Index / 171

Preface

Indigenous legal traditions have a long and rich history in North America, stretching back hundreds, if not thousands of years. Living together in societies long before the arrival of the first Europeans, Aboriginal peoples developed complex systems of law based on social, spiritual, and political values expressed through the teachings of knowledgeable and respected individuals and elders. Enunciated in rich stories, ceremonies, and traditions within Native communities, Indigenous legal systems represent the accumulated wisdom and experience of Aboriginal peoples.

Because these were ignored, banned, or overruled by non-Indigenous laws under colonialism, their influence has been greatly eroded. Despite this legacy, many Indigenous communities across Canada, maintaining and developing their own traditions, continue to be guided by them in the governance of their communities, the environment, and their relationships with people. Others are exploring ways to reclaim their customs and legal traditions and to restore their place in the governance of their communities. Canadian society also has begun to recognize the importance of Indigenous legal traditions and Aboriginal law making. With formal recognition of the inherent Aboriginal right to self-government and the observation by the Supreme Court of Canada that the customary laws of Aboriginal peoples survived the assertion of sovereignty by the Crown, Canada has begun to embrace its unique legally pluralistic identity.

The relationship between Indigenous and Canadian legal orders and the ways in which Indigenous legal traditions might be recognized and given space in the Canadian legal landscape are the common threads linking the chapters in this collection. As Andrée Lajoie notes in the Introduction, in each of the essays the authors explore "how to come out of colonialism ... from differing angles." In examining different aspects of and models for the recognition and accommodation of Indigenous legal orders, the authors also present us with several different visions of legal pluralism.

This collection is born of the legal and sociolegal research initiative jointly sponsored by the Canadian Association of Law Teachers, the Council of Canadian Law Deans, the Canadian Law and Society Association, and the Law Commission of Canada. The Legal Dimensions Initiative, which focuses on a different theme each year, seeks to stimulate critical and innovative thinking on emerging law and society issues.

The Law Commission extends its thanks to its partners, to the authors of the essays, and to Andrée Lajoie, the author of the Introduction, who also acted as discussant when the original papers were presented in Harrison Hot Springs in June 2005.

Indigenous Legal Traditions

Introduction: Which Way Out of Colonialism?

Andrée Lajoie

The expression "Aboriginal legal traditions" refers to a large corpus of rules, mostly *implicit* and *inferential* as Rod Macdonald would qualify them, that apply not only to Aboriginal dispute resolution systems but more generally to their governance process.[1] Deeply rooted in Aboriginal culture, yet constructed, as Karim Benyekhlef and others have shown,[2] and therefore evolutive, they are transmitted either orally or through precedent or pictograms, from generation to generation. The importance of these legal traditions for the preservation of the political autonomy of Aboriginal nations cannot be overstated. Aboriginal nations have not been conquered and have not surrendered (except some that have signed treaties, the validity of which in some cases is questionable). Hence the interest of the exercise in which the Law Commission of Canada has invited Aboriginal and non-Aboriginal scholars to participate, in which the complex phenomenon of disentangling colonial ties has been analyzed.

It is no secret that, during colonization, these legal traditions were deemed invalid by Canadian laws and are even nowadays deprived of effectiveness through the same means. However, as Ted Palys, Wenona Victor, and Paulette Regan show in Chapters 1 and 2, some Aboriginal nations, including the Stó:lō and the Gitxsan, covertly kept them alive or are reviving them now, even if the Canadian judiciary is far from ready to recognize them entirely, as Minnawaanagogiizhigook (Dawnis Kennedy) demonstrates in her Chapter 3 analysis of the Supreme Court case law on the subject.

Yet, this is not the only way in which Aboriginal nations are trying to get out from under colonialism. In Chapter 4, Perry Shawana studies the place of traditional knowledge in the maze of colonial/traditional/hybrid legal systems in Canada. And in Chapter 5, Ghislain Otis outlines an innovative solution as he reflects on the possibility of another kind of federalism, one based not only on territorial but also on personal links.

Although I want to thank the Law Commission for the opportunity to comment on the interesting case studies analyzed here and the occasion it provided for me to learn about West Coast Aboriginal customs and contemporary law, I am even more grateful for the interesting insights into legal theory thus offered. The essays display a convergent preoccupation with how to come out of colonialism, approaching the subject from differing angles. The "unified variety" of these angles sheds a great deal of light and opens several vistas on this difficult subject.

Below, I will summarize the five chapters gathered in this book, show their common threads and differences, and outline their contribution to legal theory, more particularly to that regarding pluralism, personal federalism, and the qualification of various stages of the evolution of normative forms as they are transited through colonization/decolonization.

The Essays

The chapters will be summarized here in the order they are mentioned above, as this reflects a progression from partial and judicial to political and more global ways out of colonialism, which can serve as a basis for further analysis.

In Chapter 1, Ted Palys and Wenona Victor provide us with an analytic description of the Qwi:qwelstóm justice project. This project is grounded in the ancestral traditions and values of the Stó:lō Nation, and is an exercise in self-determination as well as a response to an unjust and externally imposed justice system. The authors describe how, after several fruitless attempts by the Canadian government over the last four decades to "indigenize" Aboriginal justice, the Stó:lō government decided to take responsibility for justice issues in relation to its people.

Grounded in the realization that, if Aboriginal justice is not given its meaning by Aboriginal peoples, it cannot claim to be truly Aboriginal, the Qwi:qwelstóm program of justice is based on Stó:lō culture, customs, and traditions, supported by the Stó:lō communities, and driven by the Stó:lō people. In order to achieve this, the Stó:lō persuaded the Canadian government to give a "mandate" to a traditional institution of their nation, the House of Justice, to act through a devolution from the Department of Indian Affairs, "empowering" it to develop and implement alternative justice programs to help the nation re-establish healthy communities. This in itself is a great innovation on which I will comment below. But the authors stress that the Stó:lō government went even further, giving the House of Justice powers not envisaged by the delegation from the Canadian state. These included accepting referrals not only from government agencies but also from community members, as well as self-referrals, imposing preconditions deriving from Stó:lō culture for acceptance of cases, and introducing the participation of healing circles working orally in the Stó:lō language, with the collaboration of specially trained helpers in the community and a special role for elders and families.

In Chapter 2, Paulette Regan also deals with Aboriginal alternative dispute-resolution mechanisms, but more specifically in relation to Indian residential schools and reconciliation. Describing a Hazelton feast that focused on reconciliation, she draws the lessons learned from this encounter, which makes space for Indigenous law, conflict resolution, and peacemaking traditions by also addressing the colonial legacy of Indian residential schools in Canada. Rooted in the concept of reconciliation as a process inscribed in an ongoing relationship, such an encounter suggests that the space for acknowledgment of the past and envisioning of the future is necessary in order to reframe the present. Regan shows that in the second phase in this process, the Hazelton Apology Feast, the participants moved from meeting Western criteria for reconciliation to an Indigenous encounter of reconciliation, thus creating a fulcrum point for decolonizing and rebalancing the relationship between the Gitxsan and non-Aboriginal Canadians. Such political recognition of Indigenous law and especially one of its institutions, as well as respect for Indigenous legal expertise, thus shifts the balance of power and control from Western hands to Indigenous hands; the colonial taking of space is reversed in the making of space that is key to decolonization.

Yet, however important these first steps in decolonizing Aboriginal judicial processes may be, they have not fully reached the Canadian courts, which continue to interpret Indigenous traditions for the benefit of the dominant Canadian legal order. This we learn in detail in Minnawaanagogiizhigook's Chapter 3 analysis of the Canadian judicial process. She shows how Canadian Aboriginal rights doctrine installs a form of neo-colonialism. Her chapter converges with the previous ones to complete the picture of the difficult transitional stage in which we find ourselves as we emerge from judicial colonialism.

She reveals how the Supreme Court, and especially its then Chief Justice Antonio Lamer, skirts the question of Indigenous traditions whenever possible or treats them as discoverable facts that are, moreover, frozen in time, rather than as (as I have written elsewhere more than once) evolutive systems of law produced by legal orders dating from pre-colonial times but still in force. Especially interesting is her demonstration that the Supreme Court's interpretation is not at all consistent with section 35 of the *Constitution Act, 1982;* the section *recognizes* and *affirms* existing Aboriginal rights, which by definition pre-exist and have originated outside the Canadian Constitution and which are rooted in pre-contact Aboriginal legal orders, not in pre-contact frozen practices.

Yet, the hybridization of colonial and Aboriginal structures and law does not occur only in the justice system, as Perry Shawana's chapter shows through its analysis of the place of traditional knowledge in the maze of colonial/traditional/hybrid legal systems in Canada, which he correctly characterizes as a weak form of legal pluralism.[3] His discussion introduces another element of tradition – "medicine knowledge." In approaching this, the author crosses over the border from judicial to legal tradition, broaching the rules that govern the use of such knowledge both inside and outside the communities where it is produced. Drawing on the context of the Carrier people, Shawana argues that Indigenous legal systems not only exist but are best suited to govern knowledge generated from within Indigenous communities, stressing how the application of dominant Western legal norms has negatively impacted and influenced Indigenous peoples' innovations, creations, and discoveries. As we shall see, his theorization of this problem can serve not only for the justice programs analyzed by the previous contributions but also for any other sector of norms in transition from precontact traditional, to colonial, to postcolonial popular law, if and when it reaches that stage.

In Chapter 5, Ghislain Otis explores a further step in the decolonization process of legal traditions, aiming not only at specific sectors (dispute resolution, reconciliation, medicine knowledge) or systems (judicial or normative) but also at the whole jurisdiction of legal orders. He examines the option of the "personality of laws" or "personal federalism," a type of legal organization in which the laws or norms applied to individuals, and consequently to their participation in a legal tradition's culture, are predicated not exclusively upon their link to a territory but also upon their link to a group, community, or nation. He thus puts in perspective the fact that Indigenous governance can and should connect with territoriality outside territorialized legal orders. Yet, although in some instances it does not exclude purely personal jurisdiction, such a model is not intended to be exclusively personal, hence the term "personal *federalism,*" in reference not to formal federalism involving a division of powers between territorial legal orders, such as Canadian federalism, but simply to the fact that some matters are governed on a territorial basis and others on a personal one.

Common Threads and Differences

Obviously, all these contributions share a common preoccupation with colonialism and the quest for various ways out – or rather "almost out" – of it. Yet, major differences arise, concerning not only the scope of the normative sectors the authors are trying to recover in Indigenous legal traditions, but also how far – and fast – they want to run away from colonial domination.

Whether they proceed from case studies, as do Ted Palys and Wenona Victor (alternative dispute resolution in the Stó:lō Nation), Paulette Regan (reconciliation practices in the Gitxsan tradition), and Perry Shawana (medicine knowledge in Carrier norms), or from the analysis of whole systems, such as the judicial system viewed from the Supreme Court (Minnawaanagogiizhigook) or the whole normative system, viewed from the angle of personal federalism (Ghislain Otis), all the contributors to this book are looking at ways by which Indigenous legal traditions can escape the trap of colonialism. Some do so by stressing the deleterious effects on Indigenous legal traditions of their control by Canadian courts (Minnawaanagogii-zhigook), their domination by Canadian norms (Perry Shawana), or the inadequacy of their link with territory (Ghislain Otis), implicitly calling for the elimination of such external constraints on Indigenous traditional rules. Others prefer institutional solutions whereby an Indigenous institution, already endowed by Canadian authorities with certain powers, is attributed additional powers, this time by Indigenous authorities (Ted Palys and Wenona Victor), or whereby Canadian authorities are driven to adopt and participate in Indigenous institutions (Paulette Regan). But all are trying to find how to evolve out of colonialism towards a more autonomous status, be it through the recognition by Canadian authorities of Indigenous norms (Ted Palys and Wenona Victor, Paulette Regan, Minnawaanagogiizhigook), emancipation in a new kind of federalism (Ghislain Otis), or co-existence of Indigenous and Canadian territorial legal orders of equal status (Perry Shawana).

You will have noticed that all but Shawana (Chapter 4) and Regan (Chapter 2) favour solutions that do not take the Indigenous legal orders completely out of the Canadian state. This is a first and important difference, but one can find others in the gradation of solutions proposed by the authors. Thus, even though the first three chapters deal with case studies of sectorial scope and analyze institutional solutions, the reconciliation practices Regan describes in the Gitxsan Nation, which impose an Indigenous institution on the colonizer, and Shawana's option for independent legal orders seem bolder and further away from colonialism than even the addition of powers to the House of Justice of the Stó:lō Nation analyzed by Palys and Victor (Chapter 1). By comparison, the solution implicit in Minnawaan-agogiizhigook's (Chapter 3) denunciation of the Supreme Court's case law and Otis' (Chapter 5) proposition of personal federalism are both wider in scope but less invasive of the colonial state than the others.

Contributions to Legal Theory

However important they may be, the inroads these essays make into colonialism are not their only contribution, as the development they induce in legal theory is quite worthwhile as well. But before I can assess these contributions, it is important to document some legal theories that I have already mentioned as particularly relevant to this field and that will both apply to and be enriched by the chapters in this book. These are pluralism, personal federalism, and the categorization of normative forms in the colonial context. So it is with each of these legal theories as a backdrop that I will specify the advances that the chapters represent for these theoretical approaches.

Pluralism

Of course, it is pluralism that first comes to mind when Indigenous traditions are analyzed within the context of colonialism, even in its "post"-colonial form. I will not go into all the complexities this theory has developed, some of which find no application here,[4] but it is important first to define pluralism and to distinguish between at least two of its better-known forms.

Legal pluralism – as distinct from social and political pluralism[5] – is a theory that recognizes a multiplicity of legal orders functioning on the same territory at a given time, and takes into account the fact that "the state, as it exists in Canada and Quebec, does not sociologically enjoy the monopoly of legal regulation."[6] It should not be confused with the plurality of status that characterizes most legal systems in which, for instance, women and minors are treated differently from men and adults.[7] It applies only when parallel legal orders, issuing, interpreting, and applying norms, exist either within or outside the state.

The first of these forms, conceived by Max Weber within the scope of legal positivism, and qualified as "weak pluralism" by John Griffith, acknowledges the existence of only those normative powers that are distinct from those of the state and sometimes in command of better enforcement mechanisms: this form is referred to as intra-state pluralism.[8] On the contrary, the second form, extra-state pluralism, or "strong pluralism" in Griffith's language, contests the state's positivist definition of law in the name of a pluralist and decentralized formulation of democracy itself.

Against this background, one can see which form of this theory is applied by the authors of this book, and how they contribute to its evolution. After a thorough review of both the literature and the case law on the subject of pluralism, in which he detects the colonial traps embedded in weak pluralism, Shawana (Chapter 4) chooses as a solution the kind of strong pluralism characterized by the co-existence, independence, and complementarity of Indigenous and Canadian legal orders. He thus demonstrates the relevance of this theory through its application to Carrier medicine knowledge normativity.

Although they do not cross the boundary into strict extra-state pluralism, in which Indigenous legal orders are completely equal and not at all subordinate, Palys and Victor's and Regan's case studies (Chapters 1 and 2) interact very interestingly with pluralism, as they show examples of the emergence of a new hybrid pattern of governance.

In the first instance, a pre-existing traditional Indigenous institution, the Stó:lō House of Justice, was empowered by the Canadian state through delegation to develop and implement alternative justice programs to help the nation re-establish healthy communities. It was then given other powers that were not envisaged in the initial delegation, but this time by the Stó:lō authorities. The hybrid institution that resulted from this double infusion of powers certainly does not constitute pure extra-state pluralism, since it retains the powers given by Canadian authorities. But, no less certainly, it escaped the realm of pure intra-state pluralism, as it derived first its existence and later some of its powers from Indigenous authorities.

Regan's chapter has perhaps an even more important implication for theories of legal pluralism. She shows that, though the Gitx̱san legal order is not removed from the Canadian state, one of its institutions, the Hazelton Apology Feast, not only exists independently of Canadian law but binds the Canadian authorities, who have agreed to submit to its rituals.

In a different way, Minnawaanagogiizhigook's Chapter 3 analysis of Supreme Court case law contributes to debunking the myth that Aboriginals are well treated by our judicial system, which refuses to recognize both the existence and the application of their legal traditions.

Personal Federalism
As Otis himself writes in so many words (Chapter 5), personal federalism could qualify, in a way, as a yet different kind of pluralism, as it posits the co-existence of different legal orders on the same territory. Yet it differs from other kinds of pluralism due to the fact that such different legal orders, based not only on territory but on ethnicity, share jurisdiction over the same normative objects.

Personal federalism is a very complex system based on the postulate that multicultural governance implies the disjunction of territory and political authority and puts in perspective the fact that Indigenous governance can take into account territorial concerns otherwise than by making them the sole basis of institutionalization of power within the state context. There is "personal federalism," in which several communal political entities are, as between themselves and the state, in a relationship akin to federalism. Otis' contribution to this theory, which was itself conceived in the context of the analysis of European colonialism and multinational states,[9] resides perhaps in his introduction of this approach to anglophone readers in Canada, but certainly in its first application to the Indigenous context here. He identifies various scenarios in which going beyond the territorial reference becomes a condition of effectivity of Aboriginal governance and bridges the gap between internal Aboriginal governance and Indigenous/non-Indigenous relationships.

Categorization of Normative Forms in Colonial Context
A third theoretical approach, that of Etienne LeRoy and Mamadou Wane, is useful here, although it does not define various institutionalizations of legal orders, dealing instead with the categorization of norms in the successive stages of colonization and decolonization.[10] This theory constructs four

distinct status categories for the evolving norms in colonial territories. The first is the *traditional law* of pre-colonial times, when Aboriginal populations, not being herds of deer, produced rules to govern themselves according to their own values and traditions. The second is *customary law*, an initial form of colonial law in which colonial authorities reinterpret these Indigenous traditions through colonial courts. Third comes *local law*, a second form of colonial law that is characterized by a narrow delegation of powers to Indigenous populations. Fourth is *popular law*, in which the Indigenous population reinstates its traditional law, at least in part, reinterpreting it yet again in a context now completely transformed.

Although none of our five authors mention this theory, I think at least some of their findings can be interpreted through it with great advantage and can even bring it further than it has ventured so far. Indeed, as one considers the evolving categories of norms just described, it becomes obvious that – except for the first, since pre-colonial times have passed and colonization has occurred – all of them apply to the various kinds of norms reviewed in this book. For instance, and to start therefore with the second category, customary law, in which colonial authorities interpret traditional pre-colonial law to their own advantage, clearly encompasses the Supreme Court's description of Indigenous traditions as discoverable facts frozen in time, as is implied by Minnawaanagogiizhigook's analysis. But it is mostly in the last two categories, local and popular law, or a mixture of both, that the case studies examined by Palys and Victor and Regan, as well as Shawana's and Otis' propositions for new kinds of governance, can be seen to fall.

Thus, the Palys and Victor case study in Chapter 1, involving a narrow delegation of powers by Canadian authorities to a Stó:lō institution, the House of Justice, seems at first glance to be a straightforward instance of local law, precisely characterized by such a delegation. But the fact that the Stó:lō authorities subsequently delegated other powers to this same institution, thus transforming it into a hybrid normative vehicle, brings its legal production across the border into popular law as well, or places it on the frontier between both. The incursion into that last category is even more evident for the traditions followed in the Hazelton Apology Feast described in Chapter 2 by Regan, in which it is a Gitxsan institution that is imposed on colonial authorities, a clear example if there ever was one of the reinterpretation by an Indigenous nation of its tradition in a completely contemporary context, characteristic of popular law.

This last pattern of governance is also suggested by Perry Shawana and Ghislain Otis in Chapters 4 and 5, who consequently favour the production of popular law. Shawana, who shows how Canadian intellectual property law is inadequate for the regulation of traditional knowledge, suggests instead a reappropriation of this field by Indigenous traditions adapted to contemporary situations, the very definition of popular law. For his part,

Otis envisages yet a bolder form of the same mechanism applied to numerous other fields of the whole legal system, both normative and judicial. But Shawana's solution concerns only one field (intellectual property) and Otis' only those that would be confirmed to the Indigenous authorities in whatever distribution of powers would result from a given form of personal federalism.

Consequently, in none of the contributions to this book is the reappropriation total, or complete self-government involved: Indigenous legal traditions are evolving out of colonialism, but the journey is not over and the situations analyzed or suggested in this book do not qualify as extra-state pluralism. This observation brings us back to theories of legal pluralism, showing both the links between the theoretical approaches applicable to all contributions in this book and the light this last categorization of normative forms sheds on the evolving path towards decolonization.

Notes

1 Roderick A. Macdonald, "Pour la reconnaissance d'une normativité juridique implicite et inférentielle," *Sociologie et sociétés* 18, 1 (1986): 47-58.

2 Karim Benyekhlef, *Une courte histoire de la norme, les enjeux des normativités à l'heure de la mondialisation,* forthcoming. Eric Hobsbawm, "Introduction: Inventing Traditions," in E. Hobsbawm and T. Ranger, eds., *The Invention of Tradition* (Cambridge: Cambridge University Press, 1983), 1. See also Anthony Giddens, *Runaway World: How Globalization Is Reshaping Our Lives* (London: Routledge, 2000), 57, which explores the link between traditions and myths.

3 Perry Shawana wrote a draft version of this but died before he could present it at the June 2005 Law Commission meeting in Harrison Hot Springs, BC. In this book, his text is reproduced along with comments in foreword and afterword by Minnawaanagogiizhigook (Dawnis Kennedy), Mary Teegee, and Warner Adam.

4 These include radical and stipulative pluralisms. For details, see A. Lajoie, J.M. Brisson, S. Normand, and A. Bissonnette, *Le statut juridique des peoples autochtones au Québec et le pluralisme* (Cowansville: Editions Yvon Blais, 1996), 7-12.

5 *Ibid.*

6 A. Bissonnette, "Les droits et libertés des peuples autochtones au Canada: Débats constitutionnels et identités culturelles," *Recherches Amérindiennes au Québec* 19 (1989): 9 [translated by author].

7 As J. Vanderlinden first did when he published "Le pluralisme juridique, essai de synthèse," in J. Glissen, ed., *Le pluralisme juridique,* Institut de sociologie (Brussels: Éditions de l'Université de Bruxelles, 1972), 15-56, only to retract his conclusions later in "Vers une nouvelle conception du pluralisme juridique," *Revue de la recherché juridique Droit Prospectif* 18 (1993): 573-83.

8 M. Reinstein, ed., *Max Weber on Law in Economy and Society* (Cambridge: Harvard University Press, 1955); J. Griffith, "What Is Legal Pluralism?" *Journal of Legal Pluralism* 24 (1986): 1.

9 S. Pierré-Caps, *La multination: L'avenir des minorities en Europe centrale et orientale* (Paris: Éditions Odile Jacob, 1995); N. Rouland, S. Pierré-Caps, and J. Poumarède, *Droits des minorities et des peoples autochtones* (Paris: PUF, 1996).

10 Etienne LeRoy and Mamadou Wane, "La formation des droits non-étatiques," in *Encyclopédie juridique de l'Afrique* (Abidjan: Nouvelles Éditions Africaines, 1982), 1:353.

1
"Getting to a Better Place": Qwi:qwelstóm, the Stó:lō, and Self-Determination

Ted Palys and Wenona Victor

> To be able to practice our own cultural ways and to live and express ourselves within our own worldview is important to our sense of self-worth and well-being; it is a vital part of our healing journey.
>
> – Stó:lō elder Amy Victor, 2005, as told to Wenona Victor

Indigenous Rights and Justice

The contemporary effort by many First Nations communities to regenerate their own justice systems has roots in at least three different aspects of their experience. First and foremost, it is grounded in what many First Nations people and others believe to be an *inherent* right to be self-determining.[1] As an inherent right, this is not dependent upon, granted, or given by any external source. Many, however, argue that it is protected by section 35 of the Canadian Constitution. The right is also reflected in the fundamental right of self-determination that is guaranteed to all peoples in article 1 (section 2) of the *Charter of the United Nations*. More recently, Indigenous peoples' right to self-determination has been affirmed in the *Draft Declaration on the Rights of Indigenous Peoples,* which was formulated by the United Nations Working Group on Indigenous Populations (1994) in concert with Indigenous delegates who contributed to its drafting and redrafting over a twelve-year period.[2] The right to create or re-create justice systems reflecting Indigenous tradition, clearly one manifestation of the broader right of self-determination, is mentioned specifically in three articles within the declaration:

> Article 4. Indigenous peoples have the right to maintain and strengthen their distinct political, economic, social and cultural characteristics, as well as their legal systems, while retaining their rights to participate fully, if they so choose, in the political, economic, social and cultural life of the State.

...

Article 26. Indigenous peoples have the right to own, develop, control and use the lands and territories, including the total environment of the lands, air, waters, coastal seas, sea-ice, flora and fauna and other resources which they have traditionally owned or otherwise occupied or used. This includes the right to the full recognition of their laws, traditions and customs, land-tenure systems and institutions for the development and management of resources, and the right to effective measures by States to prevent any inter-ference with, alienation of or encroachment upon these rights.

...

Article 33. Indigenous peoples have the right to promote, develop and main-tain their institutional structures and their distinctive juridical customs, traditions, procedures and practices, in accordance with internationally rec-ognized human rights standards.[3]

According to a second rationale, the First Nations regeneration of their own justice "ways" is a necessary response to an externally imposed justice system whose *in*justice to and inappropriateness for Aboriginal peoples has been recognized not only by the Supreme Court of Canada (in *R. v. Gladue*) but also by so many committees and commissions of inquiry that it now ranks at the level of a cultural truism.[4] The list of reports detailing the del-eterious effects of the criminal justice system on Aboriginal peoples and their communities begins in the 1960s with a Canadian Corrections Asso-ciation publication entitled *Indians and the Law,* and has been reaffirmed since then in at least a dozen commissions and inquiry reports produced by provincial authorities, the federal government, and independent experts.[5]

A third rationale grounds the search for Aboriginal justice in ancestral traditions and values that, after a significant period of suppression, are re-surfacing and reconnecting themselves to broader community governance processes. In this view, "Aboriginal justice" is what First Nations people do because it is a fundamental part of who they are. Denying Aboriginal com-munities the right to practise "justice" in ways that are meaningful to those communities and peoples is tantamount to denying and suppressing their right to be themselves, exactly the failed policy of assimilation that we all now recognize must be left behind.

Achieving Aboriginal justice is easier said than done, however. Canadian governments have tended not to view Aboriginal peoples exercising their responsibilities over their own people in the area of justice as "community building," "healing," "restoration of balance and harmony," or a part of building a healthier Canada by ensuring that each of its constituent ele-ments thrives. Rather, Canada's federal and provincial governments appear to have viewed jurisdictional power as a zero-sum game in which any Aboriginal jurisdictional gains regarding justice over their own people must somehow be a threat to federal sovereignty, and thus something to be re-sisted.[6] Certainly, this would explain the glacially slow progression in the form of "Aboriginal justice" initiatives that have occurred since the 1970s, first through the Ministry of the Solicitor General and more recently through the Department of Justice's Aboriginal Justice Directorate and Aboriginal Justice Strategy. These initiatives ranged from the "indigenization" strate-gies of the 1970s and '80s, to the "accommodation" strategies of the 1980s and '90s, and, finally, to the beginnings of what can be called "parallel systems" in the late 1990s and early 2000s.[7]

Although each successive strategy is designed to be slightly more palat-able to Aboriginal communities than the last, common to every one is the fact that it is the *federal government* that brings it forward, sets the rules, decides what the options will be, and allocates the funds.[8] But, to para-phrase Donna Greschner, it is almost oxymoronic to talk of non-Aboriginal conceptions of Aboriginal justice; if Aboriginal justice is not given its mean-ing by Aboriginal peoples, how can it claim to be truly Aboriginal?[9]

The rest of this chapter focuses on the efforts of the Stó:lō government to "*be* Stó:lō" in the area of justice and to take responsibility for justice issues in relation to its people. We describe the processes through which and the principles by which the Stó:lō justice program was developed. More specifi-cally, we examine how traditional justice practices and processes were re-spected and given contemporary form, what was done to ensure community involvement in and commitment to the program, and the lessons that have been learned about what Canada and the provinces can do to better create space for the Stó:lō and other First Nations who wish to pursue the develop-ment of culturally appropriate, meaningful, and effective systems of justice in their communities.[10]

The Stó:lō

Traditional Stó:lō territory, extending along both sides of the Fraser River from the Langley area through to Yale, British Columbia, includes twenty-four different Stó:lō communities. The Stó:lō people are Indigenous to this territory, now referred to as the Fraser Valley. The Stó:lō know this land as S'ólh Téméxw, which, like most Halq'eméylem terms, is difficult to trans-late directly into English without losing invaluable meaning. It means much more than the English words "land" or "territory." S'ólh Téméxw is a holis-tic phrase that envelops all that is sacred, referring not only to the soil beneath our feet but also to the air, the earth, the wind, the mountains, the waterways, and so on. It includes material resources as well as all the nonphysical things we cannot see or touch but which are vital to Stó:lō survival.

For the Stó:lō, S'ólh Téméxw is embodied with spirit and includes the past, present, and future. Although it denotes "Our World," the Halq'eméylem phrase requires a deeper understanding that epitomizes the holistic world-view of the Stó:lō. In fact, the renewal of the Halq'eméylem language and phrases such as S'ólh Téméxw are integral to the true meaning of Stó:lō culture and practices. The importance of language and its tie to culture and worldview forms the subject matter of a dissertation by Ethel Gardner (Stelómethet). In exploring the importance of language to a people, she came to understand Stó:lō culture at a level unattainable to strictly English-speaking researchers. She recognized

> how deep the term "S'ólh Téméxw" is embedded in who we are as Stó:lō people ..., how we make meaning of Our World, of *"S'ólh Téméxw."* It was a great beginning in my exploration of how our land, our language, our culture and we, the People, are interconnected and interrelated. I am discovering that *"S'ólh Téméxw"* is not just words, not simply a representation of the physicality of the World, but a representation of a holistic concept that binds the People spiritually to the physical world, to each other and to all our ancestors, and is expressed best through our Halq'eméylem language. These interrelationships define our culture, define who we are as Stó:lō people, and in other words, define our worldview.[11]

It is the connection and relationship to S'ólh Téméxw that has guided the Stó:lō and defined their worldview since time immemorial.

The word "Stó:lō" basically translates into English as "river," and so the Stó:lō are also referred to as the "People of the River." As well, they refer to themselves as Xwélmexw, which loosely translates to "those who share a language." Both terms originate from the Stó:lō, as opposed to being terms imposed via the colonial process. There are approximately five thousand Stó:lō people. From 1993 to 2004, governance of the Stó:lō was shared among three Houses:[12] the Lalems Ye Siyolexwe (House of Elders), the Lalems Ye Stó:lō Sí:yá:m (House of Leaders), and the House of Justice. The House of Justice is comprised of two members from the Lalems Ye Siyolexwe, two members from the Lalems Ye Stó:lō Sí:yá:m, the *Stó:lō Yewal Siyá:m* (chiefs' representative), and the *Tes Ste'a Siyá:m* (elders' representative), and is provided with technical support by justice staff members. In 1993 the House of Justice was "empowered with the mandate to develop and implement alternative justice programs to help the Stó:lō Nation re-establish healthy communities and achieve the full potential of all Stó:lō citizens."[13]

Stó:lō governance was reorganized in 2004 under two tribal councils representing nineteen of the twenty-four Stó:lō communities. Five Stó:lō communities remain independent and unaffiliated with either tribal council but receive some of the services. The governance of any one of the twenty-four Stó:lō bands is looked after by the community itself, the Stó:lō Tribal Council (STC), the Stó:lō Society (SS), or a combination of any of the three.

Qwi:qwelstóm, the focus of this chapter, is one of the few programs that is available to all twenty-four communities.

Along with Xyolhemeylh, the Child and Family Services, the SS and the STC employ almost three hundred people. As the Stó:lō assert more and more independence, the need and use for a Department of Indian Affairs has decreased substantially. Over the years, the responsibilities of the tribal councils have grown dramatically and now include delivery of programs and services such as community development, education, economic development, Aboriginal rights and title, and health and social services, as well as child and family services to the twenty-four affiliated bands.

False Beginnings, First Lessons

In May of 1999, Wenona Victor was hired by the Stó:lō Nation to assist with the development and implementation of an "alternative justice" program for the Stó:lō. This opportunity was timely, as it occurred while she was also conducting research for her MA thesis on traditional forms of Stó:lō "justice." It is noteworthy, however, that her initial job description was not "to implement traditional ways of doing 'justice'" but rather to implement a program called Family Group Conferencing (FGC). Wenona was informed that this model of justice had been developed by the Maori, the Indigenous people of New Zealand. With such a pedigree, it was expected that FGC, or an adaptation thereof, might serve the Stó:lō well. Wenona's job supervisor provided her with contact information for the woman who would be coming to Stó:lō territory to train her and her colleagues in this model of conflict resolution.

Later, Wenona wrote about her experience:

> Although she was affiliated with the RCMP, I did not notice that anything was out of order. I obediently arranged for her to come and without hesitation paid the few thousand dollars she requested for her fee. I also booked a training room at the local Hotel and recruited some 30 Stó:lō community members and employees to take the three day training course.
>
> On the first day we all eagerly awaited her arrival. We were somewhat surprised to see an extremely "White" looking lady enter the room; however, we have blonde blue-eyed and even red-headed Stó:lō among us, and so, too, we presumed, must the Maori. However, it did not take us long to come to realize this lady was not Maori and was in fact *Xwelítem*.[14] Ah, the Maori had sent a *Xwelítem*; okay, we do that, too, on occasion. It is one of the many ironies of colonization whereby *Xwelítem* often become our teachers, even in relation to learning about our own culture. There are times when it is a *Xwelítem* who is recognized as the Stó:lō "expert" and therefore, is the one talking even when there are Elders present. But by the end

of the three day training course I was convinced the Maori had lost their minds! There was absolutely nothing Indigenous about this model of justice whatsoever![15]

The irony was compounded when the Stó:lō later learned that not even the Maori believed in the model of Family Group Conferencing that had been exported and was being sold to other Indigenous peoples in their name! This exported model of FGC, effectively appropriated by the state, allegedly in the interests of cultural sensitivity and respect, did nothing for the Maori but take their symbols, undermine their autonomy, and feed them back governmentally sanitized versions of practices they could no longer recognize as their own.[16]

Back to the drawing board the Stó:lō went; they decided to involve themselves in the training for peacemaking circles that was being offered by Judge Barry Stuart and Mark Wedge. Judge Stuart had become well known for his decision in the Yukon case of *R. v. Moses,* in which, after finding Philip Moses guilty on charges of possessing a weapon, theft, and breach of probation, he took the courageous and then unprecedented step of asking the community to take part in a sentencing circle.[17] Everyone, including the victim and offender, participated in order to develop community consensus on what to do with Philip Moses.

Sentencing circles were a significant step at the time; they are limited, however, in that they represent an accommodation strategy that, though it incorporates some vestiges and symbols of Aboriginal justice – the circle, in this instance, along with some community involvement – reserves all effective power within the Canadian justice system. Aboriginal elders and the community are relegated to the role of advisors whose advice may or may not be heeded.[18] Nevertheless, peacemaking circles seemed to be more in line with what the Stó:lō were looking for.

Again, Wenona was asked to organize the training. As she recalls,

I was pleasantly surprised when Judge Stuart expressed some hesitancy about holding the training session at a local hotel. He asked if there was a more "traditional" building we could use instead. So on the first day of this training session over 50 Stó:lo‾ people gathered at the Yakweakwioose Longhouse.

We sat in a circle in the middle of the Longhouse floor and began our round of introductions. This first round took four hours. I was so engrossed with what was being shared I did not even notice the time. At the end of introductions it was time to break for lunch. There were a few grumblings, but for the most part there was a shared feeling about what had just occurred. Circle does not operate according to a linear clock. Circle is guided by spirit. We felt good. What had just happened felt right. We felt connected to one another, a sense of kinship, belonging, caring and sharing. None of this would have occurred sitting in a circle at the Holiday Inn.

Our experience at the Longhouse taught me a valuable lesson – that we have all that we need right here. I mean no disrespect, but we don't need the Maori, we don't need a fancy hotel to legitimize what we are learning, and no disrespect, but we don't need a judge either to "teach" us about circle.[19] We have our own culture, our own teachers, our own Elders, our own language and our own learning environment. This was a valuable lesson that showed me the degree to which "how" and "what" we learn is influenced by our surroundings. The message was clear: If you are going to revitalize your culture don't do it in the *Xwelítem* world. Our experience and what we learned was more in-depth, more sincere and more valuable because we were in a Longhouse – at home, surrounded by our ancestors and with Mother Earth under our feet.[20]

This was the beginning of a process of rediscovery and community development for the Stó:lō that continues to this day, one that resulted in the formation of the justice program that is the focus of this chapter. At this point the Stó:lō did not know exactly what their own program would look like, but they knew what they did not want: one that mirrored the current Canadian justice system. Nor did they want to have their way co-opted (a valuable lesson learned from the Maori experience), and they knew it absolutely had to be their own! So the Stó:lō made a commitment to three principles, determining that their program would be

- based on Stó:lō culture, customs, and traditions
- supported by the Stó:lō communities
- driven by the Stó:lō people.

At the heart of the Stó:lō justice program is the desire that it reflect the Stó:lō people's aspiration to be self-determining and, by implication, that it realize their right to experience "justice" according to Stó:lō customs and traditions. Doing so means bringing "justice" back to the people by giving them an opportunity to play meaningful roles not only in the problem but also in its solution. For the Stó:lō, developing a justice system is about *being responsible* in a number of different ways, which ultimately is what "self-determination" is really all about.[21] In general terms, a person who has caused harm is given the opportunity to take responsibility within a forum that focuses on maintaining family ties and community connections. All of this occurs in a context in which the community takes responsibility for dealing with the troubles that exist among its people and in its external relations with other communities. To that extent, the objective is very clear. But how does a nation get there?

The Role of Language

The importance of language in directing the development and implementation of traditional forms of justice cannot be stressed enough.[22] Two separate but related dimensions can be distinguished. The first involves the use of Indigenous languages whenever possible to describe Indigenous programs, practices, traditions, and so on. The second is sensitivity to the way in which certain English terms and phrases explicitly or implicitly entrench colonial relations that perpetuate Eurocentric notions and simultaneously silence the worldview of Indigenous peoples.

With respect to the first dimension, the Indigenous language of the Stó:lō, which is known as Xwélmexwqel or Halq'eméylem, is currently being revived. Only a handful of fluent speakers are still alive. The Stó:lō believe that the very essence of who they are as a people is embedded in their language.[23] Accordingly, it is important to them to use their own language whenever possible, not only to facilitate a realization of self-determination but also to ensure that what they do is grounded in the Stó:lō worldview rather than in simply meeting the demands of the Canadian criminal justice system.

The second dimension came to the attention of the justice team in relation to the name of the program, which originally was the "Stó:lō Nation Alternative Justice Programme." This seemed reasonable and went unquestioned until the day Elder Amy Victor asked why the program was being described as an "alternative" when it was clearly *not* an alternative for the Stó:lō. Referring to their own cultural way of resolving conflict as "alternative" simply reinforced and perpetuated colonial relationships. Recognizing this and asserting the Stó:lō way as "the" way is an important step in freeing minds from the "cognitive prisons" that are one legacy of colonialism.[24]

Thinking further along these lines, the elders requested that the Stó:lō justice staff refrain from using the word "mainstream" when referring to the Canadian criminal justice system, as this implied that the Stó:lō were not the focus, even within their own frame of reference. This, too, was a very concrete reminder of whose eyes they had been looking through and how ingrained the colonial mentality can be. Removing the words "alternative" and "mainstream" represented a small decolonizing step in asserting a Stó:lō point of view.

At the same time, it was noted that the word "justice" had no exact equivalent in Halq'eméylem; thus, if the community were to feel a sense of ownership of and belonging to the program, it clearly needed a Halq'eméylem name. Elders from the Stó:lō language program were approached, the objectives of the "justice" program were explained to them, and a formal request was made for advice on a name that would capture that sense of purpose within a Stó:lō worldview.

As is customary, the elders took the time they needed to discuss and think things over. The answer was several months in coming, but their patience was rewarded. The elders came back and began teaching those in the program about Qwi:qwelstóm kwelam t' ey. A close, but incomplete, translation is "they are teaching you, moving you toward the good" (oral tradition, Elders Yamolot and Ts'ats'elexwot). Qwi:qwelstóm reflects a "way of life" that incorporates balance and harmony – a way of helping one another to survive and to care and share amongst all people. As a form of justice, it focuses on relationships and the interconnectedness of all life.

With their Halq'eméylem name in hand, the justice staff embarked upon a journey of discovery and rediscovery – an exciting journey of coming to understand what exactly Qwi:qwelstóm kwelam t' ey means, not only to their ancestors but to the Stó:lō of today, especially in relation to contemporary issues. It was from within this context of rediscovery that Wenona's MA thesis on traditional Stó:lō justice would contribute. Her project involved a search through archival materials and, most importantly, interviews with elders regarding the way that justice was done.

Asking the Elders

How was peace and harmony achieved and maintained among the Stó:lō? What would happen when someone behaved improperly and hurt another? Prior to the arrival of courts, judges, and police in S'ólh Téméxw, what did the Stó:lō do to resolve conflict within their communities? In an effort to answer these questions, Wenona approached elders who either spoke Halq'eméylem or had been taught by Halq'eméylem speakers, hoping to examine as well as could be ascertained the "uncolonized" forms of conflict resolution that existed among the Stó:lō. This meant trying to access and understand a time when Xwélmexwqel was the only language the Stó:lō knew.

Over the next year, Wenona set about visiting as many elders as she could; instead of questioning them regarding specific subjects, she used an open-ended interview style that encouraged them to share the information on their minds.[25] Each interview began with the question, "Traditionally, prior to courts coming to our territory, what did we do to resolve conflict within our communities?" From there, the interview went in whatever direction the elder deemed appropriate. In interview after interview, elder after elder spoke for hours about one thing around which all else revolved: family.

After each of the first few interviews, Wenona went home deflated. Although she had received many teachings that could guide her as a Stó:lō woman, she had learned almost nothing about "crime" and "punishment."

How could she write a thesis on "traditional forms of justice" when all the elders kept talking about was "family"? During the entire year in which she spoke to elders about Stó:lō justice, not once were the words "crime," "criminal," or "punishment" used in relation to the subject. Although grateful for all the cultural teachings that were being passed to her and honoured that the elders knew her to be "worthy" of them, Wenona worried about how she was going to complete her MA requirements. Thankfully, she had Dr. Archibald's dissertation to guide her and remind her to "trust" in the elders and how they teach.

Then, one day, that all-important paradigm shift occurred, a lesson in decolonizing one's mind, an epiphany if you will: justice to the Stó:lō within a Stó:lō worldview does not look anything like the justice one finds within the Canadian criminal justice system. The latter may focus on "crime," "prosecution," "prison," and "punishment," but to the Stó:lō "justice" is centred upon the family. Four key elements here include the role of elders; the role of family, family ties, and community connections; teachings; and spirituality.[26] As we describe below, all of these elements, which operate within the context of contemporary Stó:lō governance and in accordance with Stó:lō custom and tradition, are now present in and guide the Qwi:qwelstóm process.

Qwi:qwelstóm and the Stó:lō Community

Qwi:qwelstóm as a program is accountable to two main bodies within the Stó:lō Nation governance structure: the House of Justice and the elders council for Qwi:qwelstóm. In practice, the House of Justice is the entity that provides Qwi:qwelstóm with its mandate, whereas the Qwi:qwelstóm elders council is more concerned with the day-to-day operations of the program and ensuring that Stó:lō culture and tradition are being followed. However, also in keeping with Stó:lō tradition, it was equally important to remain connected to the broader community throughout this process.

Thus, one of the first steps Wenona undertook as a Stó:lō Nation justice worker was to go to each Stó:lō community and share what she had learned at university regarding the Canadian criminal justice system and its inability to deal humanely with Aboriginal people. She also explained that the Stó:lō Nation was developing an "alternative" dispute-resolution process that would be available to all Aboriginal people living within Stó:lō territory. The importance of community involvement and assistance in developing an elders council and recruiting Stó:lō to train as *Qwi:qwelstóm ye Smómíyelhtel* was emphasized.[27]

Visiting each Stó:lō community and talking about "justice" and how to deliver it to community members in a culturally appropriate manner represented a huge step towards visualizing what it means to be self-determining. The discussions themselves were empowering. Wenona wrote,

"In community after community the people seemed to sit taller in their chairs after our discussions; I literally could see their eyes light up right in front of me as we talked about bringing back the ways of our ancestors to help us settle current disputes within our communities."[28]

Important reservations also were expressed, and the ensuing discussions regarding them were and are a vital step in the decolonizing process. They tended to revolve around the following issues and questions: perceptions that the wrongdoer would be seen as "getting off easy"; the fact that some Aboriginal people want nothing to do with their culture; whether the Stó:lō were even "allowed" to instigate such a program; whether they had enough resources and knowledgeable people to deal with the social issues; how, given that they were not "experts" themselves, they could hope to succeed; and, perhaps most importantly, how the safety of community members, especially women and children, would be ensured. Not all these concerns were resolved before implementation of the program, but the discussions were held, concerns were heard, and an ongoing dialogue had begun. For many First Nations communities, "talking" is huge. Reclaiming voice is vital.

The discussions proved enlightening. Questions were raised about what the "experts" had managed to do for the Stó:lō so far. There are ten jails in Stó:lō territory, but had they made our communities any safer? Discussion also arose regarding what Stó:lō justice processes would look like and what enacting them might produce. Consider which of the two following alternatives is easiest: sitting silent in a courtroom, watching complete strangers decide your fate and knowing that, at the end of the day and regardless of outcome, you will not be required to change your behaviour; or sitting in a circle with your close family and elders while you speak for yourself and take responsibility for what you have done. Is it easier to be punished or to heal?[29] As for the question regarding being "allowed" – "allowed" by whom? Do we really have a choice about whether we take responsibility for our own lives?

The dialogue, which continues to this day, includes quarterly community gatherings to discuss Qwi:qwelstóm and issues pertinent to Stó:lō community members. Some Stó:lō communities and community members still express some hesitancy and reservations regarding their abilities to deal with more serious offences. Internalized colonial attitudes are evident during some of the discussions.[30] Generations have been told that it is up to "others" to fix "us." Thus, some insist upon the need for outside experts such as lawyers, social workers, counsellors, and therapists. Others talk about Stó:lō's own "experts" and the role that community healers, elders, and teachers can play, saying that "it doesn't take an 'expert' to care." As mentioned, having these discussions is important; they reflect a healthy diversity.

The fact that Qwi:qwelstóm encouraged these discussions and did not silence opposing views, concerns, and reservations was probably largely responsible for the support voiced by all the visited communities for the prospective program. Most importantly, they also favoured the idea of asking the House of Justice to permit the program to expand its scope. Initially, it was intended to deal with relatively minor offences, such as barking dogs (as is allowed under the *Indian Act*) and first-time young offenders who had committed less serious offences such as theft under the value of five thousand dollars (as was being offered by provincial authorities in the context of a protocol agreement). Like those of many First Nations, Stó:lō communities are plagued with drug and alcohol addictions that are fuelling serious offences such as assaults, domestic violence, and sexual abuse. It was also clear to everyone that, as is the case in many First Nations communities, these devastating human conditions were going largely unreported. Many community members have no faith in the criminal justice system's ability to deal with these problems, and in most instances, believe from personal experience that the system only makes things worse. The general consensus was that, even if the Stó:lō failed miserably, they would probably do a better job than the Canadian criminal justice system was doing. Certainly, they could do no worse.

With the support of the communities, the House of Justice was asked to permit the program to deal with offences more serious than dogs barking after curfew. This request was significant in that permission was sought not from a foreign voice of authority – the criminal justice system – but from internal Stó:lō governance structures. This shift regarding the question of "from whom do we gain permission" is another example of mental decolonization. It challenges a further colonial-imposed "cognitive prison" in which Indigenous peoples, as a result of generations of political, economic, and social oppression, question their own ability to be responsible. These cognitive shifts are empowering; when accomplished, they are a way in which "internal sovereignty" can be achieved.[31]

Ultimately, it is community members who decide whether to call Qwi:qwelstóm or the RCMP regarding their situation. Quite often, they call both.

Qwi:qwelstóm and the Canadian Justice System

Any Stó:lō justice program must address a wide variety of problem areas identified within both the community and the Canadian criminal justice system (CJS), especially as they pertain to Aboriginal peoples. These include

- the over-representation within the CJS of Aboriginal people, from arrest to incarceration

- the under-representation of Aboriginal people in positions of authority within the CJS
- the under-reporting of family violence and sexual assaults within Aboriginal communities
- the cultural differences and misunderstandings that often prove to be detrimental to Aboriginal offenders and their ability to be dealt with fairly
- the ability to provide a safe and effective forum within which healing is encouraged
- the need to improve relations between Aboriginal communities and Euro-Canadian agencies such as the RCMP, the courts, Crown counsel, legal aid lawyers, provincial corrections, and Correctional Services Canada.

None of these problems will be resolved solely by the Stó:lō people; hence the need for establishing and maintaining protocol agreements and reasonable lines of communication between Stó:lō and Canadian governments and agencies. Accordingly, Qwi:qwelstóm works in partnership with the RCMP, probation, corrections, Crown counsel, and the Ministry of Children and Families Development.

That said, bridging the "cultural divide" between Stó:lō justice and such Euro-Canadian agencies has often proved a challenging endeavour. When this bridge is approached with mutual respect, the journey is exhilarating and promising. However, Qwi:qwelstóm workers often report having to endure colonial attitudes and racist comments that attempt to subjugate, oppress, or silence Qwi:qwelstóm teachings. The education continues.

Qwi:qwelstóm: Getting to a Better Place

Referrals

Qwi:qwelstóm accepts referrals from seven different sources: the RCMP (pre-charge), Crown counsel (post-charge), probation officers (pre-sentence), community members, self referrals from either the ones harmed or those causing harm,[32] and, more recently, from the Department of Fisheries and Oceans, as well as Xyolhemeylh and the Ministry of Children and Families Development.

To date, the Stó:lō have signed protocol agreements with the Chilliwack, Mission, Hope, and Agassiz RCMP as well as with the Abbotsford police. As an "alternative measures" program, Qwi:qwelstóm accepts referrals from the Chilliwack and Abbotsford Crown counsel offices. Protocols with the Department of Fisheries and Oceans, the Ministry of Children and Families Development, and Xyolhemeylh are currently under way, as is a historical sexual assault protocol. The Stó:lō have asked all referral sources, especially the RCMP and Crown counsel, that all Aboriginal files being considered for diversion be forwarded to Qwi:qwelstóm.

Referrals from community members and those harmed and/or those who caused harm are unique and especially important for two main reasons: they actively reflect the nation's self-determination in defining for itself which of its "problems" require attention (these are not limited simply to "crime" or to that subset of "crime" that Canadian agencies decide is appropriate to send to the community); and they reflect the community's degree of trust in the "justice" that will result.

Acceptance of Cases

Upon receiving a referral to Qwi:qwelstóm, a justice worker or a Qwi:qwelstóm Smóyelhtel must first ensure that two criteria are met. First, the person who has done the harm must be taking responsibility for his or her behaviour. Second, all relevant persons, particularly those who have been harmed are fully informed of the Qwi:qwelstóm process and are offered the opportunity to participate when ready.

Crown counsel and the RCMP have their own policies as to what types of cases they will divert to Qwi:qwelstóm. In the beginning, they tended to divert only if the crime was minor and if it involved a first-time offender.[33] However, the Stó:lō feel that such a profile does not adequately capture the Aboriginal people who would most benefit from Qwi:qwelstóm. Statistics tell us that most Aboriginal people in conflict with the law have already had prior contact with it, which means they will be under-represented in diversion and "alternative" programs that select for first offences. In practice, the stipulation that only first-time offenders can be diverted amounts to systemic discrimination, as most of those who qualify for diversion and alternative measures will not be Aboriginal.[34] Qwi:qwelstóm does, however, accept more serious cases, either in conjunction with a court order or as a referral coming directly from a community member. As well, it should be noted that the types of cases diverted to Qwi:qwelstóm from the criminal justice system depend not only upon the program's own policy but also upon how Qwi:qwelstóm is perceived by the referring agent. Some Crown counsel will refer the serious charges, whereas other Crown counsel will not; the same is true of the RCMP.

Acceptance to the Qwi:qwelstóm program is made on a case-by-case basis. In the assessment of serious cases, many factors are considered, such as

- the remorse (level of awareness) of the person who has caused harm
- the community's willingness to deal with the person
- the resources available to the person(s) who has caused harm, the person(s) harmed, and family members (that is, are there enough Stó:lō people available to help with the situation?)
- where those involved in the conflict are in their own journey of healing

- the thoughts and opinions of the harmed person(s)
- what positive actions the wrongdoer has taken since the incident.

One of Qwi:qwelstóm's objectives is to increase the reporting rates of family violence and sexual assaults within Stó:lō communities by providing an "alternative" to the punitive and adversarial criminal justice system. Family violence is under-reported largely because Stó:lō communities tend to be under-serviced by Euro-Canadian agencies; in any event, many Stó:lō feel that these agencies are not adequately equipped to deal with their problems. The high prevalence of violence within Aboriginal communities is nothing short of epidemic; families that have not been touched in some manner by violence are rare. Qwi:qwelstóm provides an opportunity to take ownership for this devastating social problem and encourages families to begin a "healing" process that will eventually end the cycle of abuse.

Qwi:qwelstóm ye Smómíyelhtel

The heart and backbone of Qwi:qwelstóm is the group of community members who have come forward to assist with the healing journey. There are approximately twenty Smómíyelhtel. All undergo an extensive training journey that includes workshops, conferences, and sessions on peacemaking circles, other Aboriginal justice initiatives, fetal alcohol syndrome, restorative justice, and conflict resolution. Each month a guest is invited to attend the Qwi:qwelstóm monthly session, which allows the Smómíyelhtel to learn about a wide variety of topics relevant to healing within Stó:lō communities. Guests have included sexual abuse counsellors, family violence counsellors, cultural advisors, spiritual healers, prison workers, and elders. As well, the Smómíyelhtel are given articles to read that address pertinent concerns and that call for a critical analysis of justice in general.

Qwi:qwelstóm ye Smómíyelhtel inform circle participants of the process and of what will be expected from them during the circle. Organizing and leading the circles, they document the proceedings and, when necessary, the resolution. Although they have guiding principles to follow, each Smóyelhtel has developed his or her own personal style of circle facilitation. Each Smóyelhtel is asked to keep the following guiding principles in mind:

- Qwi:qwelstóm is about building relations and resolving conflict "in a good way."[35]
- Qwi:qwelstóm encourages the reconnection of family members to their extended family and to their community.
- Each participant is asked to bring an elder from his or her family to share in the circle.

- Qwi:qwelstóm is about being responsible; the focus for circle work is the self.
- Qwi:qwelstóm workers are reminded to be kind and respectful, and to remember that it takes courage to ask for help and to change (that is, to heal).

One of the challenges faced by the Qwi:qwelstóm ye Smómíyelhtel when they work with Euro-Canadian agency referrals is the balancing act that is required to meet competing demands. These agencies tend to focus on the act or behaviour, whereas Qwi:qwelstóm focuses on the person. Euro-Canadian agencies emphasize individual responsibility and rely heavily on written reports and forms. Qwi:qwelstóm places the individual within a familial context and stresses feelings, relations, and restoring the balance and harmony that has been disrupted. This requires one-to-one work that is personalized and not always conducive to report writing or categorized checklists.

For example, an important part of the healing process, and therefore of the Qwi:qwelstóm process itself, is the telling of personal histories, which quite often involve painful testimonies of survival of horrific abuses. This commonly occurs at the very first meeting. Cases involving troubled youth are often found to be symptomatic of a much larger familial problem that includes parenting challenges. Because they presume a specific criminal act and a checklist of dispositions, the incident-based statistics required by the Department of Justice and the criminal justice system fail to capture Qwi:qwelstóm's more open-ended and healing-focused interest, and thereby distort the process.

The emphasis on paper records and "case processing" can also create conflicting demands that are frustrating for Qwi:qwelstóm ye Smómíyelhtel. On one occasion, for instance, a Smóyelhtel was publicly chastised by an elder for having notes written on paper in the circle. The elder reminded the circle participants that everyone there was equal and that by having written notes a Smóyelhtel could, however unintentionally, relay the message that he or she was more important than the others. The Smóyelhtel was then put in the challenging position of adhering to the elder's teaching while somehow finding a way to document the resolution, as requested by the Euro-Canadian referral source.

Qwi:qwelstóm Circle Work

Although much work must be done in preparation for the Qwi:qwelstóm process, most of the "work" undertaken occurs in circle. Circle work provides a forum that is most conducive to traditional ways of relating to one another; circle work is to Stó:lō epistemology what empiricism is to Western epistemology. Circles create the space and the place for meaningful discussion, in-depth interaction, and better understanding. The focus for circle work is "the self," just as Stó:lō epistemology places the self as the starting point in making sense of the world.

Participants who are asked to join a circle are required to come prepared to share all four sacred parts of being, namely, the physical, the mental, the emotional, and the spiritual. They are also expected to come physically prepared, that is, well-rested, fed, and drug- and alcohol-free for at least four days prior to the circle date. Participants are also asked to come mentally prepared, that is, with a strong mind, in order to make best use of the words that will be shared.

It is impossible to describe all the dynamics that evolve during circle work. Those who have taken part in circles have probably experienced the innate power and spirituality that guide such a process. We will do our best to explain why circle work touches people so deeply, albeit knowing we cannot do it full justice. The physicality of circle and participants probably plays an important role. Participants are in close proximity to one another, with nothing between them, so there is a physical connection between all. Each is an individual who in turn is part of a whole – together they all form a circle. It is impossible to tell where it starts and where it ends, which relays a sense of equality for everyone sitting in the circle. As well, each participant is equally vulnerable, as there are no books, papers, or desks to hide behind or to deflect the in-depth human interaction.

All participants are asked to involve themselves fully by actively listening, verbally sharing, or both. The extent to which each does so is left up to the individual. There is an understanding that each must have a strong mind in order to get through the work that needs to be done. Some of the words may seem harsh; people are asked to be strong-minded so they can take the good that is offered to them.

Emotions are welcome. The work does not stop if a participant is overcome with strong emotion, whether anger, joy, sorrow, or happiness. Rather, the person is encouraged to share the emotion with everyone present; through this, each participant then takes a part of that emotion. In this sense the strength of the emotion is dispersed among everyone in the circle.

Finally, circle work is inherently spiritual. Circles have always been highly sacred to the Stó:lō. To a Stó:lō mind, all of life is best understood in terms of a circle. Spirituality, especially as it relates to our ancestors, is drawn to circle work. As is the case with oral stories, circle work has "the power to protect and to heal"; in circles, as in oral stories, our "beloved ancestors and family become present with us."[36] This is especially evident when a circle is honoured with the presence of elders. Elders and "circle work" go hand in hand. Elders are especially vibrant and are a powerful presence within a circle. A circle naturally creates space for elders and invaluable teachings. For the Stó:lō, this forum of relating to others is safe and non-confrontational. Providing an equal voice to all participants, it is also inherently spiritual, which often encourages and facilitates healing.

For criminal justice system referrals, Qwi:qwelstóm circles are available for use in four different stages of the prosecuting process. A circle can be arranged to replace the trial process, to make a sentencing recommendation, to assist with reintegrating Aboriginal people who have been incarcerated back into their communities, and/or to develop a healing plan to be part of sentencing and/or probation orders.

When referrals originate from community members, most circles that result are healing circles. However, Qwi:qwelstóm also makes use of peacemaking circles to assist with family disputes, custody concerns, and divorce settlements; they improve relationships between a whole host of parties, most notably between social workers and biological parents. Quite often healing circles and peacemaking circles are used interchangeably, as they share many similarities. There are subtle differences, however, that may be important to the circle participants. For instance, preparation for the circle may differ depending on whether one is to take part in a healing or a peacemaking circle. The former are focused almost exclusively on restoring balance to an individual(s) who is out of balance due to past and present hurts. The latter, on the other hand, are focused almost entirely on achieving better understanding by all circle participants regarding a specific incident. Peacemaking circles are similar to, but different from, a mediation process. Healing circles are similar to, but different from, counselling sessions.

As well, Qwi:qwelstóm is being asked by Stó:lō people to assist in improving relations between community members and Stó:lō Nation employees, between the latter and their supervisors, and between community members and institutional employees (such as between Aboriginal students and school staff). This desire to use the Qwi:qwelstóm processes in all areas of conflict and dispute settlement, rather than confining it to what Xwelítem deem to be "criminal matters," is testament to the success an Aboriginal approach can achieve when it is directed and implemented by Aboriginal people. Unfortunately, responding to these requests is challenging, as Qwi:qwelstóm is under-funded and therefore under-staffed, which limits the Stó:lō people's ability to expand into other areas of conflict resolution.

Elders
Program personnel are often asked regarding the circumstances under which a circle might be cancelled: the bottom line is that at least one elder *must* be present to hold a Qwi:qwelstóm circle. In the rare instances in which the elder cannot attend and circle participants cannot contact another elder to

come, the circle will be rescheduled. Only this warrants the delay of a circle. Even in the event that the person who was harmed or the person who did the harm fails to appear, the circle will nonetheless proceed. Another circle may be arranged for another time, but the circle for which everyone else had prepared would continue as planned. There are several reasons for this. One is the acknowledgment of the interrelatedness of everything and the equality of all people involved. Another is the teaching of the importance of maintaining balance. People mentally, physically, emotionally, and spiritually prepare themselves for a circle; to show up, only to have it not occur can cause a disruption in one's balance, which can create friction and disharmony – whether mentally, physically, emotionally, or spiritually.

Elders are integral to the process for many different reasons. Stó:lō people tend to listen when elders speak, especially in sacred places such as a longhouse, a sweat, a circle, and so on. Elders also tend to be the best listeners – they really listen and come without their own agenda. They also have a knack for saying things in a way that is readily accepted by circle participants. Most importantly, they know how each person is tied to the community and thus are able to re-establish these connections. This ensures that the people know they belong and reaffirms their place within the community. As well, elders bring an essential part of the spirituality that guides the entire process.

Family, Family Ties, and Connections

Stó:lō people are tied to family in many ways; for them, family includes what non-Indigenous people might distinguish as "extended" family. To the Stó:lō, family includes siblings, parents, aunties, uncles, every degree of cousin, grandparents, great-grandparents, and great-uncles and great-aunties. Cousins are considered siblings. It is a central teaching that one should not place distance between family by using words such as "step," "in-law," "half," and so on. These family ties are an important part of an individual's identity. For example, the Stó:lō are quite commonly introduced to each other in terms of their family connections ("This is the late Gordon Hall's eldest granddaughter"). Family ties are re-established in circle: while attending a circle, a person who caused harm might commonly hear something like "my grandfather was your grandmother's first cousin," which immediately links him or her to the speaker. Re-establishing such connections ensures that he or she will actually listen to the speaker; in addition, it provides one more reason to change.

If the person who caused harm has an ancestral name, this may be discussed, as all such names come with responsibilities and a long history of family ties. In some cases individuals may be "stripped" of their ancestral name until they show they can carry it with responsibility and respect. So far, however, the majority of people being referred from the criminal justice system tend not to hold ancestral names. This speaks to the importance of re-establishing the ties between individuals and their family, community, and nation. Living up to the responsibilities associated with an ancestral name assists in preventing people from offending others. Those who carry such names tend to do so with much dignity and pride; mindful of the responsibility linked to their name, they are careful to behave in a manner reflective of the honour bestowed upon them.

The role of family is always recognized and never outgrown – even as adults, people still refer to their "uncles" and "aunties" as such, as a sign of respect. The recognition of family ties is also important in order for people to understand that their misbehaviour puts a bad mark on their entire family, not just on themselves. And finally, young people who are having troubles are often sent to an uncle or auntie for help; young people who do not listen to their parents will nonetheless often listen to an auntie, uncle, and/ or grandparents. This aspect of the Qwi:qwelstóm process is especially important in its ability to stop harmful behaviour. Given the importance of family and maintaining good relations, it is much easier for those who have caused harm to sit in a courtroom, saying nothing while they face a stranger such as a judge, than it is for them to sit in an intimate circle and directly tell their aunties, uncles, grandparents, sisters, brothers, and so on exactly how they caused harm.

Teachings
Teachings are a natural outcome of circle work. Most teachings afford the opportunity to learn more about the Stó:lō worldview. To receive teachings is an important part of establishing one's sense of self-worth and identity in all its mental, emotional, physical, and spiritual aspects. The circle provides a natural environment and form of communication that is conducive to the sharing of the teachings.

For example, a talking piece is always used during circle work. Each Qwi:qwelstóm Smóyelhtel has his or her own talking piece, which is sacred to him or her, given by family relations to signify his or her ability to bring people together "in a good way." A talking piece such as this is imbued with spirit and is treated with much respect by circle participants. The use of a talking piece allows participants to practise a few of the "rules" that govern an oral tradition.[37] Only the person who holds the talking piece may speak; thus, no one talks out of turn, speakers do not feel rushed or worried about being interrupted, and the pace of the discussion itself is slowed. The talking piece reminds the speaker to be honest and to speak from the heart. Heart talk allows those not speaking to really listen, as they do not need to be formulating what they will say next. Participants speak from an "I" frame of reference that personalizes the interactions in the circle. Closeness and subjectivity are encouraged, and silence is, once again, an important part of communication.

The importance of the transference of teachings during the Qwi:qwelstóm process cannot be overstated. The Stó:lō, like most Indigenous peoples, have a history of passing valuable teachings from generation to generation via their oral tradition. Such oral information is generally passed from elders to children and from elders to young adults. Our elders are our "history books"; they are our "computers." They hold all the teachings that future generations will need to achieve peace, balance, and harmony. The colonial legacy has disrupted this vital flow of information. It is up to us to reinstate it and once again place our elders where they rightfully belong within our Indigenous societies.

Spirituality

The spirituality of the circle process has already been noted above. We add here that the circle always starts and finishes with a prayer, usually done by the elder, in order to ground the participants and acknowledge Stó:lō ancestors. Sharing a meal together is also encouraged as it brings people together and promotes closeness and good feeling. Some circles will smudge, and, in accordance with Stó:lō teachings, a sacred talking piece is always used. When staff become anxious about a pending circle and its outcome or their ability to meet the timeline provided by Crown counsel, they are reminded to have trust in the process and to let "the spirits guide us." In contrast, telling Crown counsel to "trust in spirit" doesn't always go over very well.

Qwi:qwelstóm Challenges

As a formal means of dispute resolution and a diversion program, Qwi:qwelstóm is of too recent a vintage to allow for a complete analysis. Many kinks still need to be worked out, especially in "bridging that cultural divide" in order to balance the opposing needs and expectations of two different worlds. The challenges faced by Qwi:qwelstóm and the program itself are worthy of study all on their own. We offer only a brief inventory here.

One of the biggest challenges faced by Qwi:qwelstóm is the education component. It is to be expected that Euro-Canadians will not be familiar with the principles and philosophical underpinnings that guide Qwi:qwelstóm. However, one legacy of colonial policy and practice is that many Stó:lō themselves are unfamiliar with the cultural teachings that guide Qwi:qwelstóm work. Some Stó:lō people have adopted the colonizer's view of justice as punishment and still seek to have "justice" meted out by the criminal justice system. The challenge faced by Qwi:qwelstóm is to educate the Stó:lō people so that they can make decisions informed by their own cultural and spiritual traditions. This is an exciting process for Qwi:qwelstóm as part of the "decolonizing" work required before self-determination can truly be experienced.

A second challenge is for Qwi:qwelstóm to remain focused on the Stó:lō people and communities. This is not an easy task for several reasons:

- Sometimes the depth of pain and suffering within the communities can become difficult to handle and overwhelming.
- In attempting to meet CJS demands, staff can quite easily spend all their time within CJS structures.
- Resources and support provided to First Nations communities to deal with the issues of pain and suffering are lacking.
- Too few healthy people to help leads to burnout and overworking of certain individuals, especially elders.
- Staff burnout is a problem.
- Inadequate government funding means that communities are asked to do ten dollars worth of work for a dollar; this makes it difficult to keep staff, to afford to hire and keep qualified staff, and to provide necessary programs and services.
- Canada has a tendency to subordinate and subsume Indigenous "ways of being."
- Due to cutbacks in the Native courtworkers program, justice workers must now spend more time in the courtroom liaising with court staff.

A third challenge faced by Qwi:qwelstóm involves oppression. This is represented in two separate forms: dealing with the oppressors and with the oppressed. As regards the former, Qwi:qwelstóm is continually being asked by Euro-Canadians to "prove" the ability of the Stó:lō to look after themselves. This is colonial thought that perpetuates the false ideology of Western superiority. It blindly ignores that the Stó:lō have looked after their own responsibilities since time immemorial. Asking the Stó:lō for such proof is tantamount to asking them to "prove" they exist as Stó:lō people.

It is a peculiar truism of power that those who wield it can hold others to standards that they do not apply to themselves. Can the Canadian justice system live up to its own injunctions? Certainly, it cannot do so in relation to its treatment of Indigenous people, as commission after commission has revealed its abject and total failure in this respect. Stó:lō justice can certainly do no worse. But can the Canadian justice system demonstrate its effectiveness even with its own people? The Canadian citizenry seems highly dissatisfied with the way in which its justice system works, and the media seem to report weekly on some notorious injustice. The irony of asking Aboriginal people to achieve what Canada itself has been unable to achieve is not overlooked in this situation.

But the challenge of working with oppressed people cannot be dismissed so easily. We can use an analogy to describe this oppression. Imagine that the Stó:lō people are birds and that the imposed Canadian system(s) is a small wire cage in which the birds have been forced to live for quite some time. The right to be Stó:lō is freedom. What if, while kept in this cage, the birds are subjected to various forms of indoctrination that lead many of them to believe they are not worthy of freedom? What if the birds are kept in that cage for so long they begin to forget what freedom feels like? If one day the doors to the cage are opened and the birds are given the option of leaving, what will they do? Will they even remember that they have wings?

This is what oppression can do. It can take away not only a bird's flight but also a people's confidence, their trust in themselves and in each other; it can take away their dreams. Even worse, it can make people feel that they do not have the right to dream at all.

Encouraging Dreams: What Can Canada Do?

There is much that Canada can do to encourage the dreams of Aboriginal people. As a start, we suggest that the Canadian government might take the following steps:

- Recognize that it is in everyone's best interest to have healthy and thriving Aboriginal communities that can interact in positive and mutually respectful ways with the non-Aboriginal communities around them.
- Formally recognize that Aboriginal jurisdiction over Aboriginal justice is part of the inherent right to self-determination and to create space for Aboriginal justice. We also suggest that Ottawa begin negotiations with the provinces and First Nations organizations to create an Aboriginal justice authority whose mandate would be to support the development of Aboriginal justice programs in Aboriginal communities. For budgeting, we suggest that the federal and provincial governments use all the funds they currently devote to keeping Aboriginal offenders in jail, and add in the funds that are currently allocated to the Aboriginal Justice Strategy.
- Support First Nations justice initiatives without subsuming and assimilating them into the always more assertive, better-funded, and adequately staffed criminal justice system.
- Provide adequate support that includes guidance and assistance as requested and identified by the First Nation community. This does not mean assistance and guidance in helping the community duplicate the current system.
- Find ways to improve the relationships that need to be established between the two "systems."
- Accept that each First Nation community, when ready and able, will dictate both "what" and "how many" are to be dealt with.

Even with the establishment of separate Aboriginal ways of doing justice, points of "convergence" will always remain.[38] Partnerships and working together are important. This relationship can be strengthened by educating Canadian justice system personnel to view Aboriginal justice from within an Indigenous worldview. This would allow them to understand that First Nations people view "justice" as a "way of being," as a means to heal, a way to restore balance and harmony to their families and communities, a means to be responsible for their own lives.

The resurgence and use of Aboriginal ways of doing "justice" do not call into question the sovereignty of the Crown; they simply provide an opportunity for First Nations to experience justice according to their own customs and traditions. As Patricia Monture-Angus points out, "Aboriginal Peoples do not wish to displace anyone else's right to be governed by the legitimate and properly consented to laws of their nation. To do such a thing would amount to becoming oppressors ourselves. Our challenge is not a challenge to your right to be in your own unique way, but a simple desire to follow our own ways."[39]

To view justice only in terms of the Euro-Canadian definition tends to stalemate discussions and increase the "cultural divide"; this definition quite honestly does not reflect what First Nations communities are doing in their attempts to "get to that better place."

Acknowledgments
The authors would like to thank Jeffrey Huberman, Joanne Jefferson, Tyrone McNeil, Patricia Monture, Georges Sioui, Juan Tauri, and Amy Victor for their invaluable comments on earlier drafts of this chapter.

Notes
1 P. Monture-Angus, *Journeying Forward: Dreaming First Nations' Independence* (Halifax: Fernwood Publishing, 1999).
2 See S.H. Venne, *Our Elders Understand Our Rights: Evolving International Law regarding Indigenous Peoples* (Penticton, BC: Theytus Books, 1998). See also T. Palys, "Are Canada and BC Meeting International Standards regarding the Rights of Indigenous Peoples? Stó:lō Nation and Its Search for Justice" (paper presented at Stó:lō Nation Conference 2001: Bridging the Millennia, Bridging Cultural and Legal Traditions, Mission, BC, 5-7 April 2001), http://www.sfu.ca/~palys/StoLoNation2001.htm.
3 United Nations Working Group on Indigenous Populations, *Draft Declaration on the Rights of Indigenous Peoples*, 1994, http://www.cwis.org/fwdp/drft9329.html.
4 *R. v. Gladue*, [1999] 2 C.N.L.R. 231 (B.C.C.A.), [1999] 2 C.N.L.R. 252 (S.C.C.).
5 G.C. Monture, *Indians and the Law* (Ottawa: Canadian Corrections Association, 1967), a survey prepared by Canadian Corrections Association for the Honourable Arthur Laing, Minister of Indian Affairs and Northern Development; Manitoba, *Report of the Manitoba Aboriginal Justice Inquiry* (Winnipeg: Queen's Printer, 1991), http://www.ajic.mb.ca/volume.html; Canada, Royal Commission on Aboriginal Peoples, *Bridging the Cultural Divide: A Report on Aboriginal People and Criminal Justice in Canada* (Ottawa: Minister of Supply and Services Canada, 1996); and Law Reform Commission of Canada, *Report on Aboriginal Peoples and Criminal Justice: Equality, Respect and the Search for Justice: As Requested by the Minister of Justice under Subsection 12(2) of the Law Reform Commission Act* (Ottawa: Law Reform Commission of Canada, 1991).

6   During a private conversation of several years ago, a program director in the federal Department of Justice gave Ted Palys exactly this explanation when asked to account for government intransigence regarding a proposal that seemed so clearly of benefit to both Ottawa and the First Nations (not the Stó:lō) who were involved. He remarked that, as an agent of the Crown, he could not agree to anything that might be seen as diminishing its sovereignty.

7   See T. Palys, "Considerations for Achieving 'Aboriginal Justice' in Canada" (paper presented at the annual meeting of the Western Association of Sociology and Anthropology, Vancouver, BC, 1993), http://www.sfu.ca/~palys/wasa93.htm.

8   See T. Palys, "Resolving Conflicts Involving Indigenous Peoples: Lessons from the Search for 'Indigenous Justice' in Canada" (intervention to the UN Working Group on Indigenous Populations at its 22nd session, Geneva, Switzerland, 19-23 July 2004), http://www.sfu.ca/~palys/PalysWGIPSubmission2004.pdf.

9   The Greschner quote we have paraphrased is "It is almost oxymoronic to talk of non-aboriginal conceptions of aboriginal rights; if aboriginal rights are not given their meaning by aboriginal peoples, they are not truly aboriginal." D. Greschner, "Aboriginal Women, the Constitution and Criminal Justice," special issue, *University of British Columbia Law Review* (1992): 344. An excellent example of this in the justice area is the common mistake of thinking that "sentencing circles" are a form of Aboriginal justice: as succinctly put by Patricia Monture-Angus at a recent justice conference hosted by the Stó:lō, "rearranging the furniture is not Aboriginal justice." Keynote address to the Qwi:qwelstóm gathering, "Bringing Justice Back to the People," Mission, BC, 22-24 March 2004; see also Patricia Monture-Angus, "Standing against Canadian Law: Naming Omissions of Race, Culture, and Gender," in Elizabeth Comack, ed., *Locating Law: Race/Class/Gender Connections* (Halifax: Fernwood Publishing, 1999), 81.

10   Because Wenona is Stó:lō and Ted is not, we as co-authors found ourselves grappling with the issue of how to describe our relationship with the Stó:lō subjects under study. The "we, us" approach that might work for Wenona was not necessarily appropriate for Ted. In the end, we chose to use "we" when Wenona was part of the Stó:lō teachings and perspectives described; she is the "I" when the program goal and the processes that she helped create and manage are discussed. When we refer to the program or Stó:lō people in general terms, we commonly use "they" for observations that lie beyond our own experience.

11   E.B. Gardner (Stelómethet), "Tset Híkwstexw, We Hold Our Language High: The Meaning of Halq'eméylem Language Renewal in the Everyday Lives of Stó:lō People" (PhD diss., Faculty of Education, Simon Fraser University, 2002), 56.

12   This structure represented an effort to give formal shape to what the Stó:lō envisioned a contemporary self-governing body might look like. It may have been ahead of its time, however, and was dismantled and reorganized in 2004. The Stó:lō continue in their decolonizing journey and will reinstate self-governing structures when ready. The important note is that the "what," "when," and "how" of Stó:lō governance will, as always, be dictated by the Stó:lō themselves.

13   Mandate for the Stó:lō Nation House of Justice, House of Justice notes, November 1998.

14   Xwelítem is the Halq'eméylem term used by the Stó:lō to describe the first white people who arrived in their territory. It translates literally as "starving people" or "hungry people."

15   Summary taken from unpublished article written by Wenona Victor for the Stó:lō Nation newsletter, December 2000.

16   J. Tauri, "Conferencing, Indigenisation and Orientalism: A Critical Commentary on Recent State Responses to Indigenous Offending" (keynote address to the Qwi:qwelstóm gathering, "Bringing Justice Back to the People," Mission, BC, 22-24 March 2004).

17   B. Stuart, Reasons for Sentencing, *Regina versus Philip Moses*, Yukon Territorial Court, 1992, http://www.usask.ca/nativelaw/factums/moses.html. Also cited at [1992] 3 C.N.L.R. 116, (1992) 11 C.R. (4th) 357.

18   See Palys, "Considerations."

19   Although Wenona never asked him, Judge Stuart may well have understood how holding the training session in a traditional building would affect its outcome. His suggestion was probably his nice way of pointing the Stó:lō in the right direction. For this Wenona is grateful.

20 Wenona Victor, unpublished personal journal on file with author.
21 See Monture-Angus, *Journeying Forward,* and P. Monture-Angus, *Thunder in My Soul: A Mohawk Woman Speaks* (Halifax: Fernwood Publishing, 1995).
22 The term "traditional" refers to "the ways of our ancestors."
23 For details, see Gardner, "Tset Híkwstexw." The title means "we hold our language high."
24 J.Y. Henderson, "Postcolonial Indigenous Legal Consciousness," *Indigenous Law Journal* 1 (2002): 14.
25 Before beginning her research, Wenona sought guidance from those who had worked with elders, so that she would know how to conduct herself during the interview process. Dr. Joanne Archibald, a member of the Stó:lō Nation who had recently interviewed elders in connection with her education dissertation, was of great assistance in preparing her mentally and spiritually for this. For Wenona, interviewing the elders meant, in large part, stating her interests in general terms and then trusting in their ability to teach and guide her.
26 W. Victor, "Searching for the Bone Needle: The Stó:lō Nation's Continuing Quest for Justice" (MA thesis, School of Criminology, Simon Fraser University, 2001), 64, http://www.sfu.ca/cfrj/fulltext/victor.pdf.
27 Qwi:qwelstóm ye Smómíyelhtel is the Halq'eméylem phrase used to explain the responsibilities of those who will guide the Qwi:qwelstóm process while in circle. The Halq'eméylem language does not use "s" or "es" to denote plural; therefore, Qwi:qwelstóm ye Smómíyelhtel is the plural and Qwi:qwelstóm Smóyelhtel is the singular.
28 Wenona Victor, unpublished personal journal on file with the author (September 1999).
29 The healing process required to address the traumas of colonialism should not be understated or minimized, nor should the need to heal be assigned strictly to First Nation communities. See, for example, Patricia Monture-Angus, "Considering Colonialism and Oppression: Aboriginal Women, Justice and the 'Theory' of Decolonization," *Native Studies Review* 12, 1 (1999): 84.
30 "Internalized colonial attitudes" describes a condition in which colonized groups of people eventually take on the beliefs and attitudes of the colonizers. Another relevant term is "cognitive imperialism," a "form of cognitive manipulation used to disclaim other knowledge bases and values," which thus serves the colonizer's ability to "deny people their language and cultural integrity by maintaining the legitimacy of only one language, one culture, and one frame of reference." Marie Battiste, "Maintaining Aboriginal Identity, Language, and Culture," in Marie Battiste, ed., *Reclaiming Indigenous Voice and Vision* (Vancouver: UBC Press, 2000), 198.
31 The term "internal sovereignty" is used here as defined by Robert Yazzie, "Indigenous Peoples and Postcolonial Colonialism," in Marie Battiste, ed., *Reclaiming Indigenous Voice and Vision* (Vancouver: UBC Press, 2000): "Ultimately, the lesson is that we, as Indigenous peoples, must start within. We must exercise internal sovereignty, which is nothing more than taking control of our personal lives, our families, our clans, and our communities. To do that, we must return to our traditions, because they speak to right relationships, respect, solidarity, and survival. I cannot beg for political power, because I will not get it. However, I can pray for personal power and work with people around me to achieve internal sovereignty, that is our path to postcolonial existence" (47).
32 In keeping with the Halq'eméylem language and the Stó:lō worldview, Qwi:qwelstóm avoids the use of terms that label individuals, such as "offender" and "victim," as the Halq'eméylem language (and corresponding worldview) is verb- and process-oriented, rarely relying on nouns in relations to people.
33 Not surprisingly, those RCMP officers and Crown counsel who view Qwi:qwelstóm as an alternative measures program commonly equate "diversion" with "trivial offences." This continues despite numerous attempts to explain that, as an Aboriginal justice forum, Qwi:qwelstóm is much more than this.
34 C. Griffiths and C. Belleau, "Restoration, Reconciliation and Healing: The Revitalization of Culture and Tradition in Addressing Crime and Victimization in Canadian Aboriginal Communities," in E. Fattah and T. Peters, eds., *Support for Crime Victims in a Comparative Perspective* (Leuven, Belgium: Leuven University Press, 1998).

35   The Stó:lō commonly use the phrase "in a good way" to denote the importance of, above all else, maintaining good feelings between people; this is achieved by taking care to speak and behave respectfully, so as to avoid relationship-destroying words and confrontations.
36   Leslie Silko, 1996, of the Laguna Pueblo, in *Yellow Woman and a Beauty of the Spirit: Essays on Native American life Today*. As quoted in J. Archibald, "Coyote Learns to Make a Storybasket: The Place of First Nations Stories in Education" (PhD diss., Faculty of Education, Simon Fraser University, 1997), 35.
37   Just as written languages have rules of grammar, oral traditions have "rules" governing speaking, such as who speaks when, who can speak on what topic, and so on.
38   M.E. Turpel, "Reflections on Thinking Concretely about Criminal Justice Reform," in R. Gosse, J.Y. Henderson, and R. Carter, eds., *Continuing Poundmaker and Riel's Quest: Presentations Made at a Conference on Aboriginal Peoples and Justice* (Saskatoon: Purich Publishing, 1994).
39   Monture-Angus, *Thunder in My Soul*, 251.

Bibliography

Archibald, J. "Coyote Learns to Make a Storybasket: The Place of First Nations Stories in Education." PhD diss., Faculty of Education, Simon Fraser University, 1997.

Battiste, M. "Maintaining Aboriginal Identity, Language, and Culture." In Marie Battiste, ed., *Reclaiming Indigenous Voice and Vision*, 192-208. Vancouver: UBC Press, 2000.

Canada. Royal Commission on Aboriginal Peoples. *Bridging the Cultural Divide: A Report on Aboriginal People and Criminal Justice in Canada*. Ottawa: Minister of Supply and Services Canada, 1996.

Gardner, E.B. (Stelómethet). "Tset Híkwstexw, We Hold Our Language High: The Meaning of Halq'eméylem Language Renewal in the Everyday Lives of Stó:lō People." PhD diss., Faculty of Education, Simon Fraser University, 2002.

Greschner, D. "Aboriginal Women, the Constitution and Criminal Justice." Special edition, *University of British Columbia Law Review* (1992): 338-59.

Griffiths, C., and C. Belleau. "Restoration, Reconciliation and Healing: The Revitalization of Culture and Tradition in Addressing Crime and Victimization in Canadian Aboriginal Communities." In E. Fattah and T. Peters, eds., *Support for Crime Victims in a Comparative Perspective*, 169-87. Leuven, Belgium: Leuven University Press, 1998.

Henderson, J.Y. "Postcolonial Indigenous Legal Consciousness." *Indigenous Law Journal* 1 (2002): 1-27.

Manitoba. *Report of the Manitoba Aboriginal Justice Inquiry*. Winnipeg: Queen's Printer, 1991. http://www.ajic.mb.ca/volume.html.

Monture, G.C. *Indians and the Law*. Ottawa: Canadian Corrections Association, 1967.

Monture-Angus, P. "Considering Colonialism and Oppression: Aboriginal Women, Justice and the 'Theory' of Decolonization." *Native Studies Review* 12, 1 (1999): 63-94.

–. *Journeying Forward: Dreaming First Nations' Independence*. Halifax: Fernwood Publishing, 1999.

–. "Standing against Canadian Law: Naming Omissions of Race, Culture, and Gender." In Elizabeth Comack, ed., *Locating Law: Race/Class/Gender Connections*, 76-97. Halifax: Fernwood Publishing, 1999.

–. *Thunder in My Soul: A Mohawk Woman Speaks*. Halifax: Fernwood Publishing, 1995.

Palys, T. "Are Canada and BC Meeting International Standards regarding the Rights of Indigenous Peoples? Stó:lō Nation and Its Search for Justice." Paper presented at Stó:lō Nation Conference 2001: Bridging the Millennia, Bridging Cultural and Legal Traditions, Mission, BC, 5-7 April 2001. http://www.sfu.ca/~palys/StoLoNation2001.htm.

–. "Considerations for Achieving 'Aboriginal Justice' in Canada." Paper presented at the annual meeting of the Western Association of Sociology and Anthropology, Vancouver, BC, April 1993. http://www.sfu.ca/~palys/wasa93.htm.

–. "Resolving Conflicts Involving Indigenous Peoples: Lessons from the Search for 'Indigenous Justice' in Canada." Intervention to the UN Working Group on Indigenous Populations at Its 22nd Session, Geneva, Switzerland, 19-23 July 2004. http://www.sfu.ca/~palys/PalysWGIPSubmission2004.pdf.

R. v. Gladue, [1999] 2 C.N.L.R. 231 (B.C.C.A.), [1999] 2 C.N.L.R. 252 (S.C.C.).

R. v. Moses, [1992] 3 C.N.L.R. 116, (1992) 11 C.R. (4th) 357.

Stuart, B. Reasons for Sentencing. *Regina versus Philip Moses*. Yukon Territorial Court, 1992. http://www.usask.ca/nativelaw/factums/moses.html.

Tauri, J. "Conferencing, Indigenisation and Orientalism: A Critical Commentary on Recent State Responses to Indigenous Offending." Keynote address to the Qwi:qwelstóm gathering Bringing Justice Back to the People, Mission, BC, 22-24 March 2004.

Turpel, M.E. "Reflections on Thinking Concretely about Criminal Justice Reform." In R. Gosse, J.Y. Henderson, and R. Carter, eds., *Continuing Poundmaker and Riel's Quest: Presentations Made at a Conference on Aboriginal Peoples and Justice*, 173-84. Saskatoon: Purich Publishing, 1994.

United Nations Working Group on Indigenous Populations. *Draft Declaration on the Rights of Indigenous Peoples*, 1994. http://www.cwis.org/fwdp/drft9329.html.

Venne, S.H. *Our Elders Understand Our Rights: Evolving International Law regarding Indigenous Peoples*. Penticton, BC: Theytus Books, 1998.

Victor, W. "Searching for the Bone Needle: The Stó:lō Nation's Continuing Quest for Justice." MA thesis, School of Criminology, Simon Fraser University, 2001. http://www.sfu.ca/cfrj/fulltext/victor.pdf.

Yazzie, Robert. "Indigenous Peoples and Postcolonial Colonialism." In Marie Battiste, ed., *Reclaiming Indigenous Voice and Vision*, 39-49. Vancouver: UBC Press, 2000.

2

An Apology Feast in Hazelton: Indian Residential Schools, Reconciliation, and Making Space for Indigenous Legal Traditions

Paulette Regan

The Feast Hall: An Encounter Makes Space

Canada and the United Church of Canada will host a potlatch, to be organized by the Gitxsan, beginning 1:00 PM, Saturday, March 20, 2004 at the Gitanmaxx Community Hall, Hazelton, BC, to formally and publicly apologize to the Gitxsan for the internment of Gitxsan children at Indian Residential Schools ... the theme for the potlatch is "Hla Gwxhs Bekg'um" [welcome home] ... a Gitxsan term that characterizes ... symbolically reinstating the survivor into Society ... The program will include a welcome from the Gitanmaxx Simgigyat [hereditary chiefs], the serving of traditional feast soup, the usual giveaway and gifting, traditional Gitxsan drummers and singers will entertain the guests, and responses from the Simgigyat of the Gitxsan after they hear the formal apology from Canada and the United Church.[1]

What is the story behind the day that Canada and the United Church came to Hazelton to host a potlatch in the Gitxsan Feast Hall, and what might it teach us about the importance of making space for Indigenous legal traditions to address the colonial legacy of Indian residential schools in Canada? How do we, as non-Indigenous people, learn to listen to Indigenous testimonies, bearing witness to stories of trauma that unsettle us so profoundly? How do we learn to recognize and respect, without appropriating, Indigenous ways of truth-telling, making restitution and apology that are rooted in the stories, ceremonies, and symbolic rituals of Indigenous law and peacemaking practices? Most importantly, this is a story of Indian residential school (IRS) survivors, whose courage, strength, and dignity teach us humility and respect. It is a story about a nation welcoming home Gitxsan men and women who as children were torn from their families and communities and who, through no fault of their own, were unable to learn the

Gitxsan language, their nation's laws, and their people's ways of being in the world. It is a story of Gitxsan elders and simgigyat who gave their permission for non-Gitxsan to host this feast because it was what the survivors wanted and because it is how one speaks to truth, makes restitution and apology. It is how justice is achieved according to Gitxsan law. The decision to bring Canada and the United Church into the feast hall not as guests but as hosts with particular responsibilities to fulfill, is a powerful act of diplomacy and leadership that demonstrates the resilient capacity of the Gitxsan people to use their legal traditions creatively in the face of new circumstances. The story is a testament to the people of the Gitxsan Nation, who stand strong in their commitment to truth and justice for Indian residential school survivors, their families, and communities. It is also a story about institutions – about a government and a church confronting their own history and identity as colonizers and perpetrators of assimilationist policies and abuses that did irreparable harms that continue to reverberate throughout First Nations families and communities today. A very small part of the story is also mine as one of the non-Indigenous representatives of Canada who worked on the Hazelton alternative dispute-resolution (ADR) pilot project and who participated as one of the hosts in the feast that marked the end of this project.[2] Writing this essay is, in itself, an act of truth-telling and witnessing whereby I continue to fulfill my responsibilities as host. In this way, I "remember my obligation" to polish the "chain of testimony-witnessing held together by the bonds of an ethics forged in a relationship of responsibility and respect."[3] Thus, my writing represents one way of honouring, not just in words, but through my actions, this gift of testimonies that I received that day in the feast hall. Ultimately, the Hazelton feast is a story about moving from Western law to Indigenous law in coming to terms with Canada's colonial past, recognizing its ongoing legacy, and finding new decolonizing, transformative ways of working together to repair the damaged relationship that exists between Indigenous peoples and Canadians. The teachings of the feast hall enrich and deepen our thinking about how making space for Indigenous legal traditions is key to the critical pedagogical work of a national Truth and Reconciliation Commission (TRC).[4]

Stepping into the Gitxsan Feast Hall to bear witness to stories – testimonies of loss and survival – standing and speaking truthfully to this history, learning to follow the protocols, and engaging in the public ceremonies and symbolic rituals of the feast were all part of fulfilling my responsibility as one of the hosts. One by one, the IRS survivors came forward, to be met by elders and simgigyat from their Houses and clans who wrapped them in their commemorative button vests emblazoned with symbolic crests, welcoming them with traditional ceremonies and songs of lament and joy so poignant that as the sound of their voices soared upward and in the sacred silence that followed, the pain of deep loss and the evocative feeling of belonging – of coming home – hung tangibly in the air. The feast hall taught me about the power in performative acts of testimony and truth-telling, compelling me to rethink my cultural assumptions about the meanings of history, truth, justice, and reconciliation. I learned that history resides not in dusty books but lives in the stories we carry in our hearts, minds, and spirits as we struggle to understand, acknowledge, and transform our violent colonial past. I learned that truth is not only about facts but about the harsh realities of a shared colonial experience that is rooted in inequality, injustice, and damaged human relationships. I learned that justice is found not only in case law and courtrooms but in the exquisite beauty of sacred dances, symbols and songs, the strong words of elders, simgigyat, and families, and in the healing ceremonies and rituals of the feast hall that express the laws of the Gitxsan Nation. I learned that reconciliation is not a goal but a place of encounter where all participants gather the courage to face our shared history honestly without minimizing the very real damage that has been done, even as we learn new decolonizing ways of working together that shift power and perceptions. I learned that Indigenous legal traditions make space for us to reconnect powerfully with each other, making restitution and apology in ways that speak to our highest moral and ethical values as human beings of integrity – respect, honesty, trust, caring. This story is one of many that mark the first small steps in a long journey that Indigenous peoples and Canadians must take together to restore right relations, laying the groundwork for a just reconciliation between us.

Reframing the Discourse of Reconciliation in Canada
In the first part of this chapter, I reflected on my own experiential learning in the Hazelton Apology Feast, envisioning reconciliation as an encounter of shared truth-telling and testimony between Indigenous peoples and Canadians. In this way, I provide a practical example of my primary argument, that making space for Indigenous legal traditions, breathing life into constitutionally protected rights, while attending explicitly to unequal power relations, must be *integral* to the work of a national Truth and Reconciliation Commission (TRC). At the time of this writing in May 2006, a $1.9 billion Indian Residential Schools Settlement Agreement to compensate former Indian residential school students is scheduled to be implemented pending court approval in nine Canadian jurisdictions and after a five-month opt-out period for claimants. Under the terms of the agreement, all former IRS students will be eligible for a "common experience" payment awarded solely on the basis of having attended a residential school. Those who experienced sexual or serious physical abuse can pursue their claims for additional compensation in an Independent Assessment Process designed for

this purpose. Health supports and counselling services will be provided for individuals, and additional funding will enable the Aboriginal Healing Foundation to continue supporting community-based healing projects. A TRC will be established, with a budget of $60 million over five years to "[p]rovide a holistic, culturally appropriate and safe setting for former students, their families and communities as they come forward to the Commission" and to "promote awareness and public education of Canadians about the IRS system and its impacts." Funding will also be provided for commemorative events and memorials. The TRC will "undertake a series of national and community events and will establish a research centre for ongoing access to the records collected throughout the work of the Commission." A report based on the work of the TRC will also be produced.[5]

Indigenous peoples and Canadians must use this rare opportunity wisely because, as a venue for public education and research, the TRC has the potential to be either a powerful force for decolonizing, transformative change in Indigenous/Canadian relations or one that simply works to reinforce colonialism and perpetuate historical injustices. For the purposes of this chapter, I focus on two interrelated principles that will guide the TRC in fulfilling its mandate and responsibilities: according to the first, the TRC process "is a profound commitment to establishing new relationships embedded in mutual recognition and respect that will forge a brighter future"; as defined by the second, the TRC, in the exercise of its duties, will recognize "the significance of Aboriginal oral and legal traditions."[6] The critical question that lies ahead is this: how will the work of the TRC be conducted in ways that live up to the spirit and intent of these fundamental principles? I explore this question, using the Hazelton Apology Feast as a practical case study to analyze reconciliation's critical pedagogical potential as an experientially based process wherein negotiating conflicting histories supports the decolonizing and transforming of present relationships. But, for reconciliation to be an authentic truth-telling process, it must profoundly disturb a dominant culture history and mindset that "misrecognizes" and disrespects the oral histories, cultures, and legal traditions of Indigenous peoples, including their histories of peacemaking, and sanitizes the devastating impacts of past injustices that continue into the present.[7]

The TRC must provide critical pedagogical space wherein Indigenous peoples reclaim and revitalize the cultures, laws, and histories that colonizers attempted to destroy in residential schools. Through testimony and truth-telling, these "insurgent forms of remembrance" break the silence of a hitherto unspeakable past, and in so doing, call Canada, the churches, and the public to account.[8] Non-Indigenous people must also do our own truth-telling as part of making restitution and apology. Until we engage in the struggle of coming to terms with what it means to carry the history, identity, and legacy of the perpetrator, the colonizer, the oppressor, we cannot admit, even to ourselves, the hard reality and full consequences of our collective actions.[9] Within the current discourse of reconciliation, we remain stuck in a mindset of denial and guilt about past wrongs in which we problematize and pathologize Indigenous peoples, seeking legal and bureaucratic solutions to a long list of "Indian problems" and historical "claims." In doing so, we deflect attention away from the "Settler problem," our own complicity in maintaining the colonial status quo.[10] We must therefore engage in a deeply critical reflective process – as individuals and as a nation – about our role and responsibility with regard to the residential school legacy *in dialogue* with IRS survivors, their families, and communities. A good starting point for building mutual recognition and respect is to acknowledge that Indigenous oral histories, ceremonies, symbols, and rituals constitute law.[11]

In creating critical pedagogical space, the TRC must ensure that Indigenous legal traditions are not simply appropriated and used in token, superficial ways that work to replicate existing colonial relations. Within this context, a foundational principle must be that Indigenous peoples retain control and decision-making power over whether or not they choose to practise their legal traditions as part of the TRC process and under what conditions, if at all, non-Indigenous people may participate. If and when non-Indigenous people are invited to the feast, the peacemaking circle, the healing ceremony, we must bring with us a sense of humility and a genuine willingness to struggle within, and reflect upon, our own discomfort as we engage in truth-telling and the sharing of testimonies. In this way, we challenge our own national history and colonial mindset as our historical consciousness shifts. As members of the dominant culture majority, Canadians are direct beneficiaries of unequal socioeconomic privilege and unequal power relations that characterize colonialism. It is incumbent upon the TRC to ensure that these inequities are made visible, creating public education strategies and practical working tools to address this reality in a principled way. If this is not done, reconciliation processes will simply replicate the hegemonic will of the colonizer. Therefore, at this particular juncture, before the operational work of the Truth and Reconciliation Commission begins, it is both timely and critical to rethink our ideas about reconciliation.

In this section, I begin this reframing of reconciliation, critiquing a current discourse that is deeply flawed. I set out a brief overview of Canada's ADR program, which was supposed to settle IRS claims and achieve reconciliation but failed to do either. The root of the program's failure can be traced to the underlying conflicting visions of reconciliation articulated by Indigenous peoples and the federal government. I analyze the controversy over the program that erupted in 2004-5, exploring why this tort-based alternative dispute-resolution (ADR) model was an inadequate mechanism for redressing the broader sociopolitical, cultural, and psychological harms perpetrated against Indigenous peoples in residential schools. The ADR program was no doubt a sincere attempt to create a more humane, holistic alternative to litigation. But Canada's attempt to "co-narrate a chilling truth about itself"[12] was only a partial truth-telling that, ultimately, misrecognized and disrespected Indigenous visions of reconciliation, denying the legitimacy of Indigenous oral histories – testimonies as truth-telling about the totality of traumatizing residential school experiences. Indigenous legal traditions, which are constitutionally protected rights, were relegated to the status of commemoration activities. I focus on the House of Commons Standing Committee on Aboriginal Affairs and Northern Development (AANO) meetings that were convened to hear evidence with regard to the ADR program and on the subsequent report evaluating its effectiveness. The testimonies of IRS survivors and senior government officials reveal Canada's reluctance to acknowledge the whole truth about the residential school legacy. But they also demonstrate how the giving and receiving of testimony creates a pedagogical moment that can shift understanding. Throughout, I explore the tensions that surface when Indigenous legal traditions are enacted in public ceremonies. Here I reveal the dangers of tokenism and appropriation, as well as the challenges of shifting popular opinions concerning Indigenous peoples and their legal traditions, attitudes that are embedded in a colonial culture of deep denial, misrecognition, and disrespect, and that represent a significant challenge to any meaningful reconciliation.

Setting the Context: Canada's ADR Program

The long history of Indian residential schools is captured in numerous academic and government studies and in histories published by former students that stand as testimony to their experiences.[13] But this history of cultural genocide and Indigenous survival is still unknown to the majority of Canadians. Yet these are not events of the distant past – the legacy exists today in the lived experience of some ninety thousand former students, many of whom are now elderly and ill. These federally administered schools, run by various church organizations, were established in the late nineteenth century; the last Indian residential school did not close until 1996. Their purpose was to assimilate Indigenous children into the larger Canadian society by removing them, at times forcibly, from their families and communities to live in what have been described as "total institutions" where every aspect of life was controlled and supervised in order to "re-socialize" young students. Those in charge of the schools devalued Indigenous peoples, forbidding children to speak their own languages or practise their own spiritual and cultural beliefs. In this way, Indigenous children would be transformed into English-speaking citizens with Western cultural values, religious beliefs, and social practices.[14] The first comprehensive study and report on the history, policy, and legacy of the residential schools was published in 1996 by the Royal Commission on Aboriginal Peoples (RCAP). The report documented the experiences of former students, made a series of detailed recommendations, and called for a public inquiry.[15] In 1998, the federal government responded to the RCAP report in *Gathering Strength: Canada's Aboriginal Action Plan,* rejecting the RCAP recommendation for a public inquiry. Instead, the Department of Indian Affairs and Northern Development (DIAND) announced $350 million in program funding to establish the Aboriginal Healing Foundation to support community-based IRS healing projects.[16] Canada's Indian affairs minister, Jane Stewart, issued a Statement of Reconciliation, acknowledging the devastating impacts of the residential school system that "separated many children from their families and communities and prevented them from speaking their own languages and from learning about their heritages and cultures."[17] Here I note that many Indigenous peoples considered the statement to be a completely inadequate response, lacking the moral authority or political legitimacy of a public formal apology made in Parliament by the prime minister.[18]

In the face of growing litigation as former students filed individual and class action claims against the government and various church entities, DIAND began exploring the potential for using alternative dispute resolution as a mechanism to resolve IRS claims outside the courtroom in a timelier, cost-effective, and more humane manner. In 1998-99, a series of exploratory dialogues were held across Canada, involving IRS claimants, First Nations leaders, lawyers, church representatives, and government officials. A set of principles for working together was agreed upon and formed the basis for establishing twelve ADR pilot projects.[19] In 2001, a new department, Indian Residential Schools Resolution Canada (IRSRC), was set up to deal exclusively with IRS claims. In 2002, IRSRC announced a National Resolution Framework designed to resolve the majority of sexual/physical and unlawful confinement claims through an adjudicated resolution process.[20] The ADR program, based on a tort-law model, was launched in November 2003, in conjunction with a health support program administered through Health Canada and a commemoration program that was to be developed. As of April 2005, former IRS students had filed over thirteen thousand litigation claims against the federal government and various church organizations, seeking compensation for sexual and physical abuse, unlawful confinement, and cultural losses they suffered while at the schools. Although 90 percent of the claimants cited cultural loss in their claims, the federal government would not provide compensation for this critical aspect of the residential school experience because cultural loss is not recognized as a legal cause of action, and no case law currently exists. On a policy level, however, the commemoration program was a programmatic response to the issue. It would provide funding for culturally appropriate community-based initiatives to honour and remember former IRS students, support healing and reconciliation, and educate the Canadian public about the history of Indian residential schools.[21] The adjudicative ADR program was voluntary, as litigation remained an option for claimants.

The rationale for the ADR program was that it would be less adversarial than litigation in resolving residential school claims. But the ADR program, however well intentioned, came under serious attack at numerous community meetings across the country, and most notably at a national conference titled "Residential Schools Legacy: Is Reconciliation Possible?" which I attended in March 2004 at the University of Calgary. The conference was convened jointly by the Assembly of First Nations (AFN) and the University of Calgary Law Faculty. A panel of government officials made a presentation on the ADR program, outlining its advantages. But, as a member of the audience, I saw a wide disparity between the positive messaging put forward by the panel and the visceral, angry response it received from IRS survivors. The panel was peppered with statements and questions that made it absolutely clear that the audience did not share this particular government vision of healing and reconciliation. Some consistent themes emerged. The ADR program focused too narrowly on sexual and physical abuse; it did not provide either compensation or apology for the cultural loss and social harms suffered by students, who were alienated from their families and communities as a matter of government policy. The process itself was flawed – survivors found it difficult and dehumanizing to fill out a long, complicated application form. Finally, consultation with First Nations was inadequate, and the process had been unilaterally designed by non-Indigenous people. At the end of the conference, in the face of the frustration and anger expressed, government officials agreed to engage in further consultation with the AFN, but no agreement was made at this time to change the procedural or substantive aspects of the ADR program.[22] Subsequently, funding was provided for the AFN to convene a blue-ribbon panel to evaluate the ADR program and report its findings back to the government. But I left the Calgary conference with no easy answer to the question "is reconciliation possible?" Rather, the exchanges I had witnessed revealed the deep divide that exists between Indigenous peoples and Canadians about what reconciliation is and how best to achieve it.

Critiquing the Discourse of Reconciliation

Negotiation and reconciliation as defined and implemented thus far are perversions of justice in that Settler societies end up gaining legal possession of not only land and governing power, but Onkwehonwe [First Peoples] histories and identities, integrating the desirable and useful elements into their own social fabric at little or no moral or economic cost.[23]

Thus Kanien'kehaka (Mohawk) scholar and activist Taiaiake Alfred articulates the fundamental flaw in the current discourse of reconciliation. Not only are Indigenous peoples' lands, laws, and governance systems at stake but also their very existence as distinct peoples. In contrast, we Canadians stand to lose very little compared to what we have gained. Canada, like other liberal democratic states, is engaging in what American historian Elazar Barkan describes as a new "national self-reflexivity" in which "guilty nations," as perpetrators of past wrongs, engage willingly with victims in "a political negotiation that enables the rewriting of memory and historical identity in ways that both can share."[24] This public moral reckoning with the past is manifested in a proliferation of truth and reconciliation commissions, restitution programs, war crimes tribunals, peacebuilding initiatives, and public commemorative displays and events throughout the world.[25] But it is clear that Indigenous peoples and Canada have conflicting visions of what constitutes reconciliation. The government vision of reconciliation as seen in the tort-based ADR program was to achieve legal certainty by settling litigation claims and to provide programs to support First Nations' healing and commemoration. But, as the Calgary conference revealed, Indigenous people saw this vision as highly problematic. From their perspective, Canada created a strange hybrid model of reconciliation in which the litigious aspects of tort law were mixed with what amounted to little more than lip service to the importance of healing not only IRS survivors but the damaged relationship between Indigenous peoples and Canadians.

Moreover, for Indigenous peoples, the danger of being subsumed in such processes is significant and the cost too high if the non-Indigenous majority simply appropriates Indigenous legal traditions in the name of reconciliation. Cree-Saulteaux-Dunne Zah scholar Val Napoleon questions the sincerity of non-Indigenous people who talk about reconciliation and engage in ceremonies but, in the end, provide nothing of substance. She says that, "if reconciliation for Aboriginal people in Canada is ever going to move beyond rhetoric, reconciliation discussions must include substantive societal and structural changes that deal with power imbalances, land and resources." For her, the danger is that, divorced from their political, governance, and legal systems, Indigenous stories, ceremonies, symbols, and rituals are reduced to nothing more than "rhetorical window-dressing – or a pretty band-aid on a gaping wound" in reconciliation processes that remain essentially Western and do nothing to shift the colonial status quo.[26] Writing from a non-Indigenous perspective, Annalise Acorn also criticizes the token inclusion of Indigenous ceremonial practices in courtrooms, classrooms, and at

conferences as a mere exercise in "political correctness." She argues that Indigenous peoples get satisfaction from making non-Indigenous people "act"
respectfully during ceremony. We comply, making a show of respect that
costs us nothing, rather than addressing the substantive issues of compensation and rights. Acorn concludes that "either way – a white show of obei-
sance to Aboriginal ritual is not, and cannot be required to entail, authentic
respect. It is a performance of respect and thus remains a mere token."[27]
Acorn says that although Indigenous peoples can make non-Indigenous
people go through the motions, they cannot make us respect their ceremonial practices. Of course this is true. If our intent is to misrecognize and
disrespect, how could it be otherwise? Interestingly, Napoleon and Acorn
present flip sides of the same coin. Both reject the tokenism of using Indigenous ceremony as a superficial and ultimately meaningless nod to Indigenous knowledge systems, worldviews, and beliefs. But Acorn's stance is
typical of many Canadians who deny the very presence and legitimacy of
Indigenous histories, law, and peacemaking practices.

If reconciliation is to be more than just a soothing balm for white guilt,
"an escape into 'healing' the past ... [that gives] the appearance of moral
action while being burdened only by minimal cost," as Barkan describes it,
Canadians must offer more than the token "gifts" of what American critical
race theorist Eric Yamamoto calls a "cheap reconciliation."[28] At the same
time, the totality of a *just* reconciliation must encompass more than mon-
etary compensation alone. The challenge lies in how to avoid tokenism and
appropriation while according Indigenous oral histories and legal traditions
the full political recognition and respect to which they are entitled. Writing
in the American context, Chiricahua Apache legal scholar William Bradford argues that, in fact, Indigenous legal traditions should be central to
reconciliation processes because they are uniquely well suited to the deeply
transformative work of authentic reconciliation between peoples. He suggests that "two fundamental, transformative principles" must guide reconciliation between Indigenous peoples and Americans. First, there must be
compensation, remedial programs, and substantive legal reforms, including constitutional amendments and legislative protection of Indigenous
cultural and property rights. Treaties must be interpreted liberally in favour
of these rights. There must be apology and commemoration. Second, the
non-Indigenous majority must fully support Indigenous self-determination.[29]
Although the Canadian context differs somewhat from the American, Bradford's proposed reconciliation model provides a useful framework.

In Canada, reconciliation is already embedded as a foundational principle
in the constitutional, legal, and policy framework. Canadian courts provide
clear direction that the principles of reconciliation must guide the resolution of conflicts between First Nations and the Crown, and that negotiation,

not litigation, is the preferred mechanism.[30] In accordance with the constitutional, Aboriginal, and treaty rights of First Nations, the federal government has made policy commitments aimed at achieving reconciliation with Indigenous peoples.[31] But this discourse of reconciliation has proven to be overly legalistic and ultimately limiting. Even where constitutional and legal protections do exist, Indigenous peoples still face significant challenges because their rights are interpreted narrowly. Moreover, Aboriginal rights are not defined in the Constitution, so this task has been left to the courts. As Anishinabek legal scholar John Borrows points out, "[u]nfortunately, the Supreme Court of Canada's definitions of Aboriginal rights fell far short of the large, liberal, and generous interpretations of Aboriginal rights considered throughout the political process" of constitutional negotiations.[32] Within this context, Indigenous scholars Marie Battiste (Mi'kmaq) and James (Sákéj) Youngblood Henderson (Chickasaw) remind us that Indigenous knowledge systems, languages, and cultures are, in fact, constitutionally protected rights:

> Indigenous ecological order and legal systems are *sui generis* to the Canadian order, but are protected by Canadian constitutional law and the rule of law. The constitutional law of Canada provides constitutional protection to repatriation claims for cultural property, as well as to modern manifestations of Indigenous knowledge and heritage ... Little doubt exists that language ... and ceremonies are an integral and distinctive part of Indigenous knowledge and heritage.[33]

What does the need to recognize constitutionally protected Indigenous knowledge and legal systems, cultures, and languages have to do with making Indigenous legal traditions integral to addressing the legacy of Indian residential schools in a Truth and Reconciliation Commission? In June 2005, the Task Force on Aboriginal Languages and Cultures submitted its report to the minister of Canadian heritage, with recommendations for a national strategy to revitalize Indigenous languages and cultures that have constitutional status. The report points out that Canada is obliged to provide adequate program funding to help preserve and revitalize all constitutionally protected languages and cultures. Moreover, the task force made a strong connection between the cultural and language loss experienced by Indigenous children who attended residential schools and Canada's legal obligation to provide financial compensation to individuals for "the emotional and psychological trauma brought on by loss of connection to family and community."[34] But, as noted above, Canada has consistently denied legal liability for language and culture loss. It is therefore not surprising that the Indian Residential Schools Settlement Agreement does not refer specifically to compensation for collective cultural and language loss, but defines the "common experience" payment to individuals more generically as a "lump-sum payment that recognizes the experience of residing at an Indian Residential School(s) and its impacts."[35]

Although an in-depth analysis of constitutional and case law is beyond the scope of this discussion, I raise these points to suggest that the TRC provides opportunity for Indigenous peoples to address the cultural loss associated with residential schools, making their own space for Indigenous law as legitimate in its own right. Indigenous peoples are reclaiming space in powerful ways on a number of fronts in their ongoing struggle for self-determination. If Indigenous law has a highly visible role in the TRC, this would help to breathe new life into constitutionally protected Indigenous knowledge and legal systems, languages, and cultures. It would also educate the Canadian public by making more apparent the strong connections between the cultural loss experienced by Indigenous peoples in residential schools and the political reclaiming of culture, using the principles and practices of Indigenous legal traditions. At a broader level, this would also provide substantive support for First Nations' aspirations to protect and revitalize Indigenous knowledge, governance, and legal systems as integral to nation building, community development, and intergovernmental relations. In a study of the links between healing and First Nations self-government, Wayne Warry observes that culture (and, I argue, its loss) cannot be understood apart from Indigenous political, governance, and legal structures. He notes that "while direct participation in healing ceremonies can be important for individuals, the process of community healing is much broader: it is about the protection and preservation of language, political rights, and nationhood."[36] But, in the ADR program, community healing ceremonies were not recognized as the practice of Indigenous legal traditions or the living expression of constitutionally protected rights. Rather, they were relegated to the status of commemorative activities. They were cultural or ceremonial addendums to an overall ADR process that at its heart remained distinctly Western.

The language and design of Canada's ADR program reflected the dominant culture values of Western law – neutrality, fairness, timeliness, validation of claims – as key criteria for reconciliation.[37] Thus, making neutrality the indicator of fairness, timeliness the measure of effectiveness, and rationality or the collection of facts the primary criteria for validating claims excluded Indigenous criteria for reconciliation. Indigenous legal traditions invite us to move beyond an over-reliance on factual or forensic truth – the privileging of neutrality and rationality – towards a vision of reconciliation that also incorporates narrative, social, and restorative truth, the experiential engagement that characterizes Indigenous pedagogical[38] and legal practices.

When these criteria are used to evaluate the ADR program, it becomes apparent that, whereas settling individual claims in a tort-based adjudication process may have satisfied black letter law, it failed to speak to justice, healing, and reconciliation. The problem, then, was not only the corrective justice tort-based aspects of the ADR program but the underlying cultural assumptions about neutrality and truth that influence North American ADR adjudication models more generally. Here it is instructive to turn to the South African Truth and Reconciliation Commission (SATRC), which, as regards reconciliation, identified and worked with the following four concepts of truth:

- factual or forensic truth based on legal or scientific evidence or information gathered "through reliable (impartial, objective) procedures"
- personal and narrative truth of victims and perpetrators shared in a process of storytelling based on valuing strong South African oral tradition
- social or dialogue truth – that is, "the truth of experience that is established through interaction, discussion and debate"
- healing and restorative truth, "the kind of truth that places facts and what they mean within the context of human relationships – both amongst citizens and between the state and its citizens."[39]

To generalize, the ADR program addressed only one of the SATRC's four concepts of truth – factual or forensic truth.[40] As such, it constituted only a partial truth-telling about the IRS legacy. The program was rooted in a Western legal system that privileges neutrality and rationality as the criteria for establishing facts (the truth), using documents and testimony that can then be evaluated objectively by an adjudicator. These attributes are seen as culturally unbiased but are actually culturally bound beliefs that reflect dominant culture knowledge systems, worldviews, and values. In contrast, Indigenous legal traditions incorporate all four concepts of truth used by the SATRC. They privilege experiential engagement as the criterion for establishing multiple truths, using stories, ceremonies, symbols, and rituals dialogically in order to settle disputes – attributes that, from a Western perspective, are not recognized as law but understood simply as cultural practices.

Truth-Telling and Testimony: The ADR on "Trial"
In the discourse that characterizes contemporary Indigenous-Canadian relations generally, and more specifically with regard to Indian residential schools, all parties say that reconciliation is essential. It is paradoxical that although Canada's ADR program was framed using the *language* of reconciliation – healing, redress, apology, relationship – the AFN's report, commissioned after the Calgary conference and released in November 2004,

concluded that, in *substance*, the program risked "a very real danger that new harms in the relationship between First Nations, non-Aboriginal peoples, and the government will be created ... [and that] reconciliation will become impossible for the indefinite future."[41] The Canadian Bar Association (CBA) produced a separate report, released in February 2005, which also cautioned that the ADR program, which relies on "[b]lame and faultfinding, harm, wrongdoing and compensation ... concepts [that] inform tort law ... [is] not conducive to reconciliation."[42] Writing about the residential schools legacy, legal scholar Jennifer Llewellyn argues that a restorative justice approach, rather than a tort-based ADR model, is better suited to deal with the kinds of relational harms, systemic conflict, and abuses that characterize the residential school experience.[43] She also notes that restorative justice models currently being used in a criminal law context are more congruent with Indigenous methods of conflict resolution.[44] In community-based restorative justice initiatives, Canada's Aboriginal Justice Strategy supports the use of Indigenous legal traditions such as sentencing and peacemaking circles, but this same restorative justice approach was not used within the civil law context of Indian residential school claims.[45] In rejecting the ADR program, the Canadian Bar Association captured the essence of the paradox we face, saying simply that "[t]here are legal arguments and there is justice. It is time for justice."[46]

Perhaps the AFN and CBA reports might have become just two more consultation documents to be shelved and forgotten, but several other factors emerged on the political and legal fronts in conjunction with their release, casting the ADR program in an increasingly unfavourable public light. Thus, dialogue about the ADR program shifted from the conference floor onto the floor of the House of Commons, and from consultation meetings to formal meetings held by the House of Commons Standing Committee on Aboriginal Affairs and Northern Development (AANO) as it prepared a report evaluating the program's effectiveness. In December 2004, the Ontario Court of Appeal ruled that a $2.3 billion class action lawsuit brought forward by the former students of the Mohawk Institute in Brantford, Ontario, could be certified, allowing it to proceed to the next stage towards trial. In rendering this decision, the court noted that in order to meet certification requirements, plaintiffs must demonstrate that a class action is preferable to other "reasonably available means of resolving the claims."[47] Canada had argued that the ADR program did constitute a more preferable option. But the court disagreed, saying that the ADR was "unilaterally created by one of the respondents in this action and could be unilaterally dismantled without the consent of the appellants. It deals only with physical and sexual abuse. It caps the amount of possible recovery ... [i]t does not compare favourably with a common trial."[48] This decision had significant implications for a much larger national class action suit – the $12.5 billion *Baxter* class action – which was also seeking certification. Clearly, IRS claims represent a significant legal liability to the Crown.

On 9 February 2005, against this legal backdrop, as the Liberal minority government clung to power in an increasingly volatile political environment, Conservative MP Jim Prentice stood in the House of Commons to ask for the government's response to allegations that the ADR program was not working, that the costs associated with implementing the program were excessive and the results negligible. "Moreover," he said, "it is not working for the victims. Newspapers in this country are replete with stories of residential school victims who feel they are being re-victimized by the process."[49] The AANO Committee had begun the work of preparing a report to the House of Commons, evaluating the effectiveness of the ADR program. Both the AFN and the CBA made submissions to the AANO Committee, tabling the reports referred to above. In addition, the committee heard directly from a number of other witnesses, including IRS survivors, grassroots survivor organizations, the Aboriginal Healing Foundation, claimants' counsel, and senior and government officials responsible for the ADR program. On 15 February 2005, in eloquent, powerful, and moving testimony before the committee, Chief Robert Joseph, representing the Indian Residential School Survivors Society, a grassroots organization in British Columbia that provides counselling supports and public education outreach on residential schools issues, spoke to an Indigenous vision of reconciliation:

> As you can see, I was wearing my ceremonial robes as a sign of respect for your parliamentary traditions and the standing committee, of course ... There are times when we as men and women are called upon to do the extraordinary, times when we must do the honourable thing, times when we are compelled to rise above the accustomed simple solution and to struggle to reach for the hard, principled one. These are such times ... We call upon you and Canada to do this with us ... In presenting an alternative to the civil court system ADR promised to be a more humane and expedient way to receive compensation, and we find that it is. For the sick and the elderly ADR promised to expedite claims, and it appears to do so. For those who have been sexually abused and who are able to speak about their abuse ADR is indeed a better alternative to the courts. Beyond these, ADR falls far short in addressing the majority of survivor needs for comprehensive redress ... From a western and narrow legal perspective it could be said to be world class, but if it resolves little, it has little value ... For us and Canada to turn the page on this chapter of our mutual history we need a broader response than what ADR can deliver. So here we must heed the survivor voices. For the past ten years over 40,000 survivors in over a thousand focus groups and workshops in British Columbia have told us what that broader response

should be: an apology, compensation, funding for healing, and future reconciliation. With respect to an apology, survivors want and need a full apology delivered by the Prime Minister on the floor of the House of Commons ... For an apology to work, it must be understood and performed symbolically in terms of the ritual that it is. It must offer the potential for transformation of all involved ... With respect to lump sum compensation, survivors are entitled to and want financial redress for the pain and suffering – loss of language and culture, loss of family and childhood, loss of self-esteem, addictions, depression and suicide – we've endured ... By neglecting to address residential school survivors and forcing them through an onerous process like the ADR, Canada accepts the risk of being accused of institutional racism yet again ... In its statement of reconciliation, the federal government recognized that reconciliation is an ongoing process. Survivors agree. We want reconciliation, reconciliation with ourselves, with our families, with our communities – and also with Canada. While we struggle with our pain, suffering, and loss, we know that our culture and traditions are embedded in the need for balance and harmony – reconciliation.[50]

Thus we see in Chief Joseph's testimony the fundamental shortcomings of the ADR program. Although he acknowledged that the program was better for IRS survivors than a trial would be, he told the AANO Committee that it would fail to give Indigenous peoples and Canadians the reconciliation we seek. He wore his ceremonial robes as a sign of respect, and in doing so, sent a strong symbolic message to committee members that, although Indigenous legal traditions are rooted in the principles and practices of peacemaking and reconciliation, they are absent from the program's design. He pointed out that, although his organization had been consulting with IRS survivors for ten years and had consistently put forward their vision of justice and reconciliation, Canada had not listened. Instead, the government implemented a highly bureaucratic, legalistic form of ADR that would lead to further alienation, not reconciliation. In calling on parliamentarians to do the hard, principled thing, Chief Joseph asked for justice, vision, and leadership – he asked Canadians to transcend colonialism and act with honour and integrity. In words and actions, he demonstrated that, although the ADR program may have met the criteria for success from a Western, narrow legal perspective, it did not measure up to Indigenous criteria for justice and reconciliation.

On 17 February 2005, the committee also heard directly from several IRS survivors whose public testimony reinforced Chief Joseph's message, describing their own experiences both in residential schools and with the ADR program. In coming forward with their testimony, these survivors put a human face on the residential school legacy. In the recorded minutes of the meetings, Ms. Flora Merrick, an eighty-eight-year-old elder whose ADR claim award was appealed by the federal government, told the AANO Committee,

I cannot forget one painful memory. It occurred in 1932 when I was 15 years old. My father came to the Portage la Prairie residential school to tell my sister and I that our mother had died and to take us to the funeral. The principal of the school would not let us go with our father to the funeral. My little sister and I cried so much, we were taken away and locked in a dark room for about two weeks. After I was released from the dark room and allowed to be with the other residents, I tried to run away to my father and family. I was caught in the bush by teachers and taken back to the school and strapped so severely that my arms were black and blue for several weeks. After my father saw what they did to me, he would not allow me to go back to school after the school year ended. I told this story during my ADR hearing, which was held at Long Plain in July 2004. I was told that my treatment and punishment was what they called "acceptable standards of the day." I was raised in a close and loving family before I was taken away to residential school, and being strapped until I was black and blue for weeks and being locked in a dark room for two weeks, is barbaric. I was told that my experience did not fit into the rigid categories for being compensated under the ADR. However, the adjudicator, Mr. Chin, after hearing my story at my hearing, awarded me $1,500. The federal government appealed to take even this small award from me. I was willing to accept the $1,500 award, not as a fair and a just settlement, but only due to my age, health, and financial situation. I wanted some closure to my residential school experience, and I could use the money, even as small as it was. I am very angry and upset that the government would be so mean-spirited as to deny me even this small amount of compensation. I instructed my lawyer ... to withdraw me from the ADR, not to appeal, and to place me in the national class action suit once it was certified. I'm very angry and upset, not only for myself, but for all the residential school survivors.[51]

I quote Ms. Merrick at length because her testimony conveys to the reader a sense of the power of testimony and truth-telling to teach Canadians about the residential school legacy in ways that reading studies or reports simply cannot. Her testimony reveals that beneath the rhetoric of reconciliation as it was framed in the ADR program lies a dark heart of colonial violence that is still being perpetrated against Indigenous peoples, made all the more insidious because it is cloaked in a language of healing and reconciliation. When Ms. Merrick speaks to the AANO Committee, they, like the adjudicator, respond to the profound injustice that has been perpetrated, both in the original offence and in her experience with the ADR program. Regardless of whether or not the government deemed its appeal of Ms. Merrick's claim justifiable in strictly legal terms, in the court of public opinion, its actions are deemed indefensible. Her IRS claim is one of thousands that will not meet the strict criteria of compensability under tort law, yet as human beings we know instinctively that a deep injustice has occurred that must be made right.

Thus, the giving and receiving of testimony represents a powerful peda- gogical moment in which AANO Committee members were deeply moved and unsettled by the testimony they heard. For example, MP Carol Skelton said, in part, "Tuesday's committee and today's committee have been the hardest days of testimony I have sat through in this House of Commons, because I feel the last two days have shown me how much injustice has been done to each of you. From the bottom of my heart, I say how sorry I am for that."[52] MP Bernard Cleary touched on the importance of truth- telling, saying that "[t]he primary concern of elders in discussing this mat- ter is that they be offered an apology, if only to comfort them. Money is fine, but the satisfaction it gives someone when what they have been say- ing all their life is recognized as true is worth much more ... I could have sobbed like a child earlier, listening to this story, because I could feel how terribly difficult it was for the witnesses to recall memories they would rather forget, but are unable to."[53] MP Gary Lunn said that "[t]he stories we heard this morning were just horrific ... We had better act very quickly to correct this crisis and identify the problems ... Every single member on this com- mittee ... will concur about what we heard ... I will say that, based on some of the most credible testimony that I've heard in seven years as a parliamen- tarian, this process has failed miserably."[54] Finally, MP Pat Martin spoke to the need for public truth-telling and education about the residential school legacy for all parties: "The Assembly of First Nations is calling for a truth and reconciliation healing process, not only for you to tell your story and hopefully tell the world what happened, but for us too, for the general popu- lation, for Canadians to be a part of the healing process. I think I can safely say that if you could get these stories to average Canadians, you would tap into a great deal of goodwill, because no one in this room will ever forget what we've heard today."[55]

Survivors' stories – the giving of testimony that constitutes truth-telling about what happened – must necessarily be received by those who have inflicted the harms, either as individuals or collectively as a society. Here it is helpful to turn to Dominick LaCapra's work on the role of empathy in confronting historical trauma. He argues that perpetrators of wrongs must be self-critical and reflective, must recognize that empathy is essential for developing ethical relations with those whom they have harmed. What he identifies as "empathetic unsettlement," or the "working through" of his- torical trauma via an exchange of testimony, is linked to broader social and political action and change.[56]

After hearing the testimony of survivors, who delivered a strong message that the ADR program was fundamentally flawed, the AANO Committee heard a very different perspective from Deputy Prime Minister and Minister of Indian Residential Schools Resolution Canada Anne McLellan, who appeared before them on 22 February 2005. She declared that "[o]ur ADR approach is groundbreaking, a culturally based humane and holistic way to provide additional choices for former students who are seeking compensation for sexual and physical abuses." She pointed out that the government was in the process of consulting with the AFN concerning the recommendations made in its November 2004 report. She said that the government's goals "included opening pathways to healing and reconciliation." McLellan concluded by saying that "[a]ll you have heard from every witness argues in favour of approaches that are flexible and which demonstrate a willingness on the part of all parties to listen."[57] Yet both the testimony of IRS survivors who appeared before the AANO Committee and the negative response to the ADR program in First Nations communities and organizations suggest that the government was telling only a partial truth to itself, to First Nations, and to the Canadian public. What was the public perception of the controversy over the ADR program?

Media coverage provides a sense of the complex political, legal, and fiscal concerns that characterized debate on the residential school issue during this time period. In a 23 February 2005 *Toronto Globe and Mail* article, journalist Bill Curry proclaimed "McLellan under attack over native-school redress." Reporting on the AANO Committee meetings, he captured the essence of the debate played out in a convoluted mix of national non-Indigenous politics, legal complexities, and the requirement for fiscal accountability vis-à-vis the needs of IRS survivors and their call for material and symbolic justice to be done:

> Sandwiched between emotional testimony from aboriginals who say Ottawa is taking a heartless approach to compensating residential school victims, Deputy Prime Minister Anne McLellan told a Commons committee that the government's "groundbreaking" program is working well ... Opposition MPs lashed out at the minister, pointing out that previous testimony from former students and organizations such as the Canadian Bar Association, shows that the government's plan does not work and that far more is being spent on bureaucracy than on payouts ... Calling it "the most disgraceful, harmful, racist experiment ever conducted in our history," the normally subdued chief [AFN national chief Phil Fontaine], struggled to discuss the topic ... "I know what over 150,000 of my people lived through, and I resent the need to tell our heart-wrenching stories over and over again to convince you of their truth. I resent being told that Canada can't afford to

pay survivors the compensation we are owed" ... Conservative MP Jim Prentice said Ms. McLellan appears to be the only person who thinks the government's plan works. "What we have heard as a committee has moved us, appalled and shamed us" ... Other Opposition MPs offered similar comments.[58]

Clearly, the government was on the defensive, facing significant political pressure in addition to the considerable legal liability that stemmed from the large number of claims and the class action suits described above. The AANO Committee was now evaluating the program's effectiveness, and serious questions were being raised in both the House of Commons and the media about the monies allocated to a "bloated bureaucracy" versus the relatively small number of settlements actually awarded to residential school survivors. Equally important, the minister's claim that the ADR was a culturally appropriate, humane, and holistic program that would open pathways to healing and reconciliation seemed completely at odds with what was happening on the ground. This disconnect had serious implications for the future of the ADR program.

Consequently, it came as no surprise that the AANO Committee was unconvinced by McLellan's reassurances about the virtues of the ADR program. The report tabled in the House of Commons on 7 April 2005 was scathing in its condemnation. The committee recommended that sweeping changes be made. These included terminating the existing ADR program, replacing it with court-supervised and court-enforced settlements for compensation for validated claims, and establishing a national Truth and Reconciliation Commission.[59] In producing the report, the committee itself became embroiled in political wrangling as its Liberal members refused to endorse the report, and the NDP fought to have lump sum payments and an apology included. Thus, the final report represents a compromise on the part of Opposition members, who, despite their own political differences, agreed that this critical issue must be brought before the public in the House of Commons.[60] The committee relied upon the comprehensive reports submitted by the AFN and the CBA, and made clear the relative weight it assigned to the testimonies of IRS survivors vis-à-vis Minister McLellan:

> The Committee took particular note, in formulating the recommendations below, of the written and oral evidence of the former students and the representatives of former students and survivor organizations regarding their personal experiences in the residential schools and in the Indian Residential Schools Resolution Canada ADR process. The witnesses were compelling for their candour and integrity about their experiences as inmates in the residential school system and fair, frank and persuasive on matters of

public policy ... The Committee took particular note, in formulating the recommendations below, of the written and oral evidence of the Minister ... The evidence was contradictory with respect to financial and case-resolution performance numbers of the Indian Residential Schools Resolution Canada ADR process ... More disconcerting, however, the Minister's evidence was unapologetic and self-congratulatory with respect to both the underlying framework and the results of the ADR process. It disclosed her apparent disconnectedness from the experience of the survivor witnesses, for whom she has a particular duty of care and to whom she is not listening.[61]

Moreover, the report also noted that the ADR program "is strikingly disconnected from the so-called pilot projects that preceded it" and that "it is using a model of dispute resolution that ... revictimizes former students." Furthermore, it said that the application process "imposes an egregious burden of proof on the applicants," the consultation process was insufficient, the program was too exclusionary and too slow, and the compensation amounts awarded were inadequate. The committee concluded that the program was "an arbitrary administrative solution that is subject to political whim." Most importantly, "former students do not trust the process."[62] On 12 April 2005, following a heated debate the previous day, the committee's report was adopted in the House of Commons.[63] That such a strong condemnation of the ADR program was now a matter of public record put the government under increasing pressure to respond substantively to the criticisms that had been levelled. In this account of the controversy generated by the program, we see how conflicting visions of reconciliation play out in a complex politically charged environment that pits managing legal risk and implementing policy through bureaucratic practices against the relational and ethical importance of truth-telling and testimony.

On 30 May 2005, as media gathered to record the ritual, the Government of Canada and the Assembly of First Nations announced that they had reached a political agreement with regard to the residential school issue. The event was solemnized symbolically in two ways: the smoking of a peace pipe and the signing of a Political Agreement in which both parties "committed to reconciling the residential schools tragedy in a manner that respects the principles of human dignity and promotes transformative change." Furthermore, the parties "recognize[d] that the current ADR process does not fully achieve reconciliation between Canada and the former students of residential schools."[64] The government announced the appointment of the Honourable Frank Iacobucci, former justice of the Supreme Court of Canada, as the federal representative tasked with negotiating with all the parties. He was to make recommendations to Cabinet by 31 March 2006 on "a settlement package that will address a redress payment for all former students ... a truth and reconciliation process, community based healing, commemoration, an appropriate ADR process that will address serious abuse, as well as legal fees."[65] Before exploring the public response more closely, I note here that the Political Agreement began several months of intense negotiations. On 23 November 2005, an agreement-in-principle was reached, and finally, on 10 May 2006, the Indian Residential Schools Settlement Agreement was announced. Given the legal and political complexities involved, Mr. Justice Iacobucci's appointment was perhaps predictable, as was the fact that the announcement about the Political Agreement met with mixed response in the media. It is important to note that some coverage presented a sympathetic view, profiling IRS survivors' stories. However, some was aimed squarely at those non-Indigenous people, members of the Canadian public, who are unsympathetic, even hostile towards Indigenous peoples. Two articles from the 31 May 2005 *National Post* will suffice. On that day, the paper's front-page headline read, "Billions for Natives"; in the accompanying story, reporter Cristin Schmitz observed that, "after a ceremony at the national press theatre [that] began with an aboriginal elder passing around a 'reconciliation pipe' ... Mr. Fontaine extolled it as a historic and healing moment." In "A How-to on Getting Liberal Money," editorialist Don Martin described how "a full retreat on settlement policy and a compensation resolution with a potentially massive price tag were rolled out yesterday to the triumphant smoking of a peace pipe for the cameras."[66] The bracketing of Indigenous legal traditions, both literally, as in "reconciliation pipe," and figuratively, by describing the smoking of the peace pipe in front of the cameras as "triumphant," suggests, as Acorn observes, that a deeply ingrained misrecognition and disrespect for Indigenous peoples' legal traditions and protocols is deemed acceptable, even justifiable to many Canadians. If the response of the AANO Committee members to the testimonies of IRS survivors represents a pedagogical moment of truth-telling, the media coverage indicates that we are a very long way from achieving any meaningful reconciliation. But what if we were to reframe reconciliation as an encounter conducted according to Indigenous legal traditions, meeting Indigenous criteria for making restitution and apology? In the remainder of this discussion, I return to the Gitxsan Feast Hall.

The Feast Hall as Paradox

From Western Law to Gitxsan Law: Preparing for the Feast

Just as it is in the courthouse, there is also protocol in the Feast Hall – everyone has their place and time to speak. Just as the judge has a gavel, we have a talking stick. It is or would be a most favourable place to deal with whatever has happened ... There isn't anything saying that both systems cannot be partnered ... In the Feast Hall, the wrong would be addressed. People and/or family members are witness to the steps taken when payment has been made to the persons harmed, along with an apology ... In this form, it gives both parties opportunity to heal or at least [to] open the door.[67]

In the words above, Gitxsan elder Matilda Daniels, who was the Hazelton Apology Feast coordinator, explains how the practices and protocols of the feast hall are well suited to the pedagogical work of reconciliation. The story of the Hazelton Apology Feast began as IRS survivors, elders, chiefs, and government and church officials planned and prepared for the potlatch feast. In doing so, we moved from Western law to Gitxsan law. The Gitxsan's decision to hold the feast constitutes what John Paul Lederach defines as an act of moral imagination. By this he means "the capacity to imagine and generate constructive responses and initiatives that, while rooted in the day-to-day challenges of violent settings, transcend and ultimately break those destructive patterns and cycles."[68] In a similar vein, Napoleon describes how reconciliation might require new applications of old laws and emphasizes the importance for the Gitxsan of working within their own legal systems:

Many Gitxsan laws have been violated by both Gitxsan and non-Gitxsan, and this contributes to a cultural paralysis ... reconciliation here would mean either an explicit acknowledgment of, and agreement to, the changes in Gitxsan law to fit contemporary circumstances, or application of Gitxsan laws to deal with transgressions ... It would be difficult to force participation by the transgressor, but nonetheless, the process of dealing with the transgression through the Gitxsan system, even without the transgressing parties, would be healthy and constructive for the Gitxsan.[69]

Within the context of the Hazelton feast, the Gitxsan connect the cultural loss experienced by IRS survivors to a powerful reclaiming of culture, family, community, and nation, bringing the transgressors – Canada and the United Church – into the feast hall, not as guests but as hosts with very particular responsibilities to fulfill. This had never been done before. There is a rich historical irony in the fact that the very institutions responsible for banning the potlatch came full circle to embrace it, making restitution and apology according to Gitxsan law – a fitting symbolic act that speaks to finely honed Gitxsan diplomatic skills. In writing about the feast, I do not attempt to provide an in-depth analysis of Gitxsan potlatch law or feast protocols. To do so would be inappropriate. Rather, I write about my own experience, my empathetic unsettling, as one of the hosts. Within this context, I note that legal scholar Natalie Oman describes the feast hall as a place where international diplomatic relations are forged; legitimized and recorded in the oral history of the potlatch, "[b]y exposing witnesses to diverse perspectives on the same incidents, this telling is designed to inspire reflection ... on the multiplicity of their truths."[70] Writing in 1994 from a Gitxsan perspective, Mas Gak (Don Ryan) explains that "eagle down is used ritually in our system of conflict resolution and mediation. Restitution and compensation are key features in any ceremony in which eagle down is used ... [we] have yet to use eagle down in [our] dealings with the Crown in Canada."[71] In the pedagogical space of the feast hall, truth-telling and testimonies are exchanged, and acts of wrongdoing are made right through highly symbolic acts of restitution and apology that are embedded in the laws and protocols of the potlatch.

In giving the government and church responsibilities as hosts, the Gitxsan use their legal system to address the violent legacy of residential schools. They seek a way to reintegrate into Gitxsan society those who have been lost. They break down old ways of interacting so that all who are involved in the feast take on a multiplicity of roles and responsibilities. For the representatives of perpetrator institutions – government and church – this means being willing to enter the feast hall as hosts in order to make amends according to Gitxsan law. Acknowledging that unequal power relations are inevitable in colonial relations, the parties took concrete steps to ensure that power and control shifted from Western hands to Gitxsan hands. The Gitxsan set the mandate for the feast, assigned responsibilities, and determined how the process would unfold. This required innovation because, of course, Canada and the church have no legitimacy, no standing, in the feast hall, so some of the usual protocols could not be followed. As Gitxsan and non-Gitxsan worked together, our respective roles became less defined by our institutional identities. We began to see one another through new eyes as an intercultural team with a collective responsibility to ensure that the feast was conducted properly – transforming ourselves, each other, and our relationship in the process. As we moved from Western law to Gitxsan law, our previous working relationships altered: the IRS survivors were empowered, the broader community became involved as elders and chiefs guided the feast preparations, government and church representatives learned to follow, not lead, and the feast coordinator worked as a liaison to ensure the whole team stayed on track.

In all of the preparations leading up to the feast, and in the feast hall itself, I learned experientially by listening, watching, and doing. This at times was challenging, scary, mystifying, and frustrating as I felt completely out of my depth – a humbling experience that I would now describe as deeply unsettling. I had to step outside my usual comfort zone, take off my cultural blinders, surrender a need to control, and place my trust in the IRS survivors, elders, and chiefs with whom I worked in an environment and language that was foreign to me. But my experience was by no means a negative one; it was also exciting to see the feast take shape. As we navigated the labyrinth of often conflicting requirements of Gitxsan, government, and church, maintaining good humour and the ability to laugh was essential. At other times, our meetings were very emotionally moving as, together, we shared our feelings, our fears, and our hopes for the day of the feast. In some ways it is difficult for me to articulate all that I learned in this process – much of it is intangible. But the shift in our relationship was striking. In thinking about how to work within an ethics of recognition and respect, I draw on Lederach's idea that in working in spaces of reconciliation, one must focus less on learning skills and techniques, and more on developing "qualities of process and practice ... [to] support the complex challenge of authentic reconciliation," or what he calls "relational reconciliation."[72] Drawing on this, I summarize my understanding of the principles and practices that guided the Hazelton team as we prepared for the feast:

- Relationship- and trust-building: Being consistent, transparent, and accountable. Keeping our commitments, communicating openly and quickly when problems arose, and problem-solving together to resolve them. Willingness to "roll up our sleeves and pitch in" at the community level to do a variety of tasks that were necessary.
- Authenticity: Being genuinely and deeply committed to the group and to the feast. Willingness to work and learn together with respect, caring, and good humour.
- Humility: For non-Gitxsan, learning to listen, being open to new ways of doing things, and not assuming that we already knew the answers. Being honest with the group and sharing our feelings (fear, anxiety, sadness, confusion, excitement). Thinking creatively, reflecting on our experience, and staying flexible.
- Engaging community: In moving from Western law to Gitxsan law, the larger community became involved as the circle expanded to include elders and chiefs, families, and witnesses in the feast hall. Approximately 450 people attended the feast.

Teachings of the Gitxsan Feast Hall

The lessons learned came when both the church and government recognized that we do have a system and that it is ours to use and has worked wonders for one's wellness, especially those who had survived residential school ... It would take "generations" before the wrong done to the people involved could be restored. We can't just put a bandage on it and hope that it would go away. We have to work together to take responsibility for everyone's well being – to take that step to put closure to such an ordeal and to open another door to a nation's wellness ... acknowledgment; acceptance; responsibility; harmony.[73]

Here, reflecting on what we might learn from the Hazelton Apology Feast, Gitxsan elder Matilda Daniels identifies how recognition and respect are crucial to the truth-telling work of reconciliation. On 20 March 2004, the Gitxsan Feast Hall was a place of reconciliation – an intercultural encounter of truth-telling and testimony in which restitution and apology were made according to the criteria of Gitxsan law. In the feast hall, there is no token use of ceremony; rather, it is embedded in, and integral to, the practise of Indigenous legal traditions. Senior officials from Canada and the United Church offered apologies to which simgigyat gave formal responses. Here I note that Canada's failure to issue a formal apology from the prime minister to all Indigenous peoples in Canada is highly problematic. Such an apology, as Chief Joseph pointed out in the AANO Committee hearings, would constitute an important symbolic act of recognition and respect. Accordingly, many Indigenous people say that apologies extended by lesser officials are inadequate substitutions.[74] Writing in the *United Church Observer* in June 2004, Keith Howard, who was one of the witnesses at the Hazelton feast, noted that the apologies were not necessarily accepted wholeheartedly and that "[w]ithin the Gitanmaxx feast hall there remains a sense of wait-and-see – for the church, Canada and the survivors. Maybe if our lives reflect our words, forgiveness might be offered."[75] In other words, our actions will speak louder than our words. Many of the simgigyat who responded to the apologies delivered by former United Church moderator Marion Best and, on behalf of Canada, by director-general of IRSRC Shawn Tupper, said as much. The apologies may not have been spoken in Parliament as part of the formal record, but in Gitxsan territory, they are evaluated according to Indigenous criteria for making restitution and apology. They become part of the Gitxsan oral history, spoken in the feast hall, accepted or rejected by the simgigyat assembled there, and duly witnessed by all those who attended.

The feast hall taught me that knowing our history (and its injustices) is not simply about the intellectual and interpretive study of the past – the factual or forensic truth through which we gain *knowledge* about our sociopolitical world. Rather, history, within the context of Indigenous-Canadian relations, must be a *critical pedagogical practice* – an experiential tool that we use to engage in deep dialogue about historical injustices through acts of truth-telling and witnessing, and the use of ceremony and symbolic ritual.[76] Writing about the relationship between history and trauma, LaCapra tells

us that the power of testimony in truth-telling goes far beyond a mere reci-
tation of narrative facts as history. Rather, it helps to "work through post-
traumatic symptoms in the present in a manner that opens up possible
futures ... [B]y bearing witness and giving testimony, narrative may help
performatively to create openings ... that did not exist before."[77] Story, ceremony, symbol, and ritual engage all of our senses powerfully, moving us in
ways we do not fully understand. This is why the experiential engagement
– the pedagogical practise of Indigenous legal traditions – is critical to reconciliation. It opens up intercultural possibilities for what Roger Simon calls
"an ethical learning that impels us into a confrontation and 'reckoning' not
only with the stories of the past but also with ourselves as we *are* (historically, existentially, ethically) in the present."[78] In this way, reconciliation as a
place of encounter links past, present, and future – a delicate chain of testimony and witnessing that forges new bonds of mutual recognition and
respect.

In the feast hall that day, many people spoke out in righteous anger about
the injustices that had been done – to them, to their families, to their communities, and their nation. This too is testimony. In an act of remembrance
and honouring, the names of all the Gitxsan children who had attended
the Edmonton Indian Residential School and who had since died were read
out. It was a long list, marked solemnly by a drumbeat after each name –
testament to how many lives, now lost to their families and nation, were
changed irrevocably by those who in their cultural arrogance thought that
their ways were better. This truth-telling spoke to me as a non-Indigenous
person, a Canadian who must come to terms with my own identity and history as colonizer. As I stood in the feast hall to receive these living testimonies, etched in the human faces of a history that we Canadians have hidden
so well from ourselves – denial was simply not possible. This is the deep
unsettling of a dominant culture history that must occur if non-Indigenous
people are to move from a culture of denial to an ethics of authentic recognition and respect of the Indigenous peoples whose lands they now share.
Without this profound disturbing of a colonial status quo, reconciliation
will remain fundamentally flawed. At times that evening, I felt overwhelmed
by the damage we have wrought upon Indigenous peoples. As I remembered the stories of each of the men and women who came forward to be
welcomed home, I thought about the legacy of pain and loss that began for
them when, as children, they were taken from their homes to the residential school. Yet I also knew that their stories are powerful testaments to
resilience, dignity, and quiet courage – the individual and collective strength
of the Gitxsan people. As I fulfilled my responsibilities as one of the hosts –
distributing the feast soup, gifting, offering xgweekxw (money) as payment
to the guests for witnessing the feast – in all of these things I was taught by

Gitxsan men and women who guided me with an unfailing spirit of generosity and kindness.[79] They were at once victims, IRS survivors, and proud people of the Gitxsan Nation. I was at once representative of a perpetrator nation, host, and a willing non-Indigenous learner.

This is the true pedagogical potential of reconciliation as encounter – victims are empowered, perpetrators are humbled. Reflecting back, I now understand the paradoxical richness of the feast hall. It is where we discovered the full complexity of our multiple identities and our shared humanity. It is where, for a brief moment in time, all those present could envision what it might be like if we could nurture and grow this small seed of trust, recognition, and respect that was planted there. One of the simgigyat who formally responded to the apologies reminded us that although this feast was a good thing, it was only a beginning. Many more Gitxsan are waiting for their truths to be heard, for moral justice to be done – and as Chief Robert Joseph said – for reconciliation to begin between us. The Gitxsan Feast Hall is one of many places of public memory where Indigenous legal traditions have been practised since time immemorial. My experience in this place of encounter taught me that establishing new relationships embedded in mutual recognition and respect must necessarily be done in ways that create substantive space for Indigenous legal traditions. It taught me the limitations of relying on Western ADR models to address the history of violence and injustice that is still alive in Canada today. It taught me that my responsibility as host did not end on the day of the feast but continues as I repolish the chain of testimony, truth-telling, and witnessing that was forged that day. It taught me that the challenge for Canadians is to listen deeply and to simply acknowledge with humility that Western knowledge is but *one* way – not *the* way of knowing the world. Our responsibility as non-Indigenous people to the Indigenous peoples of this land, to "those who arrive facing us; who ... draw near, demanding – not just apology, memorialization, and reparation – but something of our time, energy, and thought," requires nothing less of us.[80] As Ms. Daniels tells us, the teachings of the Gitxsan Feast Hall might open a door to a nation's well-being. And so, the story of the Hazelton Apology Feast and the principled teachings that it holds for us to fulfill both the spirit and intent of the TRC's work, both ends and begins here.

Acknowledgments

I dedicate this essay to the IRS survivors of the Edmonton Indian Residential School who participated in the Hazelton ADR pilot project and to the people of the Gitxsan Nation. In my capacity as resolution manager, IRSRC, I was deeply honoured to work in partnership with IRS survivors, their advisory group, elders, simgigyat, and the feast coordinator Matilda Daniels, as well as my colleagues Deanna Sitter, resolution manager, IRSRC, Robert Hay, senior policy and strategic analyst, IRSRC, and Brian Thorpe, senior advisor, Residential

Schools Steering Committee, United Church of Canada. I thank the Law Commission of Canada for providing research funding for this study through its Legal Dimensions Initiative, and Frederica Wilson, senior research officer, for her editorial advice. I extend special thanks to Dr. Maggie Hodgson, (Carrier) special advisor, IRSRC, who attended the feast, and to my colleague Leigh Ogston. Their incisive comments on earlier drafts of this chapter strengthened it significantly.

The research in this chapter is based on my doctoral dissertation: see especially "An Apology Feast in Hazelton: A Settler's 'Unsettling' Experience," in Paulette Regan, "Unsettling the Settler Within: Canada's Peacemaker Myth, Reconciliation, and Transformative Pathways to Decolonization" (PhD diss., University of Victoria, 2006), chap. 5. The views expressed herein are solely those of the author and do not necessarily represent the opinions of the Hazelton ADR pilot project participants, the Gitxsan Nation, the Government of Canada, Indian Residential Schools Resolution Canada, or the United Church of Canada. I want to acknowledge the contribution of Matilda Daniels, both in her capacity as the Hazelton feast coordinator and as co-presenter of "An Apology Feast in Hazelton" (draft paper presented at the Canadian Association of Law Teachers [CALT] annual conference, Law's Paradoxes, University of British Columbia, Vancouver, BC, 22-24 June 2005).

Notes

1 Gitxsan Chiefs' Office, "Apology to Gitxsan for IRS Internment," news release, 18 March 2004, http://tools.bcweb.net/gitxsan/news.shtml?x=3533&cmd{67}=x-66-3533.
2 The Hazelton ADR pilot project was one of twelve projects that were established across Canada to resolve IRS claims using the philosophy and principles of alternative dispute resolution, or ADR. It is important to distinguish between the ADR pilot projects, which were established prior to the ADR program that was launched by Indian Residential Schools Resolution Canada (hereafter IRSRC) in November 2003.
3 Here I draw on the metaphor of polishing the Iroquois Covenant Chain. The Iroquois treaty alliances during the Encounter era, known as the Covenant Chain, were constantly renewed, or polished – "a chain of friendship ... too strong ever to be broken, and polished and brightened so pure as never to rust." Mohawk speaker, quoted in Robert A. Williams Jr., *Linking Arms Together: American Indian Treaty Visions of Law and Peace, 1600-1800* (New York: Oxford University Press, 1997), 121. On remembrance as an ethical obligation, see Roger Simon and Claudia Eppert, "Remembering Obligation: Witnessing Testimonies of Historical Trauma," in Roger Simon, *The Touch of the Past: Remembrance, Learning, and Ethics* (New York: Palgrave Macmillan, 2005), 51.
4 I refer to both Western and Indigenous critical theory and pedagogy as anti-oppressive, experiential teaching/learning that links critical reflection, dialogue, and social action (praxis) to transform social relations and historical consciousness. Indigenous critical pedagogical theory and practice as a "method of learning is really one of transformation, and it is experiential, observational, and practical." Taiaiake Alfred, *Wasase: Indigenous Pathways of Action and Freedom* (Peterborough, ON: Broadview Press, 2005), 149. These pedagogical practices are rooted in the stories, ceremonies, and symbolic rituals – the oral and legal traditions of Indigenous peoples across what is now North America. See also Vine Deloria Jr. and Daniel R. Wildcat, *Power and Place: Indian Education in America* (Golden: Fulcrum Resources, 2001), 35-36. On critical pedagogical practices in public deliberative spaces, see Daniel Schugurensky, "Transformative Learning and Transformative Politics: The Pedagogical Dimension of Participatory Democracy and Social Action," in Edmund V. O'Sullivan, Amish Morrell, and Mary Ann O'Connor, eds., *Expanding the Boundaries of Transformative Learning: Essays on Theory and Praxis* (New York: Palgrave, 2002), 59-76.
5 Indian Residential Schools Settlement Agreement, Schedule "N" *Mandate for the Truth and Reconciliation Commission,* 1, 2. The Settlement Agreement and supporting documentation are available online at Indian Residential Schools Resolution Canada, http://www.irsr-rqpi.gc.ca/english/news_10_05_06.html.
6 Schedule "N" 1, 5.
7 I define "misrecognize" as the systemic denial of Indigenous oral histories, cultures, and knowledge systems, including their governance and legal traditions, in Canada's national history and in the various conflict resolution and negotiation processes that are currently

in place. This "misrecognition" is rooted in non-Indigenous attitudes of cultural superior-ity, racism, and moral indifference towards Indigenous peoples. I discuss the hidden his-tory of Indigenous diplomacy and peacemaking in my dissertation: see "Benevolent Peacemakers/Indigenous Diplomats: Myth, Ritual and History," in Paulette Regan, "Unset-tling the Settler Within: Canada's Peacemaker Myth, Reconciliation, and Transformative Pathways to Decolonization" (PhD diss., University of Victoria, 2006), chap. 3.

8   Roger Simon, "The Pedagogy of Remembrance and the Counter-Commemoration of the Columbus Quincentenary," in Simon, *supra* note 3. Here Simon identifies "insurgent and transformative forms of remembrance" as "a practice of pedagogy [that] requires the recog-nition that there are alternative and conflicting ways of constituting [historical memory's] lessons, each with a distinct pedagogical and political character" (16). He links the act of historical remembering, and the reclaiming of Indigenous histories, to the struggles for political recognition and self-determination. On breaking the silence with regard to the residential school legacy, see Dian Lynn Million, "Telling Secrets: Sex, Power and Narrative in the Rearticulation of Canadian Residential School Histories" (PhD diss., University of Berkeley, 2004).

9   Regan, *supra* note 7, "History Is Alive: Perpetrator Denial, Indigenous Testimonies, Trauma and Truth-telling," chap. 5. On national identity, perpetrator guilt, and denial, see Bernhard Giesen, "The Trauma of Perpetrators: The Holocaust as the Traumatic Reference of German National Identity," in Jeffrey C. Alexander et al., eds., *Cultural Trauma and Collective Identity* (Berkeley: University of California Press, 2004), 112-54.

10 Roger Epp, "We Are All Treaty People: History, Reconciliation and the 'Settler Problem,'" in Carol A.L. Prager and Trudy Govier, eds., *Dilemmas of Reconciliation: Cases and Concepts* (Waterloo: Wilfrid Laurier University Press, 2003), 228.

11 John Borrows, *Recovering Canada: The Resurgence of Indigenous Law* (Toronto: University of Toronto Press, 2002). Borrows explains that the principles and practice of Indigenous law "are enunciated in the rich stories, ceremonies, and traditions within First Nations ... [which] serve as sources of normative authority in dispute resolution" (13).

12 Million, *supra* note 8 at 155.

13 It is beyond the scope of this chapter to provide a comprehensive history of Indian residen-tial schools in Canada, but the literature is extensive. See John S. Milloy, *"A National Crime": The Canadian Government and the Residential School System, 1879-1986* (Winnipeg: Univer-sity of Manitoba Press, 2001); J.R. Miller, *Shingwauk's Vision: A History of Native Residential Schools* (Toronto: University of Toronto Press, 1996); Canada, Royal Commission on Ab-original Peoples, *Report of the Royal Commission on Aboriginal Peoples*, vol. 1, *Looking For-ward, Looking Back* (Ottawa: Canada Communications Group, 1996), chap. 10; Elizabeth Furniss, *Victims of Benevolence: The Dark Legacy of the Williams Lake Residential School* (Van-couver: Arsenal Pulp Press, 1992); Celia Haig-Brown, *Resistance and Renewal: Surviving the Indian Residential School* (Vancouver: Arsenal Pulp Press, 1988).

14 Jennifer J. Llewellyn, "Dealing with the Legacy of Native Residential School Abuse in Can-ada: Litigation, ADR, and Restorative Justice," *University of Toronto Law Journal* 52 (2002): 253-300. Llewellyn explains the impacts of the total institution: "As total institutions, Native residential schools imposed conditions of disconnection, degradation, and power-lessness on the students. The nature of these institutions permitted or even encouraged the abuse that often marked the children's experiences. Sexual abuse by caregivers and admin-istrators was rampant in the schools. So, too, were other forms of physical abuse, some-times rising to life-threatening levels ... Even students who did not suffer sexual or physical abuse were victims of subtler, institutionalized forms of abuse. It could be argued that every residential school student was subjected to abuse of one form or another ... in the form of removal from their families, isolation from their communities, and the destruc-tion of their culture, language and spirituality ... chronic underfunding left children per-petually hungry, malnourished, inadequately clothed, and forced into manual labour to support the daily costs of running the institutions" (257-58).

15 *Report of the Royal Commission on Aboriginal Peoples, supra* note 13.

16 Canada, Indian Affairs and Northern Development, *Gathering Strength: Canada's Aboriginal Action Plan* (Ottawa: Indian Affairs and Northern Development, 1998). On 23 February 2005, Canada announced additional funding of $40 million to enable the foundation to

continue financing community projects. Aboriginal Healing Foundation, "The Aboriginal Healing Foundation Welcomes Government's Announcement of Additional Funding," press release, 23 February 2005.

17 The complete text is available at Indian and Northern Affairs Canada, "Statement of Reconciliation," 1998, http://www.ainc-inac.gc.ca/gs/rec_e.html.

18 Matt James, "Wrestling with the Past: Apologies, Quasi-apologies, and Non-apologies in Canada," in Mark Gibney, Rhoda Howard-Hassmann, Jean-Marc Coicaud, and Niklaus Steiner, eds., *The Age of Apology: The West Faces Its Own Past* (Tokyo: United Nations University Press, forthcoming in 2007).

19 Canada, Indian Affairs and Northern Development, *Reconciliation and Healing: Alternative Resolution Strategies for Dealing with Residential School Claims* (Ottawa: Department of Indian Affairs and Northern Development, 2000).

20 For a full description of the National Resolution Framework, including the ADR program, see IRSRC, "Resolution Framework and ADR," 2003, http://www.irsr-rqpi.gc.ca/english/dispute_resolution_resolution_framework.html.

21 *Ibid.* For IRSRC statistics, see http://www.irsr-rqpi.gc.ca/english/statistics/html.

22 Based on the author's notes from the conference. For a more detailed analysis of the controversy over Canada's ADR program, see Regan, *supra* note 7, "Indian Residential Schools: Reconciliation as Contemporary Colonial Shapeshifting," chap. 4.

23 Alfred, *supra* note 4 at 137-38. Alfred defines Onkwehonwe as "the First Peoples of North America" (288).

24 Elazar Barkan, *The Guilt of Nations: Restitution and Negotiating Historical Injustice* (Baltimore and London: Johns Hopkins University Press, 2000), xvii-xviii. John Torpey calls this phenomenon of political negotiation over past injustices "reparations politics" and links their emergence to the "spread of human rights ideas ... that has fueled the sense that ... wrongs, no matter how acceptable they may have been deemed at the time they were committed, may now be said to have been illegitimate and must be compensated or redressed accordingly." John Torpey, "Introduction: Politics and the Past," in John Torpey, ed., *Politics and the Past: On Repairing Historical Injustices* (Boulder: Rowman and Littlefield, 2003), 4.

25 The literature on historical injustice, reconciliation, and peacebuilding is extensive. See, for example, Barkan, *ibid.;* Torpey, *ibid.;* John Paul Lederach, *Building Peace: Sustainable Reconciliation in Divided Societies* (Washington, DC: United States Institute of Peace Press, 1997); Carol A.L. Prager and Trudy Govier, eds., *Dilemmas of Reconciliation: Cases and Concepts* (Waterloo: Wilfrid Laurier University Press, 2003).

26 Val Napoleon, "Who Gets to Say What Happened? Reconciliation Issues for the Gitxsan," in Catherine Bell and David Kahane, eds., *Intercultural Dispute Resolution in Aboriginal Contexts* (Vancouver: UBC Press, 2002), 176, 184.

27 Annalise Acorn, *Compulsory Compassion: A Critique of Restorative Justice* (Vancouver: UBC Press, 2004), 58-59.

28 Barkan, *supra* note 24 at 345; Eric K. Yamamoto, *Interracial Justice: Conflict and Reconciliation in Post-civil Rights America* (New York: New York University Press, 1999), 11.

29 William Bradford, "With a Very Great Blame on Our Hearts: Reparations, Reconciliation, and an American Indian Plea for Peace with Justice," *American Indian Law Review* 27 (2002-3): 163-69, 72-75.

30 A detailed discussion of the Aboriginal law that now exists with regard to reconciling Aboriginal title and rights with the Crown is beyond the scope of this chapter, but see *Delgamuukw v. British Columbia,* [1997] 3 S.C.R. 1010; on the duty to consult with First Nations, see *Haida Nation v. British Columbia (Minister of Forests),* [2004] 3 S.C.R. 511.

31 On the importance of reconciliation as key to Canadian Aboriginal policy, see Canada, Indian and Northern Affairs Canada, "Renewal of Policies and Processes for Addressing Aboriginal and Treaty Rights: Federal Background Paper for the Negotiations Sectoral Roundtable" (paper presented at Canada-Aboriginal Peoples Roundtable, Negotiations Sectoral Follow-up Session, Ottawa, 12-13 January 2005), 3-4, http://www.aboriginalroundtable.ca/sect/ngot/bckpr/GOC_BgPaper_.pdf.

32 *Supra* note 11 at 57.

33 Marie Battiste and James (Sákéj) Youngblood Henderson, *Protecting Indigenous Knowledge and Heritage: A Global Challenge* (Saskatoon: Purich Publishing, 2000), 213. Under s. 35 of the *Constitution Act, 1982*, "The existing aboriginal and treaty rights of the Aboriginal peoples of Canada are hereby recognized and affirmed." Under s. 25 of the *Canadian Charter of Rights and Freedoms*, these rights are protected. Thus, Battiste and Henderson point out, "the Constitution of Canada explicitly protects Indigenous knowledge from the secular and religious rights and freedoms of individuals and from the laws of their elected governments. Under the rule of law, these sections settle public policy debate around these issues and create a legal shield around Aboriginal rights" (*ibid.*, 212).

34 Canada, Canadian Heritage, Task Force on Aboriginal Languages and Cultures, *Towards a New Beginning: A Foundational Report for a Strategy to Revitalize First Nations, Inuit and Metis Languages and Cultures* (Ottawa: Canadian Heritage, 2005), 81.

35 *Supra* note 5.

36 Wayne Warry, *Unfinished Dreams: Community Healing and the Reality of Aboriginal Self-Government* (Toronto: University of Toronto Press, 1998), 221-22. For an example of the integration of Blackfoot legal traditions in a community health context, see Reg Crowshoe and Sybille Manneschmidt, *Akak'stiman: A Blackfoot Framework for Decision-Making and Mediation Processes* (Calgary: University of Calgary Press, 2002).

37 IRSRC, "New Dispute Resolution Process Launched for Abuse Claims at Indian Residential Schools," news release, 6 November 2003, http://www.irsr-rqpi.gc.ca/english/news_06_11_03.html.

38 For details, see the studies cited *supra* note 4. See also Elmer Ghostkeeper, "Weche Teachings: Aboriginal Wisdom and Dispute Resolution," in Bell and Kahane, *supra* note 26 at 161-75.

39 Summarized from the Final Report of the Truth and Reconciliation Commission. Simon Fisher et al., *Working with Conflict: Skills and Strategies for Action* (London: Zed Books, 2000), 133.

40 Although claimants "tell their stories" in the ADR process, their evidence, both written and oral, is evaluated based on the narrow criteria of what is compensable according to tort law. Their narrative, social, and restorative truths are thus circumscribed by the limitations of the ADR program.

41 Assembly of First Nations, "Assembly of First Nations Report on Canada's Dispute Resolution Plan to Compensate for Abuses in Indian Residential Schools," November 2004, 14, http://www.afn.ca/Residential%20Schools%20Report.pdf.

42 Canadian Bar Association, "The Logical Next Step: Reconciliation Payments for All Residential School Survivors," February 2005, 16, http://www.cba.org/CBA/Sections/pdf/residential.pdf.

43 *Supra* note 14 at 288-90. On residential schools and the importance of reconciliation, community initiatives, and redress, see Law Commission of Canada, *Restoring Dignity: Responding to Child Abuse in Canadian Institutions* (Ottawa: Minister of Public Works and Government Services, 2000), 51-67, 267-343. On restorative justice within a broader reconciliation framework such as the one used in South Africa's Truth and Reconciliation process, see Jennifer J. Llewellyn and R. Howse, *Restorative Justice – A Conceptual Framework* (Ottawa: Law Commission of Canada, 1998).

44 *Supra* note 14 at 290-92.

45 The Aboriginal Justice Strategy provides funding for community sentencing circles, justices of the peace, and tribal courts. Department of Justice, "The Aboriginal Justice Strategy," 2005, http://canada.justice.gc.ca/en/ps/ajln/strategy.html. But see Jessie Sutherland, "Colonialism, Crime, and Dispute Resolution: A Critical Analysis of Canada's Aboriginal Justice Strategy 2002," http://www.mediate.com/articles/sutherlandJ.cfm. On restorative justice within Aboriginal contexts, see Kay Pranis, Barry Stuart, and Mark Wedge, *Peacemaking Circles: From Crime to Community* (St. Paul: Living Justice Press, 2003), and Rupert Ross, *Returning to the Teachings: Exploring Aboriginal Justice* (Toronto: Penguin Books Canada, 1996).

46 *Supra* note 42 at 20.

47   *Cloud v. Canada (Attorney General)* (2004), 274 D.L.R. (4th) 667 (C.A.), Reasons for Judgment at 18.
48   *Ibid.*, 23. The federal government sought leave to appeal to the Supreme Court of Canada, which was denied on 12 May 2005.
49   Canada, *House of Commons Debates* (9 February 2005), 1915 (Hon. Jim Prentice), http://www.parl.gc.ca/38/1/parlbus/chambus/house/debates/053_2005-02-09/HAN053-E.html.
50   Canada, House of Commons Standing Committee on Aboriginal Affairs and Northern Development, Evidence, 38th Parliament, 1st Session (15 February 2005), http://www.parl.gc.ca/infocomdoc/38/1/AANO/Meetings/Evidence/Int-1128319.
51   Canada, House of Commons Standing Committee on Aboriginal Affairs and Northern Development, Evidence, 38th Parliament, 1st Session (17 February 2005), http://cmte.parl.gc.ca/Content/HOC/committee/381/aano/evidence/ev1648068/aanoev19-e.htm#Int-1137136. I quote Ms. Merrick's testimony as a parliamentary document. As such, it is part of the public record.
52   *Ibid.*
53   *Ibid.*
54   *Ibid.*
55   *Ibid.*
56   Dominick LaCapra, *History in Transit: Experience, Identity, Critical Theory* (Ithaca: Cornell University Press, 2004), 135-37. On the importance of developing critical pedagogical tools for working through uncomfortable thoughts and emotions, see Megan Boler and Michalinos Zembylas, "Discomforting Truths: The Emotional Terrain of Understanding Difference," in Peter P. Trifonas, ed., *Pedagogies of Difference: Rethinking Education for Social Change* (New York: RoutledgeFalmer, 2003), 110-36.
57   *Supra* note 51 (22 February 2005), http://cmte.parl.gc.ca/cmte/CommitteePublication.aspx?SourceId=126503&Lang=1&PARLSES=381&JNT=0&COM=8972.
58   Bill Curry, "McLellan under Attack over Native-School Redress," *Toronto Globe and Mail,* 23 February 2005, A11. Other examples of media coverage include James Travers, "Indian Abuse Claims Turning into Fiasco," *Toronto Sun,* 17 February 2005; Paul Samyn, "School Abuse Delays: Lashed Aboriginals Suffering, Fontaine Tells MPs," *Winnipeg Free Press,* 23 February 2005; Cristin Schmitz, "Government Takes Heat for Inaction over Abuse Claims," *National Post,* 23 February 2005.
59   Canada, House of Commons Standing Committee on Aboriginal Affairs and Northern Development, *Fourth Report. Study on the Effectiveness of the Government Alternative Dispute Resolution Process for the Resolution of Indian Residential School Claims* (Ottawa: House of Commons Standing Committee on Aboriginal Affairs and Northern Development, 2005), http://cmte.parl.gc.ca/cmte/CommitteePublication.aspx?SourceId=107649.
60   *Supra* note 51 (24 March 2005), http://cmte.parl.gc.ca/cmte/CommitteePublication.aspx?SourceId=126515&Lang=1&PARLSES=381&JNT=0&COM=8972l.
61   *Supra* note 59.
62   *Ibid.*
63   For the debate, see Canada, *House of Commons Debates,* 38th Parliament, 1st Session, *Edited Hansard,* 079 (11 April 2005), http://www2.parl.gc.ca/HousePublications/Publication.aspx?Language=E&Mode=1&Parl=38&Ses=1&DocId=1751304#Int-1214189.
64   Canada, Indian Residential Schools Resolution Canada, "Political Agreement," 30 May 2005, http://www.irsr-rqpi.gc.ca/english/news_30_05_05b.html.
65   *Ibid.*
66   For an example of positive coverage, see Jason von Rassel, "Local Natives Recall Pain of Residential Schooling: Compensation Agreement 'Huge' Decision," *Toronto Sun,* 31 May 2005. For the *Post,* see Cristin Schmitz, "Billions for Natives," *National Post,* 31 May 2005, A1, and Don Martin, "A How-to on Getting Liberal Money," *National Post,* 31 May 2005, A6.
67   Matilda Daniels, personal communication, 14 May 2005.
68   John Paul Lederach, *The Moral Imagination: The Art and Soul of Building Peace* (New York: Oxford University Press, 2005), 182.
69   *Supra* note 26 at 188-89.

70 Natalie Oman, "Paths to Intercultural Understanding: Feasting, Shared Horizons, and Unforced Consensus," in Bell and Kahane, *supra* note 26 at 83.
71 Mas Gak (Don Ryan), foreword to *Eagle Down Is Our Law: Witsuwit'en Law, Feasts and Land Claims*, by Antonia Mills (Vancouver: UBC Press, 1994), xi.
72 John Paul Lederach, "Five Qualities of Practice in Support of Reconciliation Processes," in R.G. Helmick and R.L. Petersen, eds., *Forgiveness and Reconciliation: Religion, Public Policy and Conflict Transformation* (Philadelphia: Templeton Foundation Press, 2001), 184, 185-93.
73 Daniels, *supra* note 67.
74 James, *supra* note 18. See also Nicholas Tavuchis, *Mea Culpa: A Sociology of Apology and Reconciliation* (Stanford: Stanford University Press, 1991).
75 Keith Howard, "Residential School Survivors Come Home," *United Church Observer*, June 2004, 5.
76 On the use of ceremony and ritual in conflict resolution, see Lisa Schirch, *Ritual and Symbol in Peacebuilding* (Bloomfield: Kumarian Press, 2005), and Michelle LeBaron, *Bridging Troubled Waters: Conflict Resolution from the Heart* (San Francisco: Jossey-Bass, 2002), 181-282.
77 *Supra* note 56 at 121-22.
78 Roger Simon, "The Pedagogical Insistence of Public Memory," in Peter Seixas, ed., *Theorizing Historical Consciousness* (Toronto: University of Toronto Press, 2004), 187.
79 The Gitxsan media briefing distributed for the feast explains that xgweekxw "is the ground hog pelt, a traditional form of currency of the Gitxsan, now replaced by Canadian currency." Gary G. Patsey, Gitxsan Chiefs' Office, "Apology Feast to the Gitxsan," media briefing, 20 March 2004, 3.
80 Simon, *supra* note 78 at 199.

Bibliography

Acorn, Annalise. *Compulsory Compassion: A Critique of Restorative Justice*. Vancouver: UBC Press, 2004.
Alfred, Taiaiake. *Wasase: Indigenous Pathways of Action and Freedom*. Peterborough, ON: Broadview Press, 2005.
Assembly of First Nations. "Assembly of First Nations Report on Canada's Dispute Resolution Plan to Compensate for Abuses in Indian Residential Schools." November 2004. http://www.afn.ca/Residential%20Schools%20Report.pdf.
Barkan, Elazar. *The Guilt of Nations: Restitution and Negotiating Historical Injustice*. Baltimore and London: Johns Hopkins University Press, 2000.
Battiste, Marie, and James (Sákéj) Youngblood Henderson. *Protecting Indigenous Knowledge and Heritage: A Global Challenge*. Saskatoon: Purich Publishing, 2000.
Boler, Megan, and Michalinos Zembylas. "Discomforting Truths: The Emotional Terrain of Understanding Difference." In Peter P. Trifona, ed., *Pedagogies of Difference: Rethinking Education for Social Change*, 110-36. New York: RoutledgeFalmer, 2003.
Borrows, John. *Recovering Canada: The Resurgence of Indigenous Law*. Toronto: University of Toronto Press, 2002.
Bradford, William. "With a Very Great Blame on Our Hearts: Reparations, Reconciliation, and an American Indian Plea for Peace with Justice." *American Indian Law Review* 27 (2002-3): 1-175.
Canada. Canadian Heritage. Task Force on Aboriginal Languages and Cultures. *Towards a New Beginning: A Foundational Report for a Strategy to Revitalize First Nations, Inuit and Metis Languages and Cultures*. Ottawa: Canadian Heritage, 2005.
Canada. Department of Justice. "The Aboriginal Justice Strategy." 2005. http://canada.justice.gc.ca/en/ps/ajln/strategy.html.
Canada. *House of Commons Debates*. 38th Parliament, 1st Session. *Edited Hansard*, 053 (9 February 2005). http://www2.parl.gc.ca/HousePublications/Publication.aspx?Language=E&Mode=1&Parl=38&Ses=1&DocId=1616286#SOB-1115359.
–. *House of Commons Debates*. 38th Parliament, 1st Session. *Edited Hansard*, 079 (11 April 2005). http://www2.parl.gc.ca/HousePublications/Publication.aspx?Language=E&Mode=1&Parl=38&Ses=1&DocId=1751304#Int-1214189.

Canada. House of Commons Standing Committee on Aboriginal Affairs and Northern Development. Evidence. 15 February 2005. http://www.parl.gc.ca/infocomdoc/38/1/AANO/Meetings/Evidence/Int-1128319.

–. Evidence. 17 February 2005. http://cmte.parl.gc.ca/Content/HOC/committee/381/aano/evidence/ev1648068/aanoev19-e.htm#Int-1137136.

–. Evidence. 22 February 2005. http://cmte.parl.gc.ca/cmte/CommitteePublication.aspx?SourceId=126503&Lang=1&PARLSES=381&JNT=0&COM=8972.

–. Evidence. 24 March 2005. http://cmte.parl.gc.ca/cmte/CommitteePublication.aspx?SourceId=126515&Lang=1&PARLSES=381&JNT=0&COM=8972.

–. *Fourth Report. Study on the Effectiveness of the Government Alternative Dispute Resolution Process for the Resolution of Indian Residential School Claims.* Ottawa: House of Commons Standing Committee on Aboriginal Affairs and Northern Development, 2005. http://cmte.parl.gc.ca/cmte/CommitteePublication.aspx?SourceId=107649.

Canada. Indian Affairs and Northern Development. *Gathering Strength: Canada's Aboriginal Action Plan.* Ottawa: Indian Affairs and Northern Development, 1998.

–. *Reconciliation and Healing: Alternative Resolution Strategies for Dealing with Residential School Claims.* Ottawa: Department of Indian Affairs and Northern Development, 2000.

–. "Statement of Reconciliation." 1998. http://www.ain-inac.gc.ca/gs/rec_e.html.

Canada. Indian and Northern Affairs Canada. "Renewal of Policies and Processes for Addressing Aboriginal and Treaty Rights: Federal Background Paper for the Negotiations Sectoral Roundtable." Paper presented at Canada-Aboriginal Peoples Roundtable, Negotiations Sectoral Follow-up Session, Ottawa, 12-13 January 2005. http://www.aboriginalroundtable.ca/sect/ngot/bckpr/GOC_BgPaper_.pdf.

Canada. Indian Residential Schools Resolution Canada. "Indian Residential Schools Settlement Agreement." 2006. http://www.irsr-rqpi.gc.ca/english/news_10_05_06.html.

–. "Political Agreement." 30 May 2005. http://www.irsr-rqpi.gc.ca/english/news_30_05_05b.html.

–. "Resolution Framework and ADR." 2003. http://www.irsr-rqpi.gc.ca/english/dispute_resolution_resolution_framework.html.

Canada. Royal Commission on Aboriginal Peoples. *Report of the Royal Commission on Aboriginal Peoples.* Vol. 1, *Looking Forward, Looking Back.* Ottawa: Canada Communications Group, 1996. http://www.ainc-inac.gc.ca/ch/rcap/sg/sgm10_e.html.

Canadian Bar Association. "The Logical Next Step: Reconciliation Payments for All Residential School Survivors." February 2005. http://www.cba.org/CBA/Sections/pdf/residential.pdf.

Cloud v. Canada (Attorney General) (2004), 274 D.L.R. (4th) 667 (C.A.).

Crowshoe, Reg, and Sybille Manneschmidt. *Akak'stiman: A Blackfoot Framework for Decision-Making and Mediation Processes.* Calgary: University of Calgary Press, 2002.

Delgamuukw v. British Columbia, [1997] 3 S.C.R. 1010.

Deloria, Vine, Jr., and Daniel R. Wildcat. *Power and Place: Indian Education in America.* Golden, CO: Fulcrum Resources, 2001.

Epp, Roger. "We Are All Treaty People: History, Reconciliation and the 'Settler Problem.'" In Carol A.L. Prager and Trudy Govier, eds., *Dilemmas of Reconciliation: Cases and Concepts,* 223-44. Waterloo: Wilfrid Laurier University Press, 2003.

Fisher, Simon, Jawed Ludin, Steve Williams, Dekha Ibrahim Abdi, Richard Smith, and Sue Williams. *Working with Conflict: Skills and Strategies for Action.* London: Zed Books, 2000.

Furniss, Elizabeth. *Victims of Benevolence: The Dark Legacy of the Williams Lake Residential School.* Vancouver: Arsenal Pulp Press, 1992.

Ghostkeeper, Elmer. "Weche Teachings: Aboriginal Wisdom and Dispute Resolution." In Catherine Bell and David Kahane, eds., *Intercultural Dispute Resolution in Aboriginal Contexts,* 161-75. Vancouver: UBC Press, 2004.

Giesen, Bernhard. "The Trauma of Perpetrators: The Holocaust as the Traumatic Reference of German National Identity." In Jeffrey C. Alexander, Ron Eyerman, Bernhard Giesen, Neil J. Smelser, and Piotr Sztompka, eds., *Cultural Trauma and Collective Identity,* 112-54. Berkeley: University of California Press, 2004.

Haida Nation v. British Columbia (Minister of Forests), [2004] 3 S.C.R. 511.

Haig-Brown, Celia. *Resistance and Renewal: Surviving the Indian Residential School.* Vancouver: Arsenal Pulp Press, 1988.

James, Matt. "Wrestling with the Past: Apologies, Quasi-apologies, and Non-apologies in Canada." In Mark Gibney, Rhoda Howard-Hassmann, Jean-Marc Coicaud, and Niklaus Steiner, eds., *The Age of Apology: The West Faces Its Own Past.* Tokyo: United Nations University Press, forthcoming in 2007.

LaCapra, Dominick. *History in Transit: Experience, Identity, Critical Theory.* Ithaca: Cornell University Press, 2004.

Law Commission of Canada. *Restoring Dignity: Responding to Child Abuse in Canadian Institutions.* Ottawa: Minister of Public Works and Government Services, 2000.

LeBaron, Michelle. *Bridging Troubled Waters: Conflict Resolution from the Heart.* San Francisco: Jossey-Bass, 2002.

Lederach, John Paul. *Building Peace: Sustainable Reconciliation in Divided Societies.* Washington, DC: United States Institute of Peace Press, 1997.

–. "Five Qualities of Practice in Support of Reconciliation Processes." In R.G. Helmick and R.L. Petersen, eds., *Forgiveness and Reconciliation: Religion, Public Policy and Conflict Transformation,* 183-93. Philadelphia: Templeton Foundation Press, 2001.

–. *The Moral Imagination: The Art and Soul of Building Peace.* New York: Oxford University Press, 2005.

Llewellyn, Jennifer J. "Dealing with the Legacy of Native Residential School Abuse in Canada: Litigation, ADR, and Restorative Justice." *University of Toronto Law Journal* 52 (2002): 253-300.

Llewellyn, Jennifer J., and R. Howse. *Restorative Justice: A Conceptual Framework.* Ottawa: Law Commission of Canada, 1998.

Miller, J.R. *Shingwauk's Vision: A History of Native Residential Schools.* Toronto: University of Toronto Press, 1996.

Million, Dian Lynn. "Telling Secrets: Sex, Power and Narrative in the Rearticulation of Canadian Residential School Histories." PhD diss., University of Berkeley, 2004.

Milloy, John S. *"A National Crime": The Canadian Government and the Residential School System, 1879-1986.* Winnipeg: University of Manitoba Press, 2001.

Mills, Antonia. *Eagle Down Is Our Law: Witsuwit'en Law, Feasts and Land Claims.* Vancouver: UBC Press, 1994.

Napoleon, Val. "Who Gets to Say What Happened? Reconciliation Issues for the Gitxsan." In Catherine Bell and David Kahane, eds., *Intercultural Dispute Resolution in Aboriginal Contexts,* 176-95. Vancouver: UBC Press, 2004.

Oman, Natalie. "Paths to Intercultural Understanding: Feasting, Shared Horizons, and Unforced Consensus." In Catherine Bell and David Kahane, eds., *Intercultural Dispute Resolution in Aboriginal Contexts,* 70-93. Vancouver: UBC Press, 2004.

Prager, Carol A.L., and Trudy Govier, eds. *Dilemmas of Reconciliation: Cases and Concepts.* Waterloo: Wilfrid Laurier University Press, 2003.

Pranis, Kay, Barry Stuart, and Mark Wedge. *Peacemaking Circles: From Crime to Community.* St. Paul: Living Justice Press, 2003.

Regan, Paulette. "Unsettling the Settler Within: Canada's Peacemaker Myth, Reconciliation, and Transformative Pathways to Decolonization." PhD diss., University of Victoria, 2006.

Regan, Paulette, and Matilda Daniels. "An Apology Feast in Hazelton." Draft paper presented at the Canadian Association of Law Teachers (CALT) annual conference, Law's Paradoxes, University of British Columbia, Vancouver, BC, 22-24 June 2005.

Ross, Rupert. *Returning to the Teachings: Exploring Aboriginal Justice.* Toronto: Penguin Books Canada, 1996.

Schirch, Lisa. *Ritual and Symbol in Peacebuilding.* Bloomfield: Kumarian Press, 2005.

Schugurensky, Daniel. "Transformative Learning and Transformative Politics: The Pedagogical Dimension of Participatory Democracy and Social Action." In Edmund V. O'Sullivan, Amish Morrell, and Mary Ann O'Connor, eds., *Expanding the Boundaries of Transformative Learning: Essays on Theory and Praxis,* 59-76. New York: Palgrave, 2002.

Simon, Roger. "The Pedagogical Insistence of Public Memory." In Peter Seixas, ed., *Theorizing Historical Consciousness,* 181-201. Toronto: University of Toronto Press, 2004.

–. "The Pedagogy of Remembrance and the Counter-Commemoration of the Columbus Quincentenary." In Roger Simon, *The Touch of the Past: Remembrance, Learning, and Ethics,* 14-31. New York: Palgrave Macmillan, 2005.

Simon, Roger, and Claudia Eppert. "Remembering Obligation: Witnessing Testimonies of Historical Trauma." In Roger Simon, *The Touch of the Past: Remembrance, Learning, and Ethics,* 50-64. New York: Palgrave Macmillan, 2005.

Sutherland, Jessie. "Colonialism, Crime, and Dispute Resolution: A Critical Analysis of Canada's Aboriginal Justice Strategy." 2002. http://www.mediate.com/articles/sutherlandJ.cfm.

Tavuchis, Nicholas. *Mea Culpa: A Sociology of Apology and Reconciliation.* Stanford: Stanford University Press, 1991.

Torpey, John. "Introduction: Politics and the Past." In John Torpey, ed., *Politics and the Past: On Repairing Historical Injustices,* 1-34. Boulder: Rowman and Littlefield, 2003.

Warry, Wayne. *Unfinished Dreams: Community Healing and the Reality of Aboriginal Self-Government.* Toronto: University of Toronto Press, 1998.

Williams, Robert A., Jr. *Linking Arms Together: American Indian Treaty Visions of Law and Peace, 1600-1800.* New York: Oxford University Press, 1997.

Yamamoto, Eric K. *Interracial Justice: Conflict and Reconciliation in Post-civil Rights America.* New York: New York University Press, 1999.

3

Reconciliation without Respect?
Section 35 and Indigenous Legal
Orders

Minnawaanagogiizhigook (Dawnis Kennedy)

Relating to Indigenous Legal Traditions

The traditions of Indigenous peoples have existed within these lands for thousands of years. They reflect Indigenous peoples' collective understandings of creation and the roles of individuals within creation and within community. They serve to support the efforts of Indigenous peoples to maintain good relations in this world: relations within communities, relations between communities, and relations with the other beings of creation. For generations, Indigenous peoples have continued the efforts of those who came before them, efforts to maintain their communities, their traditions, and their roles within creation. These efforts have always been and continue to be of central significance to Indigenous peoples. Within my home community, it is often said that the fate of the Anishinabe people is tied to the fate of the ways that were given to the Anishinabe to carry, to work with, and to maintain.[1]

When European settlers first came to this territory, they carried with them memories of traditions developed in distant places, traditions that they also desired to maintain. The settlers sought to create for themselves a space within these lands that would provide for the establishment of their communities and the development of their traditions. However, since Indigenous peoples already governed these lands, settlers could not create such a space except by way of their relations with Indigenous peoples. Insofar as settlers sought to establish their societies through peaceable relations, it was necessary to ensure that their traditions developed in ways that were respectful of Indigenous peoples and the traditions they maintain. This chapter will speak to one aspect of relations between settler and Indigenous traditions: the relations between the legal traditions of settler societies, which form the basis of present-day Canadian legal orders, and those of Indigenous peoples, which are enmeshed within Indigenous legal orders.[2]

Canadian legal orders are defined by their relation to Indigenous legal orders, regardless of the nature of this relation. This flows from the fact that the territories in which settlers sought to establish the Canadian state and its legal orders were already governed, through Indigenous legal orders, by the peoples Indigenous to these lands. Where Canadian legal orders disregard the Indigenous laws that speak to the roles and responsibilities of settler societies within Indigenous territories, they are defined by their adverse relation to Indigenous legal orders. To be otherwise, the Canadian state and its legal orders must develop in a manner that demonstrates respect for Indigenous legal orders and the communities they sustain.

Canadian history tells us that, at times, settler societies demonstrated respect for Indigenous legal orders. History holds accounts of settler societies, the Crown, and, later, the Canadian state acting in accordance with Indigenous peoples' ways of law making, relation building, and renewal.[3] In particular, many Indigenous-settler treaty relationships are understood, at least by some, to be relations wholly or partially created by and governed through Indigenous law. According to such understandings, treaty relations affirm the continued co-existence of Indigenous and Canadian legal orders.[4] However, neither the treaty relations nor the instances of demonstrated respect for Indigenous legal orders were sufficient to ensure that Canadian legal orders developed in a manner that showed respect for Indigenous legal orders. State practice eventually became directed towards the destabilization, rather than the affirmation, of Indigenous legal orders.[5] Also, Canada's official understanding of the treaties between Indigenous peoples and the Crown shifted. Treaties came to be understood, at best, as constituting a burden upon the state rather than as the foundation of its legitimate existence within these lands. When considered alongside Canada's history to date, the instances in which settler societies, the Crown, or the Canadian state demonstrated respect for Indigenous legal orders appear to be deceptive or singular events that have been too often forgotten, belittled, or denied.

Similarly, there are moments in which Canadian law has accorded Indigenous laws a limited measure of recognition.[6] However, these moments are overshadowed by Canadian law's numerous efforts to deny the existence, relevance, and legitimacy of Indigenous legal orders. Indigenous legal orders have at different times been understood from within Canadian law as having never existed at all,[7] as having been wholly displaced by Canadian law,[8] or as existing only within and according to the terms set by Canadian law.[9] Canadian law's tendency to deny the existence and significance of Indigenous legal orders demonstrates disrespect for these legal orders.

Indigenous legal orders are also accorded a limited measure of recognition by colonial law.[10] Much of Canadian state practice and jurisprudence has been inconsistent with the standards found within colonial law. Moreover, colonial law does not generally meet the standards that Euro-derived international law applies to international relations not involving Indigenous peoples.[11] However, applying even the most generous interpretation of co-lonial laws regarding Indigenous legal orders does not ensure that respect for these legal orders is demonstrated. The doctrines of colonial law, includ-ing their recognition of Indigenous law, were developed primarily in order to facilitate the process of colonialism. Although colonial law may offer Indigenous laws and legal orders a severely restricted role within Euro-derived legal orders, this role is affirmed only when it is in accordance with colonial law. Therefore, to affirm the role colonial law would provide In-digenous legal orders is more accurately to affirm colonial law, not to dem-onstrate respect for Indigenous legal orders themselves. Similarly, applying Euro-derived international laws regarding international relations does not guarantee that Indigenous legal orders are respected. There is more at stake than the relations between the Canadian state and Indigenous peoples. The development of the Canadian state and its legal orders *within Indigenous territories* is at issue; thus, this development should demonstrate respect for Indigenous ways of creating and maintaining relations between peoples and legal orders, rather than forcing them to participate in forms of relation based on Euro-derived statist models.[12]

It is clear that the overall development of the Canadian state and its legal orders has fallen far short of demonstrating respect for Indigenous commu-nities and the legal orders they maintain. This has had a considerable im-pact upon the lives of all who now inhabit Indigenous territories, an impact that persists. Canada has benefited, and continues to benefit, from its abil-ity to maintain its communities, laws, and traditions within Indigenous lands, but this benefit has been gained at the expense of Indigenous legal systems, traditions, and communities.[13] To ensure that Canadian legal or-ders do not continue operating to the detriment of their Indigenous coun-terparts, they must find ways to participate in the establishment of respectful relations with them.[14]

The development of Canadian law's adverse relations with Indigenous legal orders coincided with and was reinforced by the increasing tendency to turn exclusively to Euro-derived law to understand relations between Canadian and Indigenous legal orders. Although it may offer Indigenous law a severely restricted measure of recognition *within* Canadian legal or-ders, Euro-derived law is ill-equipped to provide the means that will enable Canadian legal orders to participate in establishing respectful relations *with* Indigenous legal orders. Determining the rights of Indigenous people accord-ing to Canadian or European-derived law is not the equivalent of establish-ing respectful relations with Indigenous peoples. Likewise, the status held by Indigenous legal orders *within* Canadian law does not determine what respectful relations *between* Indigenous and Canadian orders should entail. Indigenous legal orders also speak to the nature of such relations; indeed, they are integral to understanding what constitutes respectful relations with

Indigenous peoples and their legal orders. Looking solely to Canadian law to determine the nature of Canada's relation to Indigenous peoples and their legal orders evades, rather than resolves, the complex issues that arise from the establishment of the Canadian state within Indigenous territories and from the co-existence of multiple legal orders.

To establish respectful relations with Indigenous legal orders, Canadian law must renounce its previous attempts to deny the existence, relevance, and legitimacy of Indigenous law. It must acknowledge that such laws exist within dynamic legal orders that continue to operate in Indigenous communities. It must also recognize that these laws are integral to understanding what constitutes respectful relations between Indigenous and Canadian legal orders. Thus, to fully extricate themselves from their current adverse relations with Indigenous legal orders, Canadian legal orders must go beyond applying more generous interpretations of Canadian, or Euro-derived law: they must truly engage with Indigenous legal orders.

Canada's *Constitution Act, 1982* recently recognized and affirmed Aboriginal and treaty rights under section 35(1).[15] The Supreme Court of Canada has increasingly argued that section 35 is directed towards effecting reconciliation between the Canadian state and Indigenous peoples within Canadian law. In the following section, I will consider whether the Court's pursuit of this goal has enabled Canadian law to transform its adverse relations with Indigenous legal orders. If Canadian law is to guide the Canadian state in maintaining respectful relations with Indigenous peoples, it must first participate in the establishment of such relations between Indigenous and Canadian legal orders.[16]

Indigenous Law, Aboriginal Rights, and the Canadian Constitution

Since the entrenchment of Aboriginal rights in the Canadian Constitution, Indigenous legal orders and the implications they hold for Canadian law have re-emerged as significant issues in mainstream Canadian forums. It is increasingly argued that the constitutional recognition and affirmation of Aboriginal rights should facilitate the recognition, protection, or validation of Indigenous laws and legal traditions.[17] The meaning of Aboriginal rights and their constitutional affirmation is being fiercely debated within and between Indigenous and Canadian communities.[18] Though it may not be explicitly recognized, differing conceptions of Canadian law's relation to Indigenous legal orders are implicated in and responsible for many of the growing rifts within these debates.

I will review recent Supreme Court jurisprudence to examine the effect of section 35, thus far, on Canadian law's relation to Indigenous legal orders. The goal of this review is not to determine the potential of various legal doctrines for improving the position of Indigenous peoples according to

Canadian law. I am interested in the following two questions: Has the constitutional recognition and affirmation of Aboriginal rights prompted the Supreme Court to move beyond the limitations of its past understandings of Aboriginal rights? When Canadian courts contemplate the rights and status of Indigenous peoples *within* Canadian law, do they do so in a manner that allows them to participate in transforming their relations *with* Indigenous legal orders? This examination is not an effort to identify the current status of Aboriginal rights in Supreme Court jurisprudence, and I will not conduct an exhaustive or comprehensive review of the relevant case law. Rather, I will focus on four cases that lend themselves to this analysis and that span the terms of three Chief Justices of Canada: *R. v. Sparrow, R. v. Van der Peet, R. v. Mitchell,* and *R. v. Marshall; R. v. Bernard.*[19] The aspects within judgments that will be considered include the Supreme Court's understanding of section 35's effect on the concept of Aboriginal rights, the nature of the Court's engagements with Indigenous law, and the way in which the Court conceives of Canadian law's relations to Indigenous legal orders.

Developing a *Sui Generis* Approach: *R. v. Sparrow*

The constitutional affirmation of Aboriginal rights entered into Canadian law amid many instances of limited, imperfect, and fleeting recognitions of Indigenous law that co-existed with the more numerous instances of denial and disrespect. However, state practice and Canadian law were, for the most part, detrimental to Indigenous peoples and their legal orders. Aboriginal rights received recognition under the common law; however, the extent of this recognition was severely restricted.[20] Before the Supreme Court's judgment in *Calder v. Attorney General of British Columbia,* Aboriginal rights were considered wholly dependent on the will of the sovereign, vulnerable to unilateral extinguishments, and subject to government regulation.[21] As Dickson C.J.C. and La Forest J. observe in *Sparrow,* for many years prior to 1982 Aboriginal rights, "certainly as legal rights – were virtually ignored."[22] Against this history, *Sparrow* is often referred to as a landmark case for Aboriginal rights and Indigenous peoples.

Although the *Constitution Act, 1982* came into force during Bora Laskin's tenure as Chief Justice of Canada, the Supreme Court did not engage substantively with section 35 until the *Sparrow* judgment, released two months before Laskin C.J.C.'s successor, Chief Justice of Canada Brian Dickson, retired from the Court.[23] The case arose when Ronald Edward Sparrow, a member of the Musqueam Indian Band, was charged with fishing contrary to the stipulations in the band's food fishing licence. The question before the Court was whether the restrictions contained in the licence were inconsistent with section 35. The unanimous judgment of the Court, authored by Dickson C.J.C. and La Forest J., affirms that the Musqueam have an Aboriginal right to fish under section 35.[24]

Against the arguments of the federal government, the Court finds that Aboriginal rights are legally enforceable rights under Canadian law.[25] Before *Sparrow,* whether the scope of section 35 was limited to, or exceeded, the restrictive recognition of Aboriginal rights under the common law was unclear. The Court stresses that the recognition and affirmation of Aboriginal rights in section 35 "extends beyond" the effects of previous Aboriginal rights doctrine, citing the following words of Professor Noel Lyon:

> [T]he context of 1982 is surely enough to tell us that this is not just a codification of the case law on aboriginal rights that had accumulated by 1982. Section 35 calls for a just settlement for aboriginal peoples. It renounces the old rules of the game under which the Crown established courts of law and denied those courts the authority to question sovereign claims made by the Crown.[26]

In effect, the Court finds that the rights recognized and affirmed by section 35 are not dependent upon prior recognition under Canadian law.[27]

The federal government also argued that section 35 did not protect rights incompatible with previous government regulation.[28] The Court rejects this argument as well, finding that the incompatibility of an Aboriginal right with a prior regulatory regime does not in itself limit the definition of section 35 rights.[29] However, in finding that governmental regulation does not delimit the content of Aboriginal rights, the Court simultaneously endorses the position that, prior to 1982, the Crown was capable of unilaterally extinguishing Aboriginal rights solely by demonstrating a clear and plain intention to do so.[30] Moreover, the Court finds the Crown government capable of regulating the exercise of Aboriginal rights, subject to the condition that any infringement of section 35 rights be justified by a valid legislative objective and remain in keeping with the relationship between Indigenous peoples and the Crown.[31] This finding was made despite the fact that section 35, unlike the *Canadian Charter of Rights and Freedoms,* is not accompanied by a clause limiting the exercise of Aboriginal rights.[32]

When articulating the reasons for its findings regarding the relationship between Aboriginal rights and government legislative powers, the Court looks to a traditional Euro-derived notion of Crown sovereignty for endorsement. The Court insists,

> It is worth recalling that while British policy towards the native population was based on respect for their right to occupy their traditional lands, a proposition to which the Royal Proclamation of 1763 bears witness, *there was*

*from the outset never any doubt that sovereignty and legislative power, and indeed
the underlying title, to such lands vested in the Crown.*[33]

The Court relies on the claim that Crown sovereignty has never been ques-
tioned, which is factually untrue: the Crown's assertions of sovereignty over
Indigenous peoples and "under" Indigenous territories have been, and continue to be, subject to serious contestation by Indigenous peoples.[34]

Although it affirms a traditional Euro-derived notion of Crown sovereignty, the Court determines that the constitutional recognition and affirmation of Aboriginal rights demands a new approach to understanding
Aboriginal rights at Canadian law.[35] This new approach is required, the
Court tells us, because section 35 Aboriginal rights are sui generis; they are
rights that are of their own kind.[36] The Court is vague regarding the reason
behind its sui generis characterization of Aboriginal rights; however, the
Court implies that it is due to the existence of something outside Euro-
derived law, something that is nonetheless relevant to the interpretation of
section 35. This is most evident in the Court's assertion that it is crucial for
Canadian judges to be "sensitive to the Aboriginal perspective on the meaning of the rights at stake" and "careful to avoid the application of traditional common law concepts" as they "develop their understanding of the
'*sui generis*' nature of Aboriginal rights."[37] The Court does not explain what
a sui generis approach entails, other than to suggest it has something to do
with Indigenous peoples' perspectives rather than Euro-derived common
law concepts.

The Court does not indicate whether the sui generis characterization is
meant to enable courts to move the Aboriginal rights framework beyond
the limitations of Euro-derived legal paradigms or, alternatively, to deny
Indigenous peoples access to a level of recognition commensurate to that
afforded under Euro-derived legal concepts such as sovereignty and self-
determination.[38] In discussing the sui generis nature of Aboriginal rights,
the Court cites two sources: the first, an article by Professor Leroy Little
Bear, is consistent with an enabling approach to understanding Aboriginal
rights as sui generis; the second, *R. v. Guerin,* can be associated with a limiting approach.[39] Little Bear argues that the premises upon which Indigenous
peoples relate to the world cannot be understood through British concepts
"and should be given as much weight as British concepts and philosophy."[40]
However, *R. v. Guerin* seems to take a limiting approach to understanding
the sui generis interest in land held by Indigenous peoples, describing it as
more than a personal right but less than beneficial ownership.[41] The unan-
swered questions regarding how and why Canadian Aboriginal rights law
requires a new, sui generis, approach are crucial to ascertaining whether
this new approach holds transformative potential.

Under the Court's interpretation in *Sparrow*, section 35 has certainly initiated a considerable shift *within* Canadian law. However, an approach capable of transforming Canadian law's adverse relations within Indigenous legal orders requires a serious reconsideration of Canada's relationship with Indigenous peoples, the foundation of the Canadian state's existence within Indigenous territories and the purported monopoly of Euro-derived law within them. The Court's judgment fell far short of this mark, threatening any transformative potential in a sui generis approach. The potential, I believe, lies in enabling Canadian courts to engage with Indigenous legal orders as they exist in their own right, rather than engaging with Indigenous legal orders as they are constructed within Euro-derived colonial law.

Engaging with Indigenous Law: *R. v. Van der Peet*
Just months after the *Sparrow* decision was released, Dickson C.J.C. departed from the Supreme Court, and Antonio Lamer was appointed Chief Justice. Six years after his appointment, Lamer C.J.C. authored the majority decisions in what is now known as the *Van der Peet* trilogy.[42] The appellants in all three cases were charged under section 61(1) of the *Fisheries Act* for selling, or attempting to sell, their catch contrary to section 27(5) *British Columbia Fishery (General) Regulations*.[43] All appellants claimed that the regulations violated section 35 and were therefore invalid. In *Van der Peet*, Lamer C.J.C. offered his conception of the basis, nature, and purpose of section 35 rights, in addition to putting forth tests through which to define and govern those rights.[44] Although the reasoning in all three judgments is similar, I will focus on the *Van der Peet* judgment, which contains the majority of Lamer C.J.C.'s analysis.

The *Van der Peet* case arose when Dorothy Marie Van der Peet, a member of the Stó:lō Nation, was charged for selling ten salmon. Van der Peet argued that the regulations under which she was charged violated the Stó:lō people's right to their fishery, which she understood to be protected by section 35. In Lamer C.J.C.'s view, Dorothy Van der Peet failed to demonstrate an existing Aboriginal right to exchange fish for money or other goods; thus, he affirmed the Court of Appeal's restoration of Van der Peet's conviction.[45] L'Heureux-Dubé and McLachlin JJ. dissented. L'Heureux-Dubé J., who found that the Stó:lō have an Aboriginal right to fish, including "the right to sell, trade and barter fish for livelihood, support and sustenance purposes," would have sent the case back to trial on questions of extinguishment and infringement.[46] McLachlin J. would have set aside the conviction and confirmed, in principle, the existence of an Aboriginal right to sell fish for the purpose of sustenance.[47]

In *Sparrow*, the Court called for the development of a new approach based upon the sui generis nature of Aboriginal rights. However, it did not offer an explanation of how and why Aboriginal rights are to be considered sui generis; nor did it articulate what this new approach might mean for Aboriginal rights interpretation. Although Lamer C.J.C. does not address these issues directly in *Van der Peet,* he does provide a basis for the sui generis nature of Aboriginal rights: the relation between section 35 rights and Indigenous laws. He determines that section 35 rights are given content by Indigenous laws. However, he fails to give effect to Indigenous law's relevancy to section 35 and does not provide an adequate explanation of the relationship between section 35 and Indigenous laws. Thus, as he continues on in his judgment – articulating the underlying purpose of section 35, developing a definitional test for section 35 rights, and determining how the exercise of Aboriginal rights should be governed – he does so without consideration of Indigenous law's relevance. The test he develops favours Indigenous peoples' practices over their laws and fails to provide mechanisms through which Canadian courts can engage respectfully with the laws of Indigenous peoples. Indeed, the framework he provides hinders the ability of Canadian courts to achieve such an engagement.

Lamer C.J.C.'s most direct consideration of the relationship between Indigenous law and section 35 occurs in his articulation of the basis of the section's Aboriginal rights. He finds that these rights have the same basis as that identified by Brennan J. for Aboriginal title, according to Australian common law: the laws and customs of the peoples Indigenous to the land.[48] He cites Brennan J.'s judgment in *Mabo v. Queensland [No. 2]:*

> Native title has its origin in and is given its content by the traditional laws acknowledged by and the traditional customs observed by the indigenous inhabitants of a territory. The nature and incidents of native title must be ascertained as a matter of fact by reference to those laws and customs. The ascertainment may present a problem of considerable difficulty, as Moynihan J. perceived in the present case. It is a problem that did not arise in the case of a settled colony so long as the fictions were maintained that customary rights could not be reconciled "with the institutions or the legal ideas of civilized society;" ... that there was no law before the arrival of the British colonists in a settled colony and that there was no sovereign law-maker in the territory of a settled colony before sovereignty was acquired by the Crown ... These fictions denied the possibility of a native title recognized by our laws. But once it is acknowledged that an inhabited territory which became a settled colony was no more a legal desert than it was "desert uninhabited" in fact, it is necessary to ascertain by evidence the nature and incidents of native title.[49]

The aspect of this passage explicitly incorporated into Canadian Aboriginal rights jurisprudence is the assertion that Aboriginal rights originate in, and are given content by, Indigenous laws and customs.[50]

Lamer C.J.C. also refers to academic works consistent with the view that section 35 rights are sui generis because of the relations to Indigenous laws. For example, he cites the following passage from Mark D. Walters:

> The challenge of defining aboriginal rights stems from the fact that they are rights peculiar to the meeting of two vastly dissimilar legal cultures; consequently there will always be a question about which legal culture is to provide the vantage point from which rights are to be defined ... a morally and politically defensible conception of aboriginal rights will incorporate both legal perspectives.[51]

Lamer C.J.C.'s engagement with this issue provides him with the prime opportunity to discuss the task of developing a sui generis approach to section 35, situate his recognition of Indigenous law's relevancy to section 35 rights, and articulate the effects of his recognition. However, he does none of these things; nor does he reflect upon Walters' statement. Indeed, his affirmation of Indigenous law's influence upon section 35 rights stands in sharp contrast with the rest of his judgment, in which Indigenous law receives virtually no mention.[52]

The underlying purpose that Lamer C.J.C. attributes to section 35's recognition and affirmation of Aboriginal rights does not reflect the relationship between section 35 rights and Indigenous law. He explains the section's dual purpose in the following way:

> [T]he aboriginal rights recognized and affirmed by s. 35(1) are best understood as, first, the means by which the Constitution recognizes the fact that prior to the arrival of Europeans in North America the land was already occupied by distinctive aboriginal societies, and as, second, the means by which that prior occupation is reconciled with the assertion of Crown sovereignty over Canadian territory.[53]

Here the unique position that Indigenous peoples hold within these lands is transformed into a focus on the cultural "distinctiveness" of Aboriginal societies. Likewise, the fact that Indigenous peoples have governed these lands, through their own laws, for thousands of years is reduced to "prior occupation" or "pre-existence." In her dissent, McLachlin J. challenges Lamer C.J.C.'s omission of Indigenous laws from the purpose he attributes to section 35. Relying upon principles from *Sparrow*, she argues that "s. 35(1) recognizes not only prior aboriginal occupation, but also a prior legal regime giving rise to aboriginal rights which persist."[54]

Lamer C.J.C. spends the majority of his judgment developing a definitional test for section 35, one that displays a marked inattention to Indigenous laws. Rather than providing a vehicle to structure Canadian law's respectful engagement with Indigenous law, the *Van der Peet* test focuses solely upon identifying the "practices" or "activities" that *were* "elements of a practice, custom, or tradition" in which Indigenous people engaged prior to contact.[55] The interveners Delgamuukw argued against a similar approach in the Court of Appeal's majority judgment, maintaining that

> it is of fundamental importance to recognize that societies are "aboriginal" because they evolved as distinct peoples with their own laws before the assertion of British sovereignty, and *not* because they conformed (or now conform) to any particular pattern of resource use. The majority was wrong in law to equate subsistence hunting and fishing with being "aboriginal." For the purposes of these appeals, the essential features of the appellants' societies at the assertion of European sovereignty were that they were organized to possess their lands, manage their resources, and govern themselves. It is the maintenance and development of those features, and not any particular pattern of resource use, which are the hallmarks of the appellants' aboriginal rights.[56]

Lamer C.J.C., however, disregards this argument, basing his definitional test upon what he considers to be the activities that were crucial to Indigenous societies before contact.[57] Ironically, he justifies his preoccupation with the past and distances himself from Indigenous law by way of the same passage through which he acknowledged Indigenous law's relevance to section 35.

Immediately after Lamer C.J.C. affirms Indigenous laws as the basis of Aboriginal rights, he argues that "[t]o base aboriginal title in traditional laws and customs, as was done in Mabo, is, therefore, to base that title in the pre-existing societies of aboriginal peoples."[58] His emphasis on the word *traditional* diverts attention from the fact that it is the traditional *laws* of Indigenous peoples that give rise to and define the content of section 35 rights.[59] This shift holds negative implications, not only for treatment of Indigenous laws within section 35 jurisprudence but also for the Court's ability to steer clear of the frozen rights approach, previously rejected by the Court in *Sparrow*.[60]

Legal orders, and therefore the laws within them, maintain a measure of continuity with the past and responsiveness to the present and future. They are therefore necessarily dynamic, whereas judicially constructed Aboriginal practices, in and of themselves, are not. To avoid rendering Aboriginal rights static by focusing on practices, the Court must find a way to engage with the laws of Indigenous peoples as dynamic and existing laws. The test developed in *Van der Peet*, however, does not enable Canadian courts to do so. The role of Indigenous laws, under the *Van der Peet* test, is confined to providing evidence of the "facts" of Indigenous existence prior to contact. Thus, Canadian judges are led to engage with Indigenous laws as though they were merely historical facts, artificially reifying what are in actuality dynamic processes. The shift of Lamer C.J.C.'s focus from Indigenous laws to practices, then, leads Canadian law towards an approach that might otherwise have been avoided.

Lamer C.J.C. seems aware that his approach takes him in this direction. He argues that this is precisely why it was necessary for him to incorporate a continuity requirement into the *Van der Peet* test. According to him, the concept of continuity is "the means by which a 'frozen rights' approach to s. 35(1) will be avoided."[61] However, the continuity requirement cannot mitigate his exclusive focus upon pre-contact societies during the definition of section 35. The concept of continuity is itself a limitation requiring claimants to prove that the activity for which they seek protection is one that has maintained continuity with the activities central to Indigenous societies pre-contact.[62] At most, the doctrine of continuity can allow for the "evolution" of the *form* of those activities, which is not sufficient to avoid a frozen rights approach.[63] Thus, though Lamer C.J.C. attempts to defrost the "activities" in which Indigenous people engaged prior to contact, his attempts fail because his test does not attend to the dynamic nature of the legal orders within which their significance is determined.

Lamer C.J.C.'s disregard for Indigenous laws also affects the frameworks he advances to govern the exercise of section 35 rights. The majority decision in *R. v. Gladstone* provides a clear example of this fact. In *Gladstone,* Lamer C.J.C. significantly broadens the grounds upon which the Canadian state could infringe section 35 rights in accordance with Canadian law.[64] However, his unwillingness to acknowledge the existence of Indigenous laws leads him to ground this expansion on an erroneous assumption. His justification relies on a distinction between rights with "internal limitations" and those without. As he explains,

> That difference lies in the fact that the right at issue in Sparrow has an inherent limitation which the right recognized and affirmed in this appeal lacks. The food, social and ceremonial needs for fish of any given band of aboriginal people are internally limited – at a certain point the band will have sufficient fish to meet these needs. The commercial sale of the herring spawn on kelp, on the other hand, has no such internal limitation; the only limits on the Heiltsuk's need for herring spawn on kelp for commercial sale are the external constraints of the demand of the market and the availability of the resource.[65]

Lamer C.J.C. focuses solely on those limits upon Heiltsuk participation in the commercial fishery that arise from market demand and supply, thus garnering support for his assertion that the Canadian state must have a greater opportunity to infringe the rights recognized and affirmed by section 35. He is unwilling to recognize that Heiltsuk participation in the commercial fishery is limited by more than market forces alone. Thus, he entirely ignores the fact that Heiltsuk law governs the engagement of Heiltsuk people in commercial fishing and that, in this way, their commercial fishing is already limited.[66] Lamer C.J.C.'s ignorance of Indigenous law leads him to accept, without deliberation, the premise that only Canadian law is capable of governing the manner in which Indigenous people exercise the rights they are found to possess at Canadian law.[67]

By directing the *Van der Peet* test solely towards identifying the crucial "activities" of Indigenous people pre-contact, Lamer C.J.C. frustrates any attempt by the Court to engage respectfully with Indigenous laws. However, Canadian courts cannot avoid engaging with Indigenous law, for the questions they are asking continually bring judges face to face with it. Lamer C.J.C.'s test does not leave room for him to engage with Indigenous laws, as laws, but rather limits the role of Indigenous laws in section 35 jurisprudence to merely documenting the "facts" of Indigenous existence prior to contact.[68] He cannot see Indigenous peoples' laws for what they really are: dynamic in nature; enmeshed within systems of interpretation, judgment, authority, and negotiation equal in complexity to Canadian legal orders; and still functioning in and relevant to the lives of Indigenous people today.[69] The problem with the *Van der Peet* test, then, is not just that it limits the scope of section 35 rights and broadens the grounds for their infringement but that it leads courts to treat Indigenous laws as though they were just another historical record. This leads to jurisprudence that is problematic, not just because Canadian judges get the "facts" of Indigenous existence wrong or because they get Indigenous peoples' laws wrong (though they often do both) but also because courts are rendered incapable of respecting or responding to the dynamic nature and continued existence of Indigenous laws and the rights to which they are said to give rise.

The reduction of the Court's consideration of Indigenous laws to "facts" entails serious consequences for Indigenous law as it is constructed within current Canadian jurisprudence. It renders Indigenous law static, artificially reifying what is experienced in community as complex and dynamic processes. It obscures the connection between Indigenous law and the legal orders and communities in which that law is embedded.[70] Indeed, it attempts to remove Indigenous law from the very context that I would argue makes it Indigenous. It also leads Canadian judges to believe that they are in a position to define, construct, and control Indigenous laws, regardless of whether they hold any knowledge, training, or authority regarding these laws. As a result, any test that depends upon constructing Indigenous laws as "facts" makes it impossible for courts to engage respectfully with Indigenous law and reduces the potential of section 35, not to protecting what is "central and integral" to Indigenous societies but to preserving a constitutional space within which Indigenous people are able to perpetuate the cultural stereotypes held by Canadian judges.

In *Van der Peet,* Lamer C.J.C. provides a reason for *Sparrow*'s sui generis characterization of Aboriginal rights: the relationship between section 35 and Indigenous law. A year later, in *Delgamuukw,* he makes the connection explicit, stating that Aboriginal title is

> *sui generis* in the sense that its characteristics cannot be completely explained by reference either to the common law rules of real property or to the rules of property found in aboriginal legal systems. As with other aboriginal rights, it must be understood by reference to both common law and aboriginal perspectives.[71]

He goes on to clarify that the source of Aboriginal rights lies not only in the prior occupation of Indigenous peoples but also in "the relationship between common law and pre-existing systems of aboriginal law."[72] However, the *Van der Peet* test fails to give effect to this relationship or to structure Canadian law's engagement with Indigenous legal orders in a respectful way. The dissonance between the recognition of Indigenous law and the *Van der Peet* test's demonstrated disregard for its relevancy was not explained by Lamer C.J.C. Furthermore, *Van der Peet* does not remedy *Sparrow*'s unconsidered endorsement of Crown sovereignty, choosing instead to build upon it. As such, rather than providing an understanding of section 35 capable of transforming Canadian law's adverse relations with Indigenous legal orders, *Van der Peet* advances frameworks that maintain them.

Relations between Legal Orders: *R. v. Mitchell*

Mitchell represents the Supreme Court's first engagement with section 35 after Beverley McLachlin was appointed Chief Justice of Canada. The case arose when Haudenosaunee Grand Chief Michael Mitchell of Akwesasne, also known as Kanentakeron, refused to pay duty charged under the *Customs Act* for transporting goods across the United States–Canada border.[73] Mitchell argued that he was exercising an Aboriginal right to bring goods for personal or collective use or consumption across the border without paying duties or taxes to the government of Canada. McLachlin C.J.C. authored the majority judgment, finding that the evidence advanced by Mitchell failed to establish the right claimed. Binnie J. (Major J. concurring) wrote a separate judgment, reaching the same result but incorporating the colonial doctrine of sovereign incompatibility into his section 35 analysis.

By virtue of this doctrine, Binnie J. argued that the right Mitchell claimed could never have come into existence, due to its incompatibility with the existence of Crown sovereignty.

The question arising out of *Van der Peet,* namely, how the Supreme Court understands the relations between Indigenous and Canadian legal orders, finds its most direct consideration in *Mitchell.* McLachlin C.J.C.'s majority judgment does not address this issue directly. Nonetheless, a close analysis reveals indications of a particular conception of these relations, what I will call the absorption model. The absorption model may provide an explanation for Lamer C.J.C.'s seemingly contradictory interpretation of section 35 rights. However, the Court did not endorse the model as a means to understand the sui generis, or inter-legal, nature of Aboriginal rights. Doing so would require the Court to reaffirm, rather than transform, Canadian law's adverse relation to Indigenous legal orders, for this model presumes that Indigenous legal orders have been assimilated into Canadian law. In contrast, Binnie J.'s judgment does not attempt to clarify Lamer C.J.C.'s claim that Aboriginal rights arise out of the relations between Indigenous and Canadian law. Rather, he disregards it completely, arguing that Aboriginal rights are derived from and limited by Canadian sovereignty. Under his analysis, it seems that Indigenous laws were not even assimilated into Canadian law – they were merely displaced.

Before addressing the majority judgment, I will review the judgment authored by Binnie J., as he comes closest to taking a position on the relationship between Indigenous and Canadian legal orders in Supreme Court section 35 jurisprudence. Indeed, McLachlin C.J.C.'s own comments regarding the relations between Canadian legal orders, Indigenous legal orders, and section 35 are, in large part, a response to Binnie J. In turn, Binnie J.'s position on the nature of the relationship between Indigenous and Canadian legal orders develops in response to the arguments advanced by Mitchell, as is evident in the following now infamous passage:

> Counsel for the respondent does not challenge the reality of Canadian sovereignty, but he seeks for the Mohawk people of the Iroquois Confederacy the maximum degree of legal autonomy to which he believes they are entitled because of their long history at Akwesasne and elsewhere in eastern North America. This asserted autonomy, to be sure, does not presently flow from the ancient Iroquois legal order that is said to have created it, but from the *Constitution Act, 1982.* Section 35(1), adopted by the elected representatives of Canadians, recognizes and affirms existing aboriginal and treaty rights. If the respondent's claimed aboriginal right is to prevail, it does so not because of its own inherent strength, but because the *Constitution Act, 1982* brings about that result.[74]

Binnie J. seems to be arguing that the *Constitution Act, 1982* is the exclusive source of section 35 rights.[75] At a later point in the judgment, however, he acknowledges that the concept of Aboriginal rights has several sources (although he fails to identify them).[76] When one considers the above passage alongside his judgment as a whole, it becomes clear that Binnie J. is not arguing that the *Constitution Act, 1982* supplanted other sources of Aboriginal rights. Rather, he is arguing that Aboriginal rights derive their legal basis from Crown sovereignty, an understanding that maximizes Euro-derived law's influence upon the definition of Aboriginal rights and curtails the corresponding influence of Indigenous legal orders.

Although Binnie J. does not identify the "several" sources of Aboriginal rights nor the relations among them, he does go into some detail regarding the relations between traditional British colonial law, common law Aboriginal rights doctrine, and section 35. He argues that the concept of Aboriginal rights under the common law was "built around" doctrines of traditional British colonial law.[77] And, although he acknowledges that the *Sparrow* Court attempted to move away from colonial and common law doctrines, he argues that "the language of s. 35(1) cannot be construed as a wholesale repudiation of the common law."[78] In his words, section 35 is a "new chapter," not a "new book."[79] Rather than using the opportunity to step back from common law Aboriginal rights or colonial legal doctrines provided by *Sparrow*, Binnie J. advocates for the incorporation of colonial and pre-1982 common law doctrines (or more accurately, their limitations on Aboriginal rights) into section 35.[80] With this background in mind, then, the question remains: what room does Binnie J. leave for Indigenous law – the law in which section 35 rights are said to originate and through which they derive their content – to influence the Court's understanding of section 35? The answer is, not much.

Under Binnie J.'s analysis, the only legal orders that are clearly relevant to the identification of Aboriginal rights are Euro-derived. Section 35 Aboriginal rights seem, in his mind, to be solely the product of Indigenous people's "pre-contact practices" and Euro-derived legal orders, as is evident in his description of the process by which judges are to identify them:

> [I]n considering whether the evidence gives rise to the claimed right, it is necessary to look at all of the evidence to determine whether, in its totality, it establishes not only a pre-contact practice that was capable of being carried forward under the new European-based legal orders but a practice that is compatible with Canadian sovereignty.[81]

Here we see the replication of Lamer C.J.C.'s focus upon "practices" and "activities," combined with an explicit directive to focus exclusively on European-derived legal orders and an added requirement of sovereign compatibility. In this, rather than countering the problematic effects of the *Van der Peet* test, Binnie J. merely exacerbates them.

Binnie J. seems to believe that Indigenous law, or at least, Indigenous law in its own right, is irrelevant to section 35. Under his analysis, it is relevant only insofar as it can be demonstrated that the Crown intended for it to be so. Thus, for Binnie J., there are no existing relations between Indigenous and Canadian law other than those created by the Crown (which is more accurately understood as the Crown's relationship to itself). For a partial explanation of why he might take such a position, we can turn to his response to the following famous passage from the US case of *Worcester v. Georgia*:

America, separated from Europe by a wide ocean, was inhabited by a distinct people, divided into separate nations, independent of each other and of the rest of the world, having institutions of their own, and governing themselves by their own laws. It is difficult to comprehend the proposition, that the inhabitants of either quarter of the globe could have *rightful* original claims of dominion over the inhabitants of the other, or over the lands they occupied; or that the discovery of either by the other should give the discoverer rights in the country discovered, which annulled the pre-existing rights of its ancient possessors.[82]

In response, Binnie J. writes, "nevertheless, this is what happened. From the aboriginal perspective, moreover, those early claims to European 'dominion' grew to reality in the decades that followed."[83] It is through this concept of European settlers' *rightful* dominion over Indigenous peoples that Binnie J. defends the position taken by Lamer C.J.C. in *Gladstone* and *Delgamuukw*: that "distinctive aboriginal societies exist within, and are a part of, a broader social, political and economic community, over which the Crown is sovereign."[84] From this perspective, Indigenous legal orders were completely displaced by Euro-derived legal orders by virtue of European settlers' right to dominion over Indigenous peoples.

Rather than supporting his assertion that Canadian dominion over Indigenous peoples is rightful, Binnie J. attempts to make this existence within Canada sound attractive: without their laws, their legal orders, or their institutions of governance, though with access to the small, but constitutionally protected, space created by *Van der Peet,* Indigenous people can pursue those practices that the Court believes are Aboriginal. He argues that because Indigenous people would be allowed to engage in "Court-certified" Aboriginal practices, this, in itself, could somehow effect "reconciliation between Canadian society and *its* aboriginal communities."[85] I would disagree with Binnie J.'s assertion that his vision of indigenous existence within Canadian sovereignty represents "partnership without assimilation."[86] I would say that the only offer made to Indigenous peoples by Binnie J. is to become partners in their own assimilation, and that the only reconciliation he proposes is for Indigenous peoples to reconcile themselves to their domination under Canadian sovereignty.[87]

Major J. alone concurred with Binnie J.; the rest of the Court endorsed McLachlin C.J.C.'s judgment. She herself did not directly address the relationship between Indigenous and Canadian legal orders. Nonetheless, in a brief passage, she mentions a particular understanding of the relations between them: the absorption model. It is unclear how she positions herself regarding this understanding of the relations between Indigenous and Canadian legal orders. However, for the following reasons, I do not believe that she meant to incorporate the absorption model into section 35 analysis: she employs a descriptive tone when discussing the absorption model, unlike in the rest of the judgment;[88] immediately after describing the model, she re-emphasizes the fact that section 35 "extends beyond the aboriginal rights recognized at common law";[89] and she uses the term "absorption" in relation to the doctrines of continuity and sovereign incompatibility, both of which she was hesitant to incorporate into section 35.[90] Despite the uncertain relation between the absorption model and section 35, the possibility that this view lies behind current Aboriginal rights jurisprudence cannot simply be discounted. McLachlin C.J.C.'s wording at the end of this passage is almost identical to that of the *Van der Peet* test.[91] Moreover, the absorption model could potentially provide an explanation for the otherwise contradictory aspects of section 35 jurisprudence, regardless of how problematic that explanation may be.[92]

Before one analyzes McLachlin C.J.C.'s description of the absorption model, it is important to pay close attention to what the model says about the relations between Indigenous and Canadian legal orders. In the beginning of her judgment, McLachlin C.J.C. writes,

Long before Europeans explored and settled North America, aboriginal peoples were occupying and using most of this vast expanse of land in organized, distinctive societies with their own social and political structures. The part of North America we now call Canada was first settled by the French and the British who, from the first days of exploration, claimed sovereignty over the land on behalf of their nations. *English law, which ultimately came to govern aboriginal rights, accepted that the aboriginal peoples possessed pre-existing laws and interests, and recognized their continuance in the absence of extinguishment, by cession, conquest, or legislation* ... Accordingly, European settlement did not terminate the interests of aboriginal peoples arising from their historical occupation and use of the land. *To the contrary, aboriginal interests and customary laws were presumed to survive the assertion of sovereignty, and were absorbed into the common law as rights,* unless (1) they were incompatible with the Crown's assertion of sovereignty, (2) they were surrendered voluntarily via the treaty process, or (3) the government extinguished them. *Barring one of these exceptions, the practices, customs and traditions that defined the various aboriginal societies as distinctive cultures continued as part of the law of Canada.*[93]

Thus, an absorption model approach to section 35 would explain the relations between section 35 rights, Indigenous law, and Indigenous and Canadian legal orders in the following way: Indigenous legal orders existed; upon the assertion of Crown sovereignty, Indigenous legal orders ceased to exist; and, simultaneously, Indigenous laws were assimilated into the law of Canada. These allegedly assimilated laws are transformed from laws that govern the ways in which Indigenous people engaged with others into "interests." These "interests" in turn become common law "rights" structuring the relationship between the Canadian state and "its" Aboriginal peoples, marking the boundary of a legally protected space within the Canadian state for Indigenous people to engage in what Canadian judges consider to be "aboriginal cultural practices."[94]

The absorption model would not reduce Indigenous laws purely to fact, as Lamer C.J.C.'s approach attempted to do in *Van der Peet*. However, under this analysis, such laws would remain historical in nature. Thus, the absorption model also limits the ability of Canadian judges to attend to the dynamic and existing nature of Indigenous laws and engage respectfully with Indigenous legal orders. Under this model, Indigenous legal orders would certainly exert more influence upon the content of section 35 rights than under the approach advocated by Binnie J. They would be understood to have been assimilated into, rather than displaced by, Canadian law upon the assertion of sovereignty. Pre-contact Indigenous legal orders would be understood not to have survived the assertion of sovereignty. However, they would continue to influence the substantive content of section 35 rights and, in this limited way, contribute to structuring the relations between Indigenous peoples and the Canadian state. As the product of their assimilation, Aboriginal rights would be defined by Indigenous law but enforceable under Canadian law.[95] Thus, the absorption model provides an explanation for the inter-legal nature of Aboriginal rights and the Court's failure to consider the implications of Indigenous legal orders' continuing existence. However, accepting this explanation would undermine any potential that section 35 may hold to transform the adverse relations between Indigenous and Canadian legal orders and work towards any meaningful form of reconciliation between existing Indigenous peoples and the Canadian state.

Under the absorption model, Canadian judges would seek to reconcile Canadian law, Crown sovereignty, and the Canadian state with the interests they attribute to Indigenous peoples as based on judicial interpretations of Indigenous law prior to the assertion of sovereignty. There are three problems with this approach. First, it reduces reconciliation to a process not unlike reconciling financial accounts.[96] Reconciliation within the absorption model is focused on attempting to find the correct number of rights to legitimate Crown sovereignty and compensate Indigenous peoples for the assimilation of their legal orders. Second, it focuses exclusively upon reconciling the interests that judges attribute to peoples prior to the assertion of sovereignty. Although today's Indigenous people may benefit from such efforts, these benefits are indirect; they are not intended to address the interests judges might otherwise attribute to Indigenous people based on existing Indigenous law.[97] Third, the adequacy of this entire approach is wholly dependent upon the non-existence of Indigenous legal orders after the assertion of sovereignty.

The absorption model is subject to the same flaw as is Binnie J.'s approach, that is, it rests upon the claim that settler societies were capable of unilaterally terminating (according to Binnie J.) or assimilating (according to the absorption model) Indigenous legal orders through the mere assertion of sovereignty. This claim has been strongly contested by Indigenous peoples, and as long as this remains so, any approach based upon it is unlikely to lead to reconciliation between Indigenous peoples and the Canadian state. Furthermore, Canadian law's refusal to recognize the continuing existence of Indigenous legal orders does not render them non-existent.[98] Indigenous legal orders have never derived their authority from Euro-derived law, and they do not require recognition by Euro-derived law to remain in existence. They continue to exist and influence the lives of Indigenous people.[99] If the absorption approach were adopted, however, Canadian law would remain unable to respond to the continuing existence of Indigenous legal orders and would further entrench its adverse relations with the legal orders Indigenous to these lands.

Retreating to the Divide: *R. v. Marshall; R. v. Bernard*

The Supreme Court's most recent consideration of the relationship between Indigenous law and section 35 occurs in the joint decision *R. v. Marshall; R. v. Bernard*.[100] These cases stem from charges laid against Joshua Bernard, from Eel Ground First Nation, and Stephen Frederick Marshall, from Millbrook First Nation. Marshall was charged with cutting timber on Crown lands contrary to Nova Scotia's *Crown Lands Act;* Bernard was charged under the New Brunswick *Crown Lands and Forest Act* for unlawful possession of logs cut by other Mi'kmaq community members, also on Crown lands.[101]

Both argued that, as Mi'kmaq, they did not require authorization to log, relying upon both Aboriginal title and the "peace and friendship treaties" negotiated between the British and the Mi'kmaq, Maliseet, and Passamaquoddy in 1760 and 1761.[102] Writing for the majority of the Court, McLachlin C.J.C. found that the respondents did not possess Aboriginal title to the cutting sites and that commercial logging activities by the Mi'kmaq were not protected under the treaties of 1760 and 1761; thus, she reinstated the convictions.[103] LeBel J. (Fish J. concurring) reaches the same result; however, he wrote a separate judgment arguing that the majority's approach focused too narrowly on common law concepts.

In *Mitchell*, the Court was directly confronted with the unresolved issues and tensions regarding the nature of the relations between Indigenous law, section 35, and various forms of Euro-derived law.[104] Under McLachlin C.J.C.'s authorship, the majority of the Court described but did not endorse the absorption model, which would explain the sui generis, inter-legal, nature of Aboriginal rights in a way that undercuts the Court's capacity to transform Canadian law's adverse relations with Indigenous legal orders. Therefore, both the relation between the absorption model and current section 35 jurisprudence and the tensions created by Lamer C.J.C.'s contradictory treatment of Indigenous law in *Van der Peet* remain unresolved.

In *Marshall and Bernard*, McLachlin C.J.C. neither endorses nor rejects the absorption model as a way of understanding relations between Indigenous law, Euro-derived law, and section 35. Instead, she attempts to sidestep these issues by disregarding the Court's earlier affirmation of Indigenous law's relevancy to Aboriginal rights. It is almost as though she went out of her way to remove any reference to Indigenous law from the text of the judgment. It leaves one with the impression that the many complicated questions regarding the relations between Indigenous law, Euro-derived law, and section 35 have somehow just vanished into thin air. In contrast, LeBel J.'s judgment challenged this omission, emphasizing these very same issues.[105] Both judgments addressed the respondents' Aboriginal title and treaty rights claims. However, I will limit my analysis to those portions of the judgment that deal with the Aboriginal title claims where the contention over the relevance of Indigenous law is more readily apparent.

In *Marshall and Bernard*, McLachlin C.J.C. simply ignores the Court's previous affirmation of Indigenous law as one of the primary sources of section 35 rights. She describes Aboriginal rights as though they were sourced exclusively in Indigenous people's prior occupancy and use of these lands,[106] diverging both from her earlier critique of Lamer C.J.C.'s overfocus on prior occupation and from his acknowledgment that Aboriginal rights are also sourced in the relationship between Indigenous legal systems and the common law.[107] Thus, rather than addressing Lamer C.J.C.'s failure to give effect to his affirmation, the Court attempts to obtain distance from the affirmation itself.

McLachlin C.J.C.'s apparent retreat from the Court's finding that Aboriginal rights are sourced in Indigenous law leads her to reformulate the role of Indigenous peoples' perspectives in the identification of section 35 rights and the reasoning behind the requirement that judges be sensitive to these perspectives. Dickson C.J.C. and La Forest J. considered it necessary for Canadian courts to be "sensitive to the aboriginal perspective ... *on the meaning of the rights at stake.*"[108] Earlier statements made by the Court indicated that this requirement flowed from the inter-legal nature of section 35 rights and the fact that the section cannot be understood solely in terms of common law concepts. Being true to the inter-legal characterization of Aboriginal rights would require McLachlin C.J.C. to engage with the very thing she is seeking to avoid: Indigenous law. Thus, in *Marshall and Bernard,* McLachlin C.J.C. restricts the role of Indigenous peoples' perspectives to providing a vantage point from which Canadian judges consider the past practice at issue, rather than the right.[109]

Under McLachlin C.J.C.'s approach in *Marshall and Bernard,* the criteria for establishing Aboriginal title are derived entirely from the common law. Indigenous laws do not give rise to Aboriginal rights or influence their nature; indeed, even the practices of Indigenous people do not. The most an Indigenous practice seems capable of doing is gaining Indigenous people access to a right that already exists under the common law. As McLachlin C.J.C. states,

> The Court must consider the pre-sovereignty practice from the perspective of the aboriginal people. But in translating it to a common law right, the Court must also consider the European perspective; *the nature of the right at common law must be examined to determine whether a particular aboriginal practice fits it* ... we are required to consider whether the practices of aboriginal peoples at the time of sovereignty compare with the core notions of *common law title to land* ... aboriginal title to land ... is established by aboriginal practices that indicate possession similar to that associated with title at common law.[110]

Absent in McLachlin C.J.C.'s analysis is any indication that Aboriginal rights are generated within the relationship between Indigenous and Canadian law. Indeed, her judgment gives one the impression that a limited number of prefabricated rights are available within the common law and that the only thing Indigenous about Aboriginal title is the people who are found to possess it. In this particular case, for example, McLachlin C.J.C. finds that the right to control the land and exclude others is "basic to the notion of title at common law."[111] She does not look to what might be basic to Indigenous conceptions of relationship to territory. Rather, she asks whether Indigenous people's practices signify exclusive possession, a central tenet within the Euro-derived conception of relation to territory, merely adjusting the standards of proof to compensate for Indigenous peoples' "world and value system[s]."[112]

By treating Indigenous peoples' philosophies as discrepancies for which Aboriginal rights law must compensate, McLachlin C.J.C. is limiting the capacity of Canadian judges to utilize section 35 to interpret Aboriginal rights in a way that demonstrates respect for Indigenous legal orders and Indigenous peoples' conceptions of their relationship to and status within their territories. The rights available to Indigenous peoples appear limited to those already available within the common law. McLachlin C.J.C. seems unwilling to consider the possibility that Indigenous peoples may have understandings of their relationship to territory that are entitled to respect even though they may differ from the common law concept of title.[113] It is unclear where this leaves the Court in relation to its earlier declaration that Aboriginal rights are sui generis. Certainly, it does not appear that McLachlin C.J.C. is interpreting the sui generis nature of Aboriginal rights as an enabling concept, but it remains to be seen whether she is rejecting the sui generis characterization of Aboriginal rights altogether. As the Court does not endorse the assertion of Aboriginal title in either case, McLachlin C.J.C. did not comment upon the content of Aboriginal title. However, it appears that the only role that the sui generis characterization of Aboriginal rights has left to play under this approach is that of limiting, or downgrading, Aboriginal rights.

In his judgment, LeBel J. takes a strong stance against McLachlin C.J.C.'s failure to give effect to the Court's earlier affirmation of Indigenous law's relevancy to Aboriginal rights. He highlights the incompatibilities between her judgment and previous section 35 jurisprudence. He emphasizes the sui generis nature of Aboriginal title and, in contrast to the majority's limitation upon the role of Indigenous peoples' perspectives in section 35 jurisprudence, he argues that

> The role of the aboriginal perspective cannot be simply to help in the interpretation of aboriginal practices in order to assess whether they conform to common law concepts of title. The aboriginal perspective shapes the very concept of aboriginal title ... aboriginal conceptions of territoriality, land-use and property should be used to modify and adapt the traditional common law concepts of property in order to develop an occupancy standard that incorporates both the aboriginal and common law approaches. Otherwise, we might be implicitly accepting the position that aboriginal peoples

had no rights in land prior to the assertion of Crown sovereignty because their views of property or land use do not fit within Euro-centric conceptions of property rights.[114]

LeBel J. takes a clear stance on the sui generis characterization of Aboriginal rights, arguing that it should be understood as a concept that enables, and indeed requires, Canadian law to recognize rights that are not grounded within Euro-derived law and that he believes would otherwise be ignored.

For LeBel J., Aboriginal title, as an Aboriginal right, is defined by its relationship to Indigenous and to Canadian law. He argues that Aboriginal title "has been recognized by the common law and is in part defined by the common law, but it is grounded in aboriginal customary laws relating to land,"[115] reminding the Court of its previous statements, which construct Aboriginal title as an inter-legal right.[116] He recognizes that "it is very difficult to introduce aboriginal conceptions of property and ownership into the modern property law concepts of the civil law and common law systems."[117] However, it is certain that he understands this to be the goal. He speaks highly of Cromwell J.A.'s judgment in the Nova Scotia Court of Appeal, endorsing his attempts to reconcile Mi'kmaq and common law perspectives on ownership, transpose Indigenous peoples' perspectives and experiences upon "the structures of the law of property," and bridge the gaps between "sharply distinct cultural perspectives on the relationship of different peoples with their land."[118]

LeBel J. advocates for interpreting the sui generis, inter-legal nature of Aboriginal rights as an enabling concept and giving Lamer C.J.C.'s recognition of Aboriginal rights as those that arise out of the relationship between Indigenous and Canadian legal orders. However, as the analysis of the absorption model discussed in connection with *Mitchell* demonstrates, this, in itself, is not enough to transform Canadian law's adverse relations with Indigenous legal orders. LeBel J., though arguing effectively against the majority's disregard of the Court's previous comments concerning the relation between section 35 rights and Indigenous legal orders, does not remedy the absorption model's inability to support respectful engagements with existing Indigenous legal orders. Nor does he provide an alternative understanding of the relationship between Indigenous legal orders, section 35, and Canadian law.

Reconciliation without Respect?
What effect has section 35 had upon Canada's relations with Indigenous legal orders, more than twenty years after its introduction into Canadian law? In *Sparrow*, it is clear that the Supreme Court modified the way in which Canadian law understands the position and status of Indigenous

peoples within Canadian Aboriginal rights law and called for Canadian judges to develop a sui generis approach to understanding Aboriginal rights. In *Van der Peet,* it was found that Indigenous laws are relevant to section 35 and inform section 35 rights. However, this finding was not given effect within *Van der Peet*'s definitional test, or in the frameworks that govern the exercise of Aboriginal rights under section 35. Moreover, as shown in the examination of the absorption model described in *Mitchell,* giving effect to the relevancy of Indigenous law to section 35, in itself, does not transform Canadian law's adverse relations with Indigenous legal orders. The Court's decisions in *Marshall and Bernard* demonstrate that the majority of the Court is attempting to avoid the issue altogether. Meanwhile, the two Justices who continue to seek to give effect to Indigenous law's relevancy to section 35 have not provided an alternative framework that can do so *and* structure the judiciary's engagement with Indigenous law in a manner that is conducive to establishing respectful relations with Indigenous legal orders.

To date, the absorption model is the only approach discussed by the Supreme Court that advances a position on the relations between Indigenous and Canadian legal orders that attends to the Court's characterization of section 35 rights as sui generis, inter-legal rights informed by Indigenous laws. However, if these relations are understood through the absorption model, section 35 would be rendered incapable of supporting the establishment of respectful relations between Indigenous and Canadian legal orders. In addition, its potential would be reduced to securing benefits for Indigenous people within Canadian law's continuing adverse relations with Indigenous legal orders.

One of the greatest limitations of the absorption model is its inability to appreciate and respect the nature and purpose of Indigenous law. Indigenous laws are not merely rules or customs that generate interests at Canadian law. They cannot be understood in this way, as if they were separate from the dynamic processes through which Indigenous peoples live their laws into the physical world. Moreover, the purpose of Indigenous legal orders is not to generate interests to define Canadian Aboriginal rights law. Indigenous legal orders are directed, first and foremost, towards supporting the efforts of Indigenous peoples to maintain good relations: relations within communities, relations between communities, and relations with the other beings of creation. Indigenous laws work to structure the roles and the responsibilities of Indigenous people in terms of these relations.[119]

For three main reasons, the absorption model provides an inadequate framework to enable Canadian courts to participate in the establishment of respectful relations with Indigenous legal orders. First, it includes a temporal limitation constraining the influence of Indigenous law and Indigenous legal orders, rendering the Court unable to acknowledge their engagement with existing Indigenous legal orders. Second, it assumes that Canadian judges have the capacity and the authority to make determinative interpretations of Indigenous laws.[120] And third, it presumes that Canadian law is capable of unilaterally determining what constitutes respectful (or just) relations between Indigenous peoples and the Canadian state, as well as between Indigenous and Canadian legal orders, ignoring the Indigenous laws that also speak to these relations. Under the absorption model, Canadian judges would attempt to define relations between the Canadian state and Indigenous peoples by assimilating the Indigenous laws that speak to the relations between Indigenous peoples and the other beings of creation (such as the land, the fish, and the trees). Ironically, the Indigenous laws regarding the nature of respectful relations between Indigenous peoples and the Canadian state are completely disregarded under this approach.

If section 35 lost even the limited potential it created to recognize, affirm, and respectfully engage with Indigenous law, this would affect much more than just the ability of Indigenous people to advance claims for the recognition of Indigenous laws by way of the section. It would frustrate any effort made by the court to participate in any process of reconciliation with anything but itself. It is a mistake to believe that Canadian courts, merely by interpreting section 35, can provide the long overdue, authoritative, and final determination of the relationship between Indigenous peoples and the Canadian state.[121] The status of Indigenous peoples and the rights they hold according to Canadian law does not determine what respectful relations between the Canadian state and Indigenous peoples should entail. Moreover, determining the status of Indigenous legal orders *within* Canadian law does not determine what respectful relations *between* Indigenous and Canadian legal orders may require.

The adoption of the absorption model would require the court to abandon its most promising inheritance in its relation to Indigenous peoples and their legal orders: all of the instances of limited, imperfect, and fleeting recognitions of Indigenous law, those within section 35 jurisprudence and those existing outside section 35. It would require Canadian courts to replace Canada's previous attempts to deny the existence or relevancy of Indigenous law with yet another denial: of the continuing existence and relevance of Indigenous legal orders. Thus, courts would effectively frustrate their ability to move beyond the detrimental relations between Indigenous and Canadian legal orders. As long as Indigenous peoples still work to maintain their own traditions, laws, and legal orders, such relations turn section 35 into yet another form of attempted assimilation.

Section 35 did not create the task that Canadian law has, as of yet, left undone, a task that will remain outstanding until respectful relations between Indigenous and Canadian legal orders are established. This task is one that Canadian legal orders cannot undertake alone. They can ensure that they are able to participate only by moving beyond the limitations of their attempts to reconcile Indigenous and Canadian law *within* Canadian legal orders and working towards fostering respect in the existing relations between legal orders. It is clear that section 35 has taken its place among the many imperfect attempts to recognize Indigenous peoples' laws. The question is – can it become something more?

Continuing to Relate through Indigenous Legal Orders

In our history it tells us of a prophecy of the seventh fire, fire representing time, eras. In that prophecy, it says that in the time of seventh fire a new people will emerge to retrace the steps of our grandfathers, to retrieve the things that were lost but not of our own accord. There was time in the history of Anishnabe people we nearly lost all of these things that we once had as a people, and that road narrowed ... But today we strive to remind our people of our stories once again, to pick up that work that we as Anishnabe people know. *It is our work and we ask no one to do that work, for it is our responsibility to maintain those teachings for our people.*[122]

These words were spoken by my uncle, Charles Nelson, when the Royal Commission on Aboriginal Peoples came to Roseau River Anishinabe First Nation. Some years have passed since then, but his words remain true. There is still much work to be done, regardless of whether Canadian courts acknowledge the continued existence and relevance of our ways of law making and governance. We, as Indigenous peoples, need not wait for recognition by the courts, or permission from the Canadian state, to pick up that work that we know to be ours. As Professors Taiaiake Alfred and Jeff Corntassel remind us, "we only need to start to use *our* Indigenous languages to frame our thoughts, the ethical framework of *our* philosophies to make decisions and to use *our* laws and institutions to govern ourselves."[123] Our legal orders, our institutions, our ways, although they have been affected by generations of attempts to destabilize them, continue to operate: within the lives of individuals, within the families, and within the communities that have continued to pick up their work as Anishinabe people.[124]

Those who continue their work – to pick up, to revitalize, and to maintain their laws, their institutions, and their ways – join with long lines of others, reaching back countless generations: others who have continued the efforts of those who came before them, efforts to maintain their communities, their traditions, and their roles within creation. We, as Anishinabe, may not always have been able to effect what we most wanted to see happen in the world, but in order to maintain our ways, our legal orders, or our governance structures, we did not need to do so. The choices available to the Anishinabe may have been severely restricted, but we have continued to make decisions among those that were available.[125] There have always been Anishinabe, and there will continue to be Anishinabe, who make these decisions according to their understanding of Anishinabe law and of the ways that we were given.

The courts may not understand the purpose of the ways that were given to the Anishinabe; they may believe that their only value is to structure our relationship to the Canadian state. That does not mean that others do not remember. The ways that were given to the Anishinabe were not given merely to aid our people in securing rights and recognition from others. They were not given to us merely so that we might retain a cultural continuity with our ancestors. The ways that were given to the Anishinabe were given to us to support our efforts to pursue good lives. They provide us with a source of strength and guidance when we commit ourselves to living good lives, lives lived in harmony with all of our relations. It is for this reason that we must continue the work of our ancestors, to continue to relate to each other and to all of Creation through the ways that we know as Anishinabe and to maintain these teachings for future generations. As is still said within my community, the fate of the Anishinabe is tied to the fate of the ways that were given to the Anishinabe to carry, to work with, and to maintain.[126]

Acknowledgments

I would like to sincerely thank Professors John Borrows, James Tully, Jeremy Webber, Lorena Fontaine, and the late Perry Shawana, in addition to Charles Yung, Josephine Nelson, Allyssa Case, and the Master of Laws students of the University of Victoria for their comments on earlier drafts of this chapter; the Canadian Association of Law Teachers, the Canadian Council of Law Deans, the Canadian Law and Society Association, and the Law Commission of Canada for financially supporting the development of this chapter and the Legal Dimensions Initiative; the University of Victoria, the British Columbia Law Foundation, and the Social Sciences and Humanities Research Council for supporting my Master's studies (during which I wrote this chapter); and my family, my community, and the Anishinabe people for supporting and sustaining me.

Notes

1   What I know of the teachings given to the Anishinabe I have learned from my family, my elders, and the people of the Three Fires Midewiwin Lodge. However, any mistakes or misrepresentations I have made are my own, for I am still very much an Anishinabe learner with a great deal left to do.
2   Western theory has a long history of attempting to draw "bright lines" that distinguish legal traditions from "non-legal" traditions. It is not yet clear to me that such delineations are understood to be as important within Indigenous communities. In this essay, I focus upon Indigenous traditions, institutions, and ways of life as they address the concerns of what many understand to be "law" and can therefore be understood as "legal." However, what I understand to be Indigenous peoples' laws, legal traditions, legal systems, and legal orders might also be understood as Indigenous peoples' traditions or institutions of governance, education, or medicine, for example.
3   See *e.g.* Mark D. Walters, "The Morality of Aboriginal Law" (2006) 31 Queen's L.J. 470 at 489-94 [Walters, "Morality"]; John Borrows, "Creating an Indigenous Legal Community"

(2005) 50 McGill L.J. 153 [Borrows, "Indigenous Legal Community"]; Robert A. Williams, *Linking Arms Together: American Indian Treaty Visions of Law and Peace, 1600-1800* (New York: Oxford University Press, 1997).

4 See *e.g.* John Borrows, "Wampum at Niagara: Canadian Legal History, Self-Government, and the Royal Proclamation" in Michael Asch, ed., *Aboriginal and Treaty Rights in Canada: Essays on Law, Equality, and Respect for Difference* (Vancouver: UBC Press, 1997) 155; James (Sákéj) Youngblood Henderson, "Empowering Treaty Federalism" (1994) 58 Sask. L. Rev. 241; Harold Cardinal and Walter Hildebrandt, *Treaty Elders of Saskatchewan: Our Dream Is That Our People Will One Day Be Clearly Recognized as Nations* (Calgary: University of Calgary Press, 2000).

5 See *e.g.* Canada, *Report of the Royal Commission on Aboriginal Peoples: Looking Forward, Looking Back,* vol. 1 (Ottawa: Supply and Services Canada, 1996) at 31-41 [Canada, *RCAP: Looking Forward*].

6 See *Connolly v. Woolrich* (1867), 11 L.C. Jur. 197 (Qc. Sup. Ct.); *R. v. Nan-e-quis-a Ka* (1889), 1 Terr. L. R. 211 (C.A.); *Re Deborah E4-789,* [1972] 5 W.W.R. 203 (N.W.T.C.A.), *(sub. nom. Kitchooalik v. Tucktoo* (1972), 28 D.L.R. (3d) 483).

7 For a recent example of this view, see *Delgamuukw v. British Columbia* (1991), 79 D.L.R. (4th) 185 (B.C.S.C.), McEachern C.J., rev'd (1993), 104 D.L.R. (4th) 470 (B.C.C.A.), rev'd [1997] 3 S.C.R. 1010 [*Delgamuukw* cited to S.C.R.] ("Gitksan and Wet'suwet'en laws and customs are not sufficiently certain to permit a finding that they or their ancestors governed the territory according to Aboriginal laws even though some Indians may well have chosen to follow local customs when it was convenient to do so." at 449).

8 For a recent example of this view, see *ibid.* ("the Aboriginal system, to the extent it constituted Aboriginal jurisdiction of sovereignty, or ownership apart from occupation for residence and use, gave way to an [sic] new colonial form of government which the law recognizes to the exclusion of all other systems ... After that, Aboriginal customs, to the extent they could be described as laws before the creation of the colony became customs ... they ceased to have any force, as laws, within the colony." at 453).

9 The following statement made by Binnie J. in his minority judgment could be interpreted as a modern example of this view: "Counsel for the respondent ... seeks for the Mohawk people of the Iroquois Confederacy the maximum degree of legal autonomy to which he believes they are entitled because of their long history at Akwesasne and elsewhere in eastern North America. This asserted autonomy, to be sure, does not presently flow from the ancient Iroquois legal order that is said to have created it, but from the Constitution Act, 1982. Section 35(1), adopted by the elected representatives of Canadians, recognizes and affirms existing aboriginal and treaty rights. If the respondent's claimed aboriginal right is to prevail, it does so not because of its own inherent strength, but because the Constitution Act, 1982 brings about that result." *Mitchell v. M.N.R.,* [2001] 1 S.C.R. 911 at para. 70, 2001 SCC 33 [*Mitchell*].

10 See *e.g.* Mark D. Walters, "British Imperial Constitutional Law and Aboriginal Rights: A Comment on *Delgamuukw v. British Columbia*" (1992) 17:2 Queen's L.J. 350 ["British Imperial"].

11 I use the term "Euro-derived law" to refer to the law of European countries, of countries such as Canada and the United States (because the development of their law was based on the law of European countries), and of international legal systems such as the United Nations. It is often assumed that Euro-derived international law is global or universal in nature. However, the vast majority of Indigenous polities are not members of this system; it is not reflective of their forms of law and does not speak to the international laws, treaties, and relations existing between Indigenous peoples. For a discussion of an inter-Indigenous treaty, see Victor P. Lytwyn, "A Dish with One Spoon: The Shared Hunting Grounds Agreement in the Great Lakes and St. Lawrence Valley Region" in David H. Pentland, ed., *Papers of the 28th Algonquian Conference* (Winnipeg: University of Manitoba, 1997) 210.

12 On the dangers of framing Indigenous peoples' political goals according to statist models, see Taiaiake Alfred, *Peace, Power, Righteousness: An Indigenous Manifesto* (Oxford: Oxford University Press, 1999) at 55-58.

13 Not all Canadians feel that the Canadian state reflects their traditions, legal or otherwise. However, for the purposes of this chapter, I focus upon the ability of the Canadian state to develop its traditions and not upon whether they reflect the diversity of its citizens.

14   Given that Canada's legal orders are implicated in attempts to eliminate Indigenous legal orders, such an effort should also include finding ways to respectfully support the revitalization of the latter.

15   Part II of the *Constitution Act, 1982*, s. 35(1), being Schedule B to the *Canada Act 1982* (U.K.), 1982, c. 11.

16   I consider the establishment of respectful relations between Indigenous and Canadian legal orders a necessary, though not sufficient, condition of establishing respectful relations between Canadian and Indigenous societies.

17   See *e.g.* Borrows, "Indigenous Legal Community," *supra* note 3; Douglas Lambert, "The Future of Indigenous Laws in the Canadian Legal System" (2006) 64 Advocate 216.

18   For some, the debate about Aboriginal rights centres upon their definition, nature, and content. However, others contest the desirability of including Aboriginal rights in the *Constitution Act, 1982*. See *e.g.* Tom Flanagan, *First Nations? Second Thoughts* (Montreal and Kingston: McGill-Queen's University Press, 2000) (Professor Flanagan argues that differentiating between the rights of Indigenous people and settlers is discriminatory) and Taiaiake Alfred and Jeff Corntassel, "Being Indigenous: Resurgences against Contemporary Colonialism" (2005) 40 Government and Opposition 497 (Professors Alfred and Corntassel argue that the *Constitution Act, 1982* represents the culmination of attempts to subordinate Indigenous peoples to an unjust relation within the construct of the colonial state).

19   *R. v. Sparrow*, [1990] 1 S.C.R. 1075 *[Sparrow]; R. v. Van der Peet*, [1996] 2 S.C.R. 507 *[Van der Peet]; Mitchell, supra* note 9; *R. v. Marshall; R. v. Bernard*, [2005] 2 S.C.R. 220, 2005 SCC 43 *[Marshall and Bernard]*.

20   See *e.g. R. v. St. Catherine's Milling and Lumber Company* (1888), 14 A.C. 46 (P.C.).

21   *Calder v. British Columbia (A.G.)*, [1973] S.C.R. 313 *[Calder]* (In this case, the prior occupation of Indigenous peoples was found to give rise to rights under Canadian law; however, the Court split on the issue of whether these rights had been extinguished by general legislation); see also Michael Asch, "From *Calder* to *Van der Peet*: Aboriginal Rights and Canadian Law, 1973-96" in Paul Havemann, ed., *Indigenous Peoples' Rights: In Australia, Canada and New Zealand* (Oxford: Oxford University Press, 1999) 428.

22   *Sparrow, supra* note 19 at 1103. See also Minister of Indian Affairs and Northern Development, *Statement of Government of Canada on Indian Policy, 1996 [The White Paper]* (Ottawa: Indian and Northern Affairs Canada, 1969) ("aboriginal claims to land ... are so general and undefined that it is not realistic to think of them as specific claims capable of remedy" at 11).

23   *Sparrow, ibid.* Although s. 35 issues were raised in three Supreme Court cases prior to *Sparrow*, these cases were decided without reference to the *Constitution Act, 1982*. See *R. v. Simon*, [1985] 2 S.C.R. 387; *R. v. Horse*, [1988] 1 S.C.R. 187; *R. v. Sioui*, [1990] 1 S.C.R. 1025 *[Sioui]*.

24   *Sparrow, ibid.* at 1099.

25   *Ibid.* at 1106-8.

26   Noel Lyon, "An Essay on Constitutional Interpretation" (1988) 26 Osgoode Hall L.J. 95 at 100 cited in *Sparrow, ibid.* at 1105-6.

27   This point was reaffirmed in later judgments. See *R. v. Côté*, [1996] 3 S.C.R. 139; *Delgamuukw, supra* note 7 at para. 136; see also *Van der Peet, supra* note 19 at para. 225.

28   See *Sparrow, supra* note 19 at 1084 and 1097.

29   *Ibid.* at 1091, affirming *R. v. Agawa* (1988), 28 O.A.C. 201, Blair J.A.

30   *Sparrow, ibid.*

31   *Ibid.* at 1109-10.

32   *Canadian Charter of Rights and Freedoms*, s. 1, Part I of the *Constitution Act, 1982*, being Schedule B to the *Canada Act 1982* (U.K.), 1982, c. 11 ("The Canadian Charter of Rights and Freedoms guarantees the rights and freedoms set out in it subject only to such reasonable limits prescribed by law as can be demonstrably justified in a free and democratic society"). Compare Part VII of the *Constitution Act, 1982*, s. 52(1) *ibid.* ("The Constitution of Canada is the supreme law of Canada, and any law that is inconsistent with the provisions of the Constitution is, to the extent of the inconsistency, of no force or effect").

33 *Sparrow, supra* note 19 at 1103 (emphasis added). For critiques of this assertion, see *e.g.* Michael Asch and Patrick Macklem, "Aboriginal Rights and Canadian Sovereignty: An Essay on *R. v. Sparrow*" (1992) 29 Alta. L. Rev. 498 at 510; John Borrows, "Sovereignty's Alchemy: An Analysis of *Delgamuukw v. British Columbia*" (1999) 37 Osgoode Hall L.J. 537.

34 See *e.g.* James Tully, "The Struggles of Indigenous Peoples for and of Freedom" in Duncan Ivison, Paul Patton, and Will Sanders, eds., *Political Theory and the Rights of Indigenous Peoples* (Cambridge: Cambridge University Press, 2000) 36.

35 *Sparrow, supra* note 19 at 1111-12.

36 *Ibid.* at 1112. On the sui generis characterization of Aboriginal rights, see John Borrows and Leonard I. Rotman, "The Sui Generis Nature of Aboriginal Rights: Does It Make a Difference?" (1997) 36 Alta. L. Rev. 9; James (Sákéj) Youngblood Henderson, "Aboriginal Jurisprudence and Rights" in Kerry Wilkins, ed., *Advancing Aboriginal Claims: Visions/Strategies/ Directions* (Saskatoon: Purich Publishing, 2004) 67.

37 *Sparrow, supra* note 19 at 1078.

38 See Tully, *supra* note 34 at 46-47 (Professor Tully argues that characterizing Aboriginal rights as sui generis unjustly precludes Indigenous peoples from making appeals to the universal general rights of liberal Enlightenment based on freedom and equality of peoples, rights that would call the adverse relations between Indigenous peoples and the Canadian state into question. Tully makes this argument in relation to the "distinctiveness" approach developed after *Sparrow;* however, the distinctiveness approach is similar to understanding the sui generis characterization of Aboriginal rights as a limiting mechanism); see also Asch, *supra* note 21.

39 *Sparrow, supra* note 19 at 1112, citing Leroy Little Bear, "A Concept of Native Title" (1982) 5:2 Can. Legal Aid Bul. 99, and *R. v. Guerin,* [1984] 2 S.C.R. 335 *[Guerin].*

40 Little Bear, *ibid.;* see also Borrows and Rotman, *supra* note 36; Henderson, *supra* note 36.

41 *Guerin, supra* note 39 at para. 93, Dickson J. A similar approach was also taken in *R. v. Sioui,* in which the Court found that treaties between Indigenous peoples and settler societies do not constitute international treaties. Rather, by virtue of their sui generis nature, Indigenous-settler treaties are thought to fall "somewhere between the kind of relations conducted between sovereign states and the relations that such states had with their own citizens." *Sioui, supra* note 23 at para. 26.

42 Including *Van der Peet, supra* note 19; *R. v. N.T.C. Smokehouse,* [1996] 2 S.C.R. 672; and *R. v. Gladstone,* [1996] 2 S.C.R. 723 *[Gladstone].*

43 *Fisheries Act,* R.S.C. 1970, c. F-14, s. 61(1); *British Columbia Fishery (General) Regulations,* SOR/1984-248.

44 See *Van der Peet, supra* note 19 at paras. 1-4.

45 *Ibid.* at para. 93.

46 *Ibid.* at para. 222.

47 *Ibid.* at para. 322.

48 *Ibid.* at para. 40; *Mabo v. Queensland [No. 2]* (1992), 175 C.L.R. 1 (H.C. Aus.) *[Mabo 2].*

49 *Mabo 2, ibid.* at 58, citing *Re Southern Rhodesia,* [1919] A.C. 211 at 233 cited in *Van der Peet, supra* note 19 at para. 40.

50 *Van der Peet, ibid.*

51 "British Imperial," *supra* note 10 at 412-13 cited in *Van der Peet, ibid.*

52 Although Lamer C.J.C. mentions Indigenous laws once more (in relation to another quotation from *Mabo 2*), he quickly replaces the term with "practices, customs, and traditions." *Van der Peet, ibid.* at paras. 42, 63.

53 *Ibid.* at para. 41; see also *ibid.* at para. 31.

54 *Ibid.* at para. 230, McLachlin J., dissenting.

55 *Ibid.* at para. 56. Lamer C.J.C. equates practices, customs, and traditions with "activities" in the following statement: "[I]n order to be an aboriginal right an activity must be an element of a practice, custom or tradition integral to the distinctive culture of the aboriginal group claiming the right." *Ibid.* at para. 46.

56 Interveners Delgamuukw et. al., *R. v. Van der Peet,* [1996] 2 S.C.R. 507 (Factum of the Interveners) at para. 15 (emphasis in original), http://www.usask.ca/nativelaw/factums/ view.php?id=164.

57 See *e.g. Van der Peet, supra* note 19 ("the test for identifying the aboriginal rights recognized and affirmed by s. 35(1) must be directed at identifying the crucial elements of those pre-existing distinctive societies. It must, in other words, aim at identifying the practices, traditions and customs central to the aboriginal societies that existed in North America prior to contact with the Europeans." at para. 44).

58 *Ibid.* at para. 40; see also *ibid.* at para. 41.

59 See Russel Lawrence Barsh and James Youngblood Henderson, "The Supreme Court's *Van der Peet* Trilogy: Naive Imperialism and Ropes of Sand" (1997) 42 McGill L.J. 993 at 1007-8.

60 *Sparrow, supra* note 19 ("the phrase 'existing aboriginal rights' must be interpreted flexibly so as to permit their evolution over time ... Clearly, then, an approach to the constitutional guarantee embodied in s. 35(1) which would incorporate 'frozen rights' must be rejected." at 1093). For critiques of Lamer C.J.C.'s approach on this basis, see *e.g.* Barsh and Henderson, *supra* note 59; John Borrows, "Frozen Rights in Canada: Constitutional Interpretation and the Trickster" (1997-98) 22 Am. Indian L. Rev. 45; Bradford W. Morse, "Permafrost Rights: Aboriginal Self-Government and the Supreme Court in *R. v. Pamajewon*" (1996-97) 42 McGill L.J. 1011; Anna Zalewski, "From *Sparrow* to *Van der Peet:* The Evolution of a Definition of Aboriginal Rights" (1997) 55 U.T. Fac. L. Rev. 435.

61 *Van der Peet, supra* note 19 at para. 64.

62 *Ibid.* at para. 63.

63 *Ibid.* ("the activities may be the exercise in a modern form of a practice, custom or tradition that existed prior to contact" at para. 64).

64 See Lisa Dufraimont, "From Regulation to Recolonization: Justifiable Infringement of Aboriginal Rights at the Supreme Court of Canada" (2000) 58 U.T. Fac. L. Rev. 1.

65 *Gladstone, supra* note 42 at para. 57.

66 See Ardith Walkem, "Constructing the Constitutional Box: The Supreme Court's Section 35(1) Reasoning" in Ardith Walkem and Halie Bruce, eds., *Box of Treasures or Empty Box? Twenty Years of Section 35* (Penticton: Theytus Books, 2003) 196 at 204-8.

67 See Borrows, "Frozen Rights," *supra* note 60.

68 See Borrows, "Indigenous Legal Community," *supra* note 3 ("Aboriginal law should not just be received as evidence that Aboriginal peoples did something in the past on a piece of land. It is more than evidence: it is actually law." at 173).

69 See *e.g. ibid.* ("Numerous indigenous legal traditions continue to function in Canada in systemically important ways. They influence the lives of indigenous and non-indigenous peoples").

70 For more on this subject, see chap. 4 in this collection, p. 128.

71 *Delgamuukw, supra* note 7 at para. 112.

72 *Ibid.* at para. 114.

73 *Customs Act*, R.S.C. 1985, c. 1 (2nd Supp.).

74 *Mitchell, supra* note 9 at para. 70. An entire book was written in response to this small passage: see Ardith Walkem and Halie Bruce, "Introduction" in Ardith Walkem and Halie Bruce, eds., *Box of Treasures or Empty Box? Twenty Years of Section 35* (Penticton: Theytus Books, 2003) 9 at 10.

75 See also *Mitchell, supra* note 9 at paras. 138-39, 141-44 (in which Binnie J. argues, first, that treaty rights are a promise made by the Crown and as such are an expression of Crown sovereignty and, second, that the recognition of Indigenous laws and customs flows solely from the presumption that the Crown intended to respect those customs and their resultant rights).

76 *Ibid.* at para. 144.

77 *Ibid.*

78 *Ibid.* at para. 150; see also *ibid.* at para. 149.

79 *Ibid.* at para. 115.

80 *Ibid.* at para. 144. The incorporation of these limitations at the definitional stage, advocated by Binnie J., would have circumvented both the requirement that the Crown demonstrate a clear and plain intention to extinguish Aboriginal rights prior to 1982 and the burden *Sparrow* placed upon the Crown to justify its infringement of Aboriginal rights. See *Sparrow, supra* note 19 at 1099, 1002.

81 *Mitchell, supra* note 9 at para. 123. See also *ibid.* at para. 73.
82 *Worcester v. Georgia,* 31 U.S. (6 Pet.) 515 at 542-43 (1832), Marshall C.J. (emphasis added). Binnie J., however, quoted only the following section: "'It is difficult to comprehend the proposition, that the inhabitants of either quarter of the globe could have rightful original claims of dominion over the inhabitants of the other, or over the lands they occupied.'" *Ibid.* at 543 cited in *Mitchell, supra* note 9 at para. 112.
83 *Mitchell, ibid.* at para. 113.
84 *Ibid.* at para. 133, citing *Gladstone, supra* note 42 at para. 73, and *Delgamuukw, supra* note 7 at para. 165; see also *Mitchell, ibid.* at para. 112-13.
85 *Ibid.* at para. 123 (emphasis added).
86 *Ibid.* at para. 130. Binnie J. describes Canadian sovereignty as a form of "merged sovereignty" within which "aboriginal and non-aboriginal Canadians together form a sovereign entity with a measure of common purpose and united effort." *Ibid.* at para. 129. Upon this basis, he attempts to unilaterally alter the *Gus-Wen-Tah,* a treaty created through many years of negotiation between the leaders of European and Haudenosaunee peoples. Some see this as positive, indicating a willingness to reinterpret Crown sovereignty in a manner favourable to Indigenous peoples. See *e.g.* Doug Moody, "Thinking outside the 20th Century Box: Revisiting 'Mitchell' – Some Comments on the Politics of Judicial Law-Making in the Context of Aboriginal Self-Government" (2003-4) 35 Ottawa L. Rev. 1. For a critique of Binnie J.'s reconceptualization of sovereignty, see Gordon Christie, "The Court's Exercise of Plenary Power: Rewriting the Two-Row Wampum" (2002) 16 Sup. Ct. L. Rev. (2d) 285 [Christie, "Rewriting the Two-Row Wampum"].
87 See *Mitchell, ibid.* at paras. 120 and 144. This view of reconciliation is akin to what Mark Walters describes as a one-sided approach to reconciliation in which Indigenous peoples' perspectives and aspirations are adapted to fit within "an otherwise fixed and immutable constitutional reality represented by the idea of Crown sovereignty." If this is so, he warns that the process of reconciliation "may become one of *resignation* rather than reconciliation: aboriginal peoples may have to resign themselves to the fact that they live under the Crown's sovereignty and adjust their expectations and aspirations accordingly." Walters, "Morality," *supra* note 3 at 501 (emphasis in original).
88 *Mitchell, supra* note 9 at paras. 8-9.
89 *Ibid.* at para. 10, citing *Delgamuukw, supra* note 7 at para. 136.
90 According to McLachlin C.J.C., the doctrine of sovereign incompatibility is sourced in the doctrine of continuity, which governs the absorption of Indigenous laws into the new legal regime. Regarding the relationship between such doctrines and s. 35, she states, "[t]his Court has not expressly invoked the doctrine of 'sovereign incompatibility' in defining the rights protected under s. 35(1) ... I would prefer to refrain from comment on the extent to which colonial laws of sovereign succession are relevant to the definition of aboriginal rights under s. 35(1) until such a time as it is necessary to do so." *Mitchell, ibid.* at paras. 63-64. See also *ibid.* at paras. 61-62.
91 See *ibid.* ("the practices, customs, and traditions that defined the various aboriginal societies as distinctive cultures continued as part of the law of Canada." at para. 10).
92 In particular, the absorption model could explain the following: the Supreme Court's automatic adherence to a traditional European conception of exclusive Crown sovereignty; the recognition of the existence of Indigenous laws (and, by implication, Indigenous legal orders) prior to European arrival; the relationship between Indigenous laws and s. 35 rights (Indigenous laws as the basis for s. 35 rights, giving them meaning and content); the inadequate engagement with Indigenous law by the Court; and the Court's failure to consider the implications that the existence of Indigenous legal orders hold for Canadian law and Canadian legal orders.
93 *Mitchell, supra* note 9 at paras. 9-10 (emphasis added, references omitted).
94 Christie refers to this approach as "compassionate colonialism," "for it envisions a complete transfer of power to the Crown, but with the *rights* of the indigenous peoples afforded the protection expected of other subjects of the Crown," as opposed to "ugly colonialism," the approach he believes the Court is moving towards. Christie, "Rewriting the Two-Row Wampum," *supra* note 86 at 300.

95   McLachlin C.J.C. makes a similar statement in *Van der Peet,* arguing that Canadian judges engaged in interpreting s. 35 "apply the common law, but the common law we apply must give full recognition to the pre-existing Aboriginal tradition." *Van der Peet, supra* note 19 at para. 232.

96   See Walters, "Morality," *supra* note 3 at 499-500 (in which he argues that "reconciliation" in the context of s. 35 means [or should mean] more than reconciling financial accounts – that it implies a moral exercise).

97   Today's Indigenous people are understood to benefit from the judicial attribution of an interest – and thus a corresponding right – to Indigenous peoples historically, because in so doing, Canadian judges also sanction the exercise of this right by current-day Indigenous people.

98   See Noel Pearson, "The Concept of Native Title at Common Law" in Galarrwuy Yunupingu, ed., *Our Land Is Our Life: Land Rights – Past, Present and Future* (St. Lucia, Queensland: University of Queensland Press, 1997) 150.

99   See *e.g.* John Borrows, "Indigenous Legal Traditions in Canada" (2005) 19 Wash. U.J.L & Pol'y 167 ("Indigenous legal traditions can have great force and impact in people's lives despite their lack of prominence in broader circles" at 174).

100   *Marshall and Bernard, supra* note 19. The Court did not directly consider the relationship between Indigenous law and s. 35 in *Mikisew Cree First Nation v. Canada (Minister of Canadian Heritage),* its most recent case to date. *Mikisew Cree First Nation v. Canada (Minister of Canadian Heritage),* [2005] 3 S.C.R. 388, 2005 SCC 69.

101   *Crown Lands Act,* R.S.N.S. 1989, c. 114, s. 29; *Crown Lands and Forest Act,* S.N.B. 1980, c. C-38.1, s. 67(1)(c).

102   Aboriginal harvesting rights were not asserted in this case.

103   *Marshall and Bernard, supra* note 19 at paras. 39, 106.

104   Particularly British colonial law, English and Canadian common law, and Canadian constitutional law.

105   Ironically, LeBel J.'s stance towards McLachlin C.J.C.'s majority judgment in *Marshall and Bernard* is strikingly similar to the stance McLachlin J. took regarding Lamer C.J.C.'s majority judgment in *Van der Peet.*

106   See *Marshall and Bernard, supra* note 19 ("Aboriginal peoples used the land in many ways at the time of sovereignty. *Some uses,* like hunting and fishing, *give rights* to continue those practices in today's world. Aboriginal title, *based on occupancy* at the time of sovereignty, is one of these various aboriginal rights." at para. 38, emphasis added, references omitted).

107   *Delgamuukw, supra* note 7 at para. 112.

108   *Sparrow, supra* note 19 at 1112.

109   See *Marshall and Bernard, supra* note 19 ("The Court must consider the pre-sovereignty practice from the perspective of the aboriginal people" at para. 48). See also *ibid.* at para. 52.

110   *Ibid.* at paras. 48, 61, 54, respectively.

111   *Ibid.* at para. 64.

112   *Ibid.* at para. 69. See also *ibid.* ("It is therefore critical to view the question of exclusion from the aboriginal perspective" at para. 64).

113   See *ibid.* ("The common law, over the centuries, has formalized title through a complicated matrix of legal edicts and conventions. The search for aboriginal title, by contrast, takes us back to the beginnings of the notion of title. Unaided by formal legal documents and written edicts, we are required to consider whether the practices of aboriginal peoples at the time of sovereignty compare with the core notions of common law title to land" at para. 61).

114   *Ibid.* at paras. 130, 127, respectively (reference omitted).

115   *Ibid.* at para. 128.

116   See *ibid.* at para. 129 (in which LeBel J. cites heavily from previous judgments regarding Indigenous law).

117   *Ibid.* at para. 128.

118   *Ibid.* at para. 130.

119   See Patricia Monture-Angus, *Journeying Forward: Dreaming First Nations' Independence* (Halifax: Fernwood Publishing, 2003).

120 As Professor Jeremy Webber attempted to warn the Australian Court, "the simple enforce-
     ment by the courts of interests held under indigenous law would produce detrimental
     results: it would displace indigenous methods of social ordering, freeze the development of
     indigenous law, and place the administration of that law in the hands of non-indigenous
     tribunals." Jeremy Webber, "Beyond Regret: Mabo's Implications for Australian Constitu-
     tionalism" in Duncan Ivison, Paul Patton, and Will Sanders, eds., *Political Theory and the
     Rights of Indigenous Peoples* (Cambridge: Cambridge University Press, 2000) 60 at 85.
121 This understanding is evident in many descriptions of s. 35 and the Canadian legal doc-
     trine of Aboriginal rights. See *e.g. Van der Peet, supra* note 19 at para. 230, dissenting (in
     which Justice McLachlin, as she was then, describes s. 35 as seeking not only "to reconcile
     these claims with European settlement and sovereignty but also to reconcile them in a way
     that provides the basis for a just and lasting settlement of aboriginal claims").
122 Canada, *RCAP: Looking Forward, supra* note 5 at 617-18. The speaker is referring to a proph-
     ecy shared by Edward Benton-Banai. See Edward Benton-Banai, *The Mishomis Book: The
     Voice of the Ojibway* (St. Paul, MN: Red School House, 1988).
123 Alfred and Corntassel, *supra* note 18 at 614 (emphasis in original).
124 In this section I refer specifically to the Anishinabe, as I myself am Anishinabe, and so it is
     to this experience that I will speak; however, it is my belief that much of what I say here is
     also true for many other Indigenous peoples.
125 See John Borrows, "Indian Agency and Taking What's Not Yours" (2003) 22 Windsor Y.B.
     Access Just. 253.
126 For more on the teachings given to the Anishinabe, see Benton-Banai, *supra* note 122.

Bibliography

Legislation
British Columbia Fishery (General) Regulations, SOR/1984-248.
Constitution Act, 1982, being Schedule B to the *Canada Act 1982* (U.K.), 1982, c. 11.
Crown Lands Act, R.S.N.S. 1989, c. 114.
Crown Lands and Forest Act, S.N.B. 1980, c. C-38.1.
Customs Act, R.S.C. 1985, c. 1 (2nd Supp.).
Fisheries Act, R.S.C. 1970, c. F-14, s. 61(1).

Jurisprudence
Calder v. British Columbia (A.G.), [1973] S.C.R. 313.
Connolly v. Woolrich (1867), 11 L.C. Jur. 197 (Qc. Sup. Ct.).
Delgamuukw v. British Columbia (1991), 79 D.L.R. (4th) 185.
Delgamuukw v. British Columbia, [1997] 3 S.C.R. 1010.
Mabo v. Queensland [No. 2] (1992), 175 C.L.R. 1.
Mikisew Cree First Nation v. Canada (Minister of Canadian Heritage), [2005] 3 S.C.R. 388, 2005
    SCC 69.
Mitchell v. M.N.R., [2001] 1 S.C.R. 911, 2001 SCC 33.
R. v. Agawa (1988), 28 O.A.C. 201.
R. v. Côté, [1996] 3 S.C.R. 139.
R. v. Gladstone, [1996] 2 S.C.R. 723.
R. v. Guerin, [1984] 2 S.C.R. 335.
R. v. Horse, [1988] 1 S.C.R. 187.
R. v. Marshall; R. v. Bernard, [2005] 2 S.C.R. 220, 2005 SCC 43.
R. v. Nan-e-quis-a Ka (1889), 1 Terr. L. R. 211 (C.A.).
R. v. N.T.C. Smokehouse, [1996] 2 S.C.R. 672.
R. v. Simon, [1985] 2 S.C.R. 387.
R. v. Sioui, [1990] 1 S.C.R. 1025.
R. v. Sparrow, [1990] 1 S.C.R. 1075.
R. v. St. Catherine's Milling and Lumber Company (1888), 14 A.C. 46 (P.C.).
R. v. Van der Peet, [1996] 2 S.C.R. 507.
Re Deborah E4-789, [1972] 5 W.W.R. 203 (N.W.T.C.A.), (sub. nom. *Kitchooalik v. Tucktoo*
    (1972), 28 D.L.R. (3d) 483).

Re Southern Rhodesia, [1919] A.C. 211.
Worcester v. Georgia, 31 U.S. (6 Pet.) 515 (1832).

Books and Chapters
Alfred, Taiaiake. *Peace, Power, Righteousness: An Indigenous Manifesto* (Oxford: Oxford University Press, 1999).
Asch, Michael. "From *Calder* to *Van der Peet:* Aboriginal Rights and Canadian Law, 1973-96" in Paul Havemann, ed., *Indigenous Peoples' Rights: In Australia, Canada and New Zealand* (Oxford: Oxford University Press, 1999) 428.
Benton-Banai, Edward. *The Mishomis Book: The Voice of the Ojibway* (St. Paul, MN: Red School House, 1988).
Borrows, John. "Wampum at Niagara: Canadian Legal History, Self-Government, and the Royal Proclamation" in Michael Asch, ed., *Aboriginal and Treaty Rights in Canada: Essays on Law, Equality, and Respect for Difference* (Vancouver: UBC Press, 1997) 155.
Cardinal, Harold, and Walter Hildebrandt. *Treaty Elders of Saskatchewan: Our Dream Is That Our People Will One Day Be Clearly Recognized as Nations* (Calgary: University of Calgary Press, 2000).
Flanagan, Tom. *First Nations? Second Thoughts* (Montreal and Kingston: McGill-Queen's University Press, 2000).
Henderson, James (Sákéj) Youngblood. "Aboriginal Jurisprudence and Rights" in Kerry Wilkins. ed., *Advancing Aboriginal Claims: Visions/Strategies/Directions* (Saskatoon: Purich Publishing, 2004) 67.
Lytwyn, Victor P. "A Dish with One Spoon: The Shared Hunting Grounds Agreement in the Great Lakes and St. Lawrence Valley Region" in David H. Pentland, ed., *Papers of the 28th Algonquian Conference* (Winnipeg: University of Manitoba, 1997) 210.
Monture-Angus, Patricia. *Journeying Forward: Dreaming First Nations' Independence* (Halifax: Fernwood Publishing, 2003).
Pearson, Noel. "The Concept of Native Title at Common Law" in Galarrwuy Yunupingu, ed., *Our Land Is Our Life: Land Rights – Past, Present and Future* (St. Lucia, Queensland: University of Queensland Press, 1997) 150.
Tully, James. "The Struggles of Indigenous Peoples for and of Freedom" in Duncan Ivison, Paul Patton, and Will Sanders, eds., *Political Theory and the Rights of Indigenous Peoples* (Cambridge: Cambridge University Press, 2000) 36.
Walkem, Ardith. "Constructing the Constitutional Box: The Supreme Court's Section 35(1) Reasoning" in Ardith Walkem and Halie Bruce, eds., *Box of Treasures or Empty Box? Twenty Years of Section 35* (Penticton: Theytus Books, 2003) 196.
Walkem, Ardith, and Halie Bruce. "Introduction" in Ardith Walkem and Halie Bruce, eds., *Box of Treasures or Empty Box? Twenty Years of Section 35* (Penticton: Theytus Books, 2003) 9.
Webber, Jeremy. "Beyond Regret: Mabo's Implications for Australian Constitutionalism" in Duncan Ivison, Paul Patton, and Will Sanders, eds., *Political Theory and the Rights of Indigenous Peoples* (Cambridge: Cambridge University Press, 2000) 60.
Williams, Robert A. *Linking Arms Together: American Indian Treaty Visions of Law and Peace, 1600-1800* (New York: Oxford University Press, 1997).

Articles
Alfred, Taiaiake, and Jeff Corntassel. "Being Indigenous: Resurgences against Contemporary Colonialism" (2005) 40 Government and Opposition 497.
Asch, Michael, and Patrick Macklem. "Aboriginal Rights and Canadian Sovereignty: An Essay on *R. v. Sparrow*" (1992) 29 Alberta Law Review 498.
Barsh, Russel Lawrence, and James Youngblood Henderson. "The Supreme Court's *Van der Peet* Trilogy: Naive Imperialism and Ropes of Sand" (1997) 42 McGill Law Journal 993.
Borrows, John. "Creating an Indigenous Legal Community" (2005) 50 McGill Law Journal 153.
–. "Frozen Rights in Canada: Constitutional Interpretation and the Trickster" (1997-98) 22 American Indian Law Review 45.

–. "Indian Agency and Taking What's Not Yours" (2003) 22 Windsor Yearbook of Access to Justice 253.

–. "Indigenous Legal Traditions in Canada" (2005) 19 Washington University Journal of Law and Policy 167.

–. "Sovereignty's Alchemy: An Analysis of *Delgamuukw v. British Columbia*" (1999) 37 Osgoode Hall Law Journal 537.

Borrows, John, and Leonard I. Rotman. "The Sui Generis Nature of Aboriginal Rights: Does It Make a Difference?" (1997) 36 Alberta Law Review 9.

Christie, Gordon. "The Court's Exercise of Plenary Power: Rewriting the Two-Row Wampum" (2002) 16 Supreme Court Law Review (2d) 285.

–. "Law, Theory and Aboriginal Peoples" (2003) 2 Indigenous Law Journal 67.

Dufraimont, Lisa. "From Regulation to Recolonization: Justifiable Infringement of Aboriginal Rights at the Supreme Court of Canada" (2000) 58 University of Toronto Faculty of Law Review 1.

Henderson, James (Sákéj) Youngblood. "Empowering Treaty Federalism" (1994) 58 Saskatchewan Law Review 241.

Lambert, Douglas. "The Future of Indigenous Laws in the Canadian Legal System" (2006) 64 Advocate 216.

Little Bear, Leroy. "A Concept of Native Title" (1982) 5:2 Canadian Legal Aid Bulletin 99.

Lyon, Noel. "An Essay on Constitutional Interpretation" (1988) 26 Osgoode Hall Law Journal 95.

Moody, Doug. "Thinking outside the 20th Century Box: Revisiting 'Mitchell' – Some Comments on the Politics of Judicial Law-Making in the Context of Aboriginal Self-Government" (2003-4) 35 Ottawa Law Review 1.

Morse, Bradford W. "Permafrost Rights: Aboriginal Self-Government and the Supreme Court in *R. v. Pamajewon*" (1996-97) 42 McGill Law Journal 1011.

Walters, Mark D. "British Imperial Constitutional Law and Aboriginal Rights: A Comment on *Delgamuukw v. British Columbia*" (1992) 17 Queen's Law Journal 350.

–. "The Morality of Aboriginal Law" (2006) 31:2 Queen's Law Journal 470.

Zalewski, Anna. "From *Sparrow* to *Van der Peet*: The Evolution of a Definition of Aboriginal Rights" (1997) 55 University of Toronto Faculty of Law Review 435.

Other Documents

Canada. *Report of the Royal Commission on Aboriginal Peoples: Looking Forward, Looking Back*, vol. 1 (Ottawa: Supply and Services Canada, 1996).

Interveners Delgamuukw et. al., *R. v. Van der Peet*, [1996] 2 S.C.R. 507 (Factum of the Interveners), http://www.usask.ca/nativelaw/factums/view.php?id=164.

Minister of Indian Affairs and Northern Development. *Statement of Government of Canada on Indian Policy, 1969 [The White Paper]* (Ottawa: Indian and Northern Affairs Canada, 1969).

4

Legal Processes, Pluralism in Canadian Jurisprudence, and the Governance of Carrier Medicine Knowledge

*Perry Shawana**

Foreword

Minnawaanagogiizhigook, Mary Teegee, and Warner Adam

This collection was to have included a chapter titled "Carrier Medicine Know-ledge, Ethics, and Legal Processes," by Perry Shawana. Although Perry did write the initial draft, he never finished the chapter itself, for on 1 June 2005, he crossed over into the spirit world, completing the draft just days before he passed away. Perry planned on substantially revising this draft after engaging more extensively with the relevant literature, particularly that relating to legal pluralism, and completing his community research regarding the governance of Carrier medicine knowledge by Carrier people through Carrier legal traditions (including the Bah'lats, or potlatch).[1]

We are both honoured and humbled to be a part of bringing his text forward into this collection. Honoured, because we greatly respected Perry Shawana and his work, humbled because we are unable to transform his initial draft into the text it would have become had Perry lived to complete his vision. We have chosen instead to publish Perry's draft much as he origi-nally wrote it, situating it within the broader research agenda he envisioned.

Perry Shawana was an Anishinabe from Serpent River First Nation who was embraced and adopted into the Carrier Nation. He learned and lived the way of the Carrier people while maintaining his connection to his own culture. Perry was proud to be adopted by the Likh C'ibu Clan of the Lake Babine Nation and was an active member of the Bah'lats. As a student of the combined Master of Laws/Doctor of Philosophy degree program at the University of Victoria, Perry focused on examining and articulating, "with

---

To provide additional context for this chapter, a foreword and afterword, written collec-tively by Minnawaanagogiizhigook (Dawnis Kennedy), Mary Teegee, and Warner Adam, appear here.

Carrier peoples, Carrier conceptions of medicine knowledge and the foundations of Carrier legal traditions in the governance of medicine knowledge" and validating "Carrier medicine knowledge as a legitimate and viable means of achieving health for all people."[2]

This chapter complimented his graduate work and is itself indicative of Perry's commitment to supporting Indigenous peoples' efforts to govern their communities by strengthening their legal institutions.[3] This draft clearly demonstrates Perry's faith in the ability of Indigenous legal traditions, knowledge systems, and communities to respond to the needs of Indigenous people today and in the future. It also reveals his skepticism regarding approaches that seem to imply otherwise.

In many ways, the form of Perry's text is consistent with his approach to life. He saw that the application of Western legal regimes was "not attentive to the unique aspects of indigenous knowledge or legal processes," did not give due recognition to the full importance of Indigenous knowledge to the future, and "rarely, if ever, cited or recognized [Indigenous laws] as legitimate means to govern [Indigenous] knowledge."[4] Seeing this, he immediately dove into the existing debate, challenging the ways in which Western legal regimes fail to validate Indigenous legal systems, in particular Carrier legal systems, as mechanisms through which to govern Indigenous knowledge.

Perry draws our attention to the problematic assumptions and implications associated with current attempts to recognize Indigenous knowledge within Western legal regimes, including attempts that purport to take a pluralist approach to the governance of Indigenous knowledge. In particular, Perry foregrounds the tendency of Western legal regimes to characterize Indigenous knowledge as exclusively "traditional"; to disregard the differences between Indigenous and Western ways of governing the use of knowledge, particularly regarding the distinctions between public and private knowledge; to misunderstand what is required to "protect" Indigenous knowledge; to commodify Indigenous knowledge; and to recognize Indigenous laws in ways that benefit dominant legal regimes rather than Indigenous legal orders.

However, it was not enough for Perry merely to challenge current modalities of thought with respect to Indigenous knowledge (although he certainly enjoyed doing so). Perry wanted to demonstrate that Carrier laws and legal processes could effectively govern Carrier medicine knowledge. Although he considered pluralist approaches laudable, he remained cognizant of their inability to ignite Indigenous people to protect their own traditional systems. He did, however, believe that it was possible for Western legal regimes to find ways of treating Carrier medicine knowledge with respect and honour. Although Perry did envision a future role for pluralist approaches in the governing of Indigenous knowledge, he did not have time to fully develop this vision in connection with Carrier medicine knowledge.

We can no longer challenge or question Perry on his particular vision of a relationship between Indigenous and Canadian legal processes that is able to avoid the pitfalls he identified and to support the effective governance of Indigenous knowledge. We can no longer ask him about the aspects of his argument that we still struggle to understand. All we can do is hold on to the insights and questions that knowing Perry brought us and find ways of carrying these gifts forward into the future. It is our hope that the generosity of Perry's loved ones, in allowing his last work to be brought forward, will enable others to do the same.[5]

Carrier Medicine Knowledge, Ethics, and Legal Processes

After more than a decade of research and publication in the fields of intellectual property rights and Indigenous knowledge, a debate has emerged regarding the governance of Indigenous knowledge systems.[6] Typically, this debate is cast in Western concepts of law, ethics, and legal processes. More recently, Indigenous scholars and others have called for a reframing of the issues within Indigenous legal processes, ethics, and laws. This study critically examines the debate that has emerged in response to this call, asking what systems and processes are best situated, and thereby appropriate, to govern Indigenous knowledge for a sustainable future: Indigenous legal orders, international and domestic legal orders, or a hybrid of these distinct orders.[7]

Focusing particularly on medicine knowledge held by Carrier people, this chapter argues that Indigenous legal systems are best situated to address Indigenous desires to govern knowledge generated from within their communities. This notion is in stark contrast to the commonly held view that Western legal processes are best able to protect, preserve, and maintain the integrity of Indigenous knowledge. Although a number of Western legal processes do recognize Indigenous knowledge, the application of dominant Western legal orders can nonetheless negatively impact and influence Indigenous peoples' innovations, creations, and discoveries. It is therefore important to seriously question whether Western legal traditions ought to govern Indigenous knowledge.

Pluralism is often seen as the answer to issues relating to the governance and protection of Indigenous knowledge. However, in pluralist democracies (such as Canada), the debate about such knowledge is primarily consumed with finding room for Indigenous ways of knowing within the larger body politic. In essence, this approach argues that, if Indigenous ways of knowing are to survive, their only hope is to be incorporated into dominant legal orders or the processes they support. By advocating for governance by Indigenous polities, I seek to validate the Indigenous, and specifically Carrier, political and legal systems that have governed medicine knowledge for generations prior to and since contact. In Indigenous societies, the debate about Indigenous knowledge is primarily concerned with the integrity of that knowledge and focuses on maintaining a way of being over time into the future.[8] Given the distinct worldviews that Western and Indigenous legal orders represent, it is important to critically examine the utility of legal pluralist traditions as a means to negotiate the intersection between legal orders that maintain discrete purposes (and, at times, cross-purposes).

In this discussion, I ultimately seek to identify the shortcomings of current understandings of legal pluralism in relation to Indigenous legal orders, particularly where such an approach expects Indigenous legal orders to fundamentally alter themselves in response to their dominant counterparts. In critically examining the assumptions that underlie some legal pluralist approaches, I wish also to offer suggestions about how the concept may reconstruct itself so as to become respectful of legal orders grounded in understandings of democracy that are not tied to liberal democratic traditions. It must be stated at the outset that I am operating from the premise that Indigenous societies maintain discrete and distinct legal orders within Indigenous polities that depend neither on the nation-state nor on recognition of their existence from other societies (whether Indigenous or non-Indigenous); rather, they are inherent in nature.[9]

Indigenous Knowledge
Indigenous knowledge covers a broad spectrum of sciences, arts, culture, literature, and all varieties of creations, discoveries, and innovations. As Stefan Matiation points out, much of the literature on Indigenous rights describes Indigenous knowledge as "tradition-based" or "traditional." He argues that this language reflects a perception among nation-state players that it is unnecessary to create room for Indigenous knowledge within intellectual property regimes, as those regimes are capable of dealing with Indigenous knowledge in their current form.[10] The "traditional" language is found in *Convention on Biological Diversity* and *International Labor Organization Convention 169*, two working documents from the World Intellectual Property Organization. Similar debates also surround the development of the *Agreement on Trade-Related Aspects of Intellectual Property Rights* (TRIPS) by a branch of the World Trade Organization, an agreement that espouses a universal international intellectual property regime.[11] The "tradition-based" or "traditional" language used in domestic and international intellectual property regimes has tended to result in the treatment of Indigenous knowledge as though it were static, developed in the distant past and handed down from generation to generation. One assumption derived from this line of thinking is that Indigenous peoples are not actively engaged in the discovery and creation of new knowledge. Nothing could be further from the truth.

Indigenous scholars, scientists, medicine people, and many others dedicate much of their personal lives and careers to the creation and discovery of new knowledge. What is unique about these individuals is that they bring an Indigenous perspective to their work, a perspective that is grounded in Indigenous understandings of the world, the environment, and the inter-relationships between all animate and inanimate matter. This is not to suggest that all Indigenous peoples share the same values and beliefs, but rather that, as in all societies, a diversity of understandings exists between and within Indigenous communities. As scholar Russel Barsh notes, "Within any community, however, people vary greatly in what they know. There are not only differences between ordinary folks and experts, such as experienced healers, hunters or ceremonialists; there are also major differences of experience and professional opinion among experts, as we should expect in any living, dynamic knowledge system that is continually responding to new phenomena and fresh insights."[12]

Indigenous knowledge systems have very practical uses; therefore, they are constantly generating knowledge relevant to current circumstances and experiences, and are dynamic in nature. For example, Indigenous medicine knowledge plays a significant role in maintaining the health of community members. Historically, this knowledge, including Carrier medicine knowledge, was used to treat tuberculosis, scarlet fever, and other diseases introduced by European settlers. More recently, it has been used to address current-day ailments experienced by Indigenous/Carrier people, including chronic diseases such as arthritis, diabetes, heart conditions, and addictions. It has also been used to address a host of other health conditions, including cancer.[13]

Indigenous knowledge is also considered by some to be an important component of the bank of human knowledge for the future well-being of all people. For example, researchers at Royal Roads University are currently seeking out Indigenous community partners to study the chemical properties of devil's club and its efficacy in the treatment of diabetes.[14] Similar initiatives have been undertaken with respect to the medicinal uses of soapberries, blueberries, strawberry root, and the inner bark of numerous tree species. Indigenous knowledge is therefore highly sought-after by non-Indigenous peoples, most often to supplement Western knowledge and advance technological developments in the name of progress.

For Indigenous people, the fact that their knowledge is in high demand means that determining how, when, where, and by whom it is used becomes critical. Such questions recognize the primary characteristics of Indigenous knowledge and its relationship to Indigenous desires for self-determination and claims to territory. Non-Indigenous interest in Indigenous medicine knowledge represents a potential threat to the integrity of that knowledge because it is often limited to the benefit of Western knowledge and can coincide with a complete disregard for Indigenous peoples' desire to maintain their own knowledge systems. This reality underlies Indigenous desires for governance of Indigenous knowledge.[15]

Indigenous knowledge is often regarded as being inherently connected to the land and the spiritual and environmental characteristics of specific territories.[16] For example, high-ranking hereditary chiefs in the Carrier Bah'lats hold hereditary names that are assigned to specific tracts of lands, names that they are expected to know. In fulfilling their obligations, they acquire an acute understanding of the territory and the philosophy associated with their name. In this sense, hereditary chiefs develop a vibrant appreciation for eco-systems, including the location of plant, animal, and aquatic life, and for the connection of these life forms to spiritual, metaphysical, and intangible ways of knowing.[17] This knowledge is critical for the preparation of medicines, the sustainability of eco-systems, and the autonomy of Carrier people. Similar systems exist for Indigenous groups around the world. Claims to territories and assertions of self-determination are therefore very much embodied in Indigenous desires to govern their knowledge. In effect, these claims and assertions are about ensuring that Indigenous perspectives survive and that their knowledge systems are not subsumed in pluralist approaches. In this way, Indigenous conceptions of knowledge, time, space, awareness, and being are preserved, protected, and maintained over time.

Indigenous Governance of Knowledge

Indigenous legal regimes are one means through which to preserve, protect, and maintain Indigenous knowledge over time. Arguments for Indigenous legal regimes as the best model to govern Indigenous knowledge are very compelling.[18] Once considered dead or dying, Indigenous legal regimes have re-emerged as a vibrant and integral aspect of Indigenous desires for autonomy and self-determination. The Carrier First Nations in northcentral British Columbia are well situated to govern the knowledge generated from within their communities.[19] An examination of Carrier legal orders regarding knowledge development provides an excellent opportunity to explore and address issues that have broader implications for Indigenous peoples throughout the world.

Integral to the Carrier people is their governing structure, the Bah'lats, or potlatch. The Bah'lats guides the individual, the community, and the nation in all aspects of life. Carrier society is matrilineal: community members identify their social standing in relation to the clan affiliation of their mother. Four primary clans make up Carrier society (Bear, Caribou, Frog, and Beaver), each with several sub-clans. Generally, each primary clan has one head clansperson, and each sub-clan is represented by a hereditary chief who holds rank in the Bah'lats as a wing chief. The role of hereditary chiefs, which is varied, includes being main spokespersons for the clan or sub-clan they represent and tending to the welfare of clan members.[20]

The Bah'lats is the core institution of the Carrier people. All formal business in the Bah'lats is conducted in an open and transparent environment in which members are witnesses to transactions such as the assigning of a chief's name, the solidifying of Carrier laws, the transfer of territory, and the granting of authority for specific uses of territory. As witnesses, individuals are expected to commit to memory the details of transactions; witnesses who are also hereditary chiefs are expected to recount the transactions in oral histories at future feasts.[21]

With regards to the governance of Carrier knowledge, Carrier legal traditions have clear conceptions of private and public knowledge. For example, upon acquiring a name, hereditary chiefs sponsor individuals from their father's clan who compose a song that best emulates the designation of the name and who design and prepare regalia for each "high" chief. Both the song and the regalia would be considered types of public knowledge in that they relate to a specific name that may be held by several individuals over several generations. Use of the song or regalia, however, is exclusive to the individual who holds the name with which they are associated. According to Western legal traditions, any individual is entitled to reinterpret public knowledge as he or she sees fit; in addition, he or she alone enjoys any benefits that might accrue from that reinterpretation. Such is not the case in Carrier legal traditions. There, only those individuals who are so designated have the right to employ, distribute, or share such knowledge and the benefits arising from it.

Carrier conceptions of public knowledge should not be interpreted to mean that private knowledge has no place in Carrier legal traditions. In the example above, a form of private knowledge development includes sponsoring individuals to compose songs or design regalia for specific hereditary names. Sponsorship in Carrier society recognizes the skill and level of understanding that an individual may have about the principles, teachings, values, and beliefs that govern Carrier society. The private sphere of knowledge is thus intricately connected to the public sphere of knowledge, whereby individuals are paid (in goods, monetarily, and/or by status) for their skill and level of understanding. It is thus understood that, as private knowledge is developed in Carrier society, one consideration is the extent to which the knowledge holder is required to consider the implications of knowledge transfer and interpretation by the public sphere. One cannot simply assume that knowledge situated in one sphere or the other (or both) entitles them to use that knowledge solely for their own benefit.

Whether dominant legal processes and traditions can play a role in supporting the desires of Indigenous people to control their knowledge is an important debate in which we must engage. If we wish simply to protect knowledge from abuses by unscrupulous prospectors who would use it for their sole benefit, perhaps Western legal traditions would be adequate to achieve that objective. It is well known that Western legal traditions have a long history of protecting proprietary interests in knowledge.[22] However, the issue is not solely one of protecting knowledge but also determining how knowledge may be documented and to what purposes and uses it may be put. Essentially, the debate is about governing knowledge and the uses of knowledge.

For several reasons, Indigenous laws and legal processes are well positioned to govern Indigenous knowledge. First, they ensure the continued transmission and reliance on Indigenous values and belief systems. Maintaining these plays a significant role in the decolonization and emancipation of Indigenous societies. By reinforcing historically relevant and contemporary forms of Indigenous knowledge, Indigenous societies are able to bring meaning and purpose for their desires of autonomy.

A second reason for supporting the Indigenous governance of knowledge is to ensure its integrity and authenticity over time. To understand fully this aspect of the emerging debate, one must distinguish between the acts of preserving, protecting, and maintaining the integrity of Indigenous knowledge, as each action, though connected, involves discrete processes and rationales. For the purposes of this discussion, "preservation" is used in its plainest meaning – to record for present and future use. As regards Indigenous knowledge, the act of preserving is not as much about reclaiming the past as it is about documenting knowledge (whether in written, oral, or other form) as it has evolved over time. Dominant Western ideology is reluctantly and slowly moving away from the old belief that, because Indigenous knowledge and peoples were dying out, it was important to preserve their cultures, practices, and traditions.[23] Today there is a greater recognition of the resiliency of Indigenous peoples and acceptance that they will be here for many generations to come.[24] The act of preserving Indigenous knowledge has therefore taken on new meanings and forms.

One of the ways in which preservation movements have evolved is in their desire to maintain the integrity of Indigenous knowledge. This involves the manner in which the knowledge is documented or preserved, so that its meaning and intention are clearly and accurately expressed. It is equally important to maintain the landscape to which Indigenous knowledge is connected. Earlier preservation movements were grounded in a desire to document Indigenous culture, practices, and traditions for the advancement of Western societies. It comes as no surprise, therefore, that most people who documented Indigenous cultures were from the West, interpreting Indigenous cultures from Western perspectives. This process has been an integral aspect of colonization movements throughout the world.[25]

In more recent times, the desire to maintain the integrity of Indigenous knowledge has been grounded in a resurgence of Indigenous pride and a realization that only those who are schooled in Indigenous ways are best situated to understand and interpret the knowledge generated by Indigenous peoples.[26] This resurgence embraces historical and contemporary forms of Indigenous innovation, creation, and discovery. In Western legal traditions, the issue is cast in terms of who owns this "new" knowledge; hence, the Western legal tradition of "protecting" knowledge for those who own it. Indigenous legal traditions cast the issue in terms of one's connection to land and community; here, "protection" is but one aspect of the appropriate treatment and use of knowledge.

It is important to recognize that simply protecting knowledge does not necessarily equate to preserving or maintaining its integrity. For the most part, protection approaches are grounded in Western legal traditions that seek to locate room for the protection of Indigenous knowledge within domestic and international legal regimes.[27] These approaches have a number of limitations, including the risk of discounting Indigenous understandings of the interplay between the private and public spheres of knowledge. This has serious implications for the integrity of Indigenous knowledge and may reshape understandings of Indigenous knowledge solely through the "protection" lens.

Understanding knowledge through such a lens results in interpreting it primarily for the purpose of economic gain. In this scenario, Indigenous knowledge, both private and public, is commodified. This would remain true even if legislation existed to protect Indigenous knowledge from being appropriated for sale by unauthorized persons, as nothing but the illegal sale of the knowledge would be affected. All other forms and uses of knowledge, ranging from a hereditary chief's vibrant appreciation of life forms on his or her territory to spiritual, metaphysical, and intangible ways of knowing, would not be afforded the same level of protection. More disconcerting, however, is the fact that this model does not grant the governance of knowledge to those who should determine what and how Indigenous knowledge may be used: the community in which the knowledge is generated.

Another consequence of adopting a singular objective of "protecting" Indigenous knowledge is its potential to drive all forms of Indigenous knowledge underground. Fear that Indigenous knowledge will be abused and/or misused for personal or financial gain could prevent its transmission, even among members of the Indigenous community. A pressing concern in Indigenous country is the secrecy that has become attached to Indigenous ways of knowing. Fear of appropriation, or that others may reify Indigenous knowledge as though it were their own, as well as a desire to ensure that such knowledge is accurately understood, has resulted in an ethos among knowledge holders that they cannot trust others with their knowledge – even if those others are from their own community. In these circumstances, questions of place, status in community, familial relations, and rights to distribute knowledge are matters of serious concern that are not typically resolved on the basis of rights but rather on Indigenous understandings of the public and private sphere of knowledge.

A growing gap between knowledge holders, leadership, and youth contributes to the fearmongering associated with the transmission of Indigenous knowledge. Unless concerted efforts are made to reconnect knowledge holders with community members, the potential will remain for Indigenous knowledge to be held underground. One way to ensure that the connection is made between knowledge holder and community (and Indigenous knowledge is thereby validated) is through the recognition of Indigenous legal institutions and systems as the means to transmit knowledge. This would necessitate a re-evaluation of the utility of Indigenous legal institutions in contemporary times.

There is a clear need to foster ways to support contemporary as well as historically relevant Indigenous knowledge. For most Indigenous peoples, this translates to reinforcing their connection to land and understandings of community, to their laws, which are grounded in an acute understanding of the environment, and to their legal processes and institutions, which in themselves are an expression of Indigenous being. In short, protecting, preserving, and maintaining the integrity of Indigenous knowledge is about being Indigenous within a worldview that is distinct and set apart from all other worldviews – a worldview that celebrates a distinct body politic that is wholly Indigenous. This is in contrast to Western-based attempts to support Indigenous knowledge by using a protection approach that is grounded in pluralist ideology.

Pluralist Approaches in Indigenous Contexts

In examining the efficacy of Indigenous legal regimes to govern Indigenous knowledge, one is faced with Western approaches steeped in pluralist ideology. The primary goal of legal pluralism is the co-existence of independent systems that are complementary to each other. In pluralist systems, each independent system is capable of existing in its own right, while at the same time each is open to incorporating new ideas and knowledge from the others.[28] This theory presents many challenges for Indigenous peoples, including the concern that, should Indigenous laws and legal processes engage in legal pluralist approaches, they will be expected to fundamentally alter their objectives to suit the needs of dominant Western legal orders.

Early conceptions of legal pluralism were very much bound up with legal anthropology, sociology, and the study of multiple legal traditions within a society. Legal anthropology in particular was influenced by the assertions that a society has one unified legal system that controls its members, that law is the exclusive domain of the state, and that all normative orderings are subordinate to the law and institutions of the state.[29] Within this framework, it was argued that sovereignty justified the state as the fundamental unit of political organization and that legal pluralism was a means to describe the reception of "customary law" in colonial settings (or dominant legal orders). Customary law was understood to include Indigenous conceptions of law and normative orderings.

In his article "What Is Legal Pluralism?" John Griffith challenged early perceptions of legal pluralism as reflecting legal centralism, or more specifically, the notion that all societies maintain a unified singular legal order. For Griffith, legal centralism frustrates the development of general theory and ignores the legal reality of an "unsystematic collage of inconsistent and overlapping parts."[30] Looking critically at legal pluralism from this perspective, Griffith distinguishes between its "strong" and "weak" variants. In the former, not all law is state law; nor is law administered by a single set of state legal institutions. In this sense, law is neither systematic nor uniform. In contrast, "weak" legal pluralism is a sub-type of centralism in which the sovereign commands different bodies of law for different groups, and all law is dependent on a single validating source.[31]

Another school of thought has developed in contrast to Griffith's conceptions of strong and weak legal pluralism. Led by Brian Tamanaha, this approach argues that there is scant legal analysis of the concept of legal pluralism. Moreover, the concept is grounded in an unstable analytical foundation, namely, the assumption that all forms of social control are law and that all law is synonymous with normative order.[32] Tamanaha posits that legal pluralism is really about a political impetus to call certain non-state normative orders "law" so as to lessen the stature of state law and its monopoly over law, while at the same time granting non-state law an equivalent footing with state law.

In challenging strong legal pluralism, Tamanaha offers two critiques, one analytical and the other instrumental. The former argues that legal pluralism has constructed a notion of law that builds a fundamental ambiguity, namely, a question as to whether the norm or the institution that enforces the norm is "law." In either case, Tamanaha argues that the concept of law is grounded in state law or state sanction of non-state law.[33] The instrumental critique holds that legal pluralism perpetuates assumptions that state law norms and institutions are involved in the maintenance of societal normative order without asking how or if legal pluralism advances the maintenance of social order. By asking the questions that legal pluralism fails to address, Tamanaha reveals that, in colonization processes, the transplanted

state legal apparatus was used as an instrument of power, not for the maintenance of societal normative order. Moreover, in postcolonial settings, state
law is better understood by way of contrast with the lived norms of social
order. Therefore, an understanding of state and non-state law is best reached
by focusing on how each influences the other rather than on their convergence into a singular unified law.[34]

Whether one accepts legal pluralism as a theory or solely as a means
through which to compare and contrast legal traditions, a significant challenge arises when one attempts to apply it to Indigenous legal orders: current understandings of legal pluralism are limited by the perception that
state law is the primary point of reference through which to determine
whether the concept is valid. When discussing legal pluralism, perceiving
state law in this manner has the potential to delegitimize and/or negatively
affect the validity of non-state legal orders. Within such an approach, the
primacy of state law over Indigenous law is simply presumed to be legitimate, and the effect of state law upon non-state legal orders is not readily
open to questioning.

Legal pluralist traditions in dominant legal regimes have tended to dis-
count the possibility of a body politic that is specific to Indigenous peoples,
independent of dominant society. This results directly from the fact that
the dominant body politic holds the balance of power, allowing it to influence the relationship between two independent systems to its own benefit.
For example, some have argued that existing international and domestic
initiatives intended to "protect" Indigenous knowledge are a means for
Western legal regimes to claim Indigenous knowledge as their own.[35] Pro-
ponents of this view hold that cultural property law is framed in terms of
the competing interests between the state and humankind, whereas intellectual property regimes attempt to balance the individual rights to knowledge as against those attributed to the universal public.

Within intellectual property regimes, the public sphere is understood to
include information to which all peoples have access and over which no
one group of peoples or an individual may claim ownership. There is no
expectation that public information or knowledge may take on differing
meanings and forms, such as the spiritual and cultural significance to a way
of life and being. In this sense, Indigenous knowledge is perceived to be
wholly within the public sphere, available to all to use for the discovery,
development, and creation of new knowledge for the "discoverer's" benefit.
Typically, this approach assumes that the private and public spheres of knowledge are the same in Western and Indigenous legal systems.[36]

This discussion raises the question of whether there are better ways for
dominant legal orders to support the wish of Indigenous people to govern
their knowledge. Several scholars have offered a variety of solutions to this

question. Many, such as Michael Halewood, have called for *sui generis* legislation that would incorporate Indigenous legal systems into a contemporary Western pluralist legal tradition.[37] Others, such as Amanda Pask, have argued for the continued existence of Indigenous legal regimes and against pluralist approaches as forms of contemporary colonial practice.[38]

One example of the adoption of a pluralist approach by dominant legal orders is in the treatment of Indigenous "customary" laws. An examination of domestic legal traditions in this regard is instructive and, as will be demonstrated, is relevant to the debate about which system and process is best situated and thereby most appropriate to govern Indigenous knowledge. The Canadian legal system has a long history of recognizing the "customary" laws of Indigenous peoples; in doing so, its courts and judges (all of whom to date have been non-Indigenous) have created rules to determine which "customary" laws are legitimate. Courts and the judiciary then interpret, apply, and develop a set of legal precedents that purport to be "customary" laws arising from Indigenous legal traditions and processes. Many reported cases support this trend.[39] One example, *Connolly v. Woolrich,* involved the estate of William Connolly, who died in the 1840s. In a Cree ceremony, he married a Métis woman named Suzanne and the two had six children; some years later, he left his family and married Julia Woolrich in a Catholic ceremony. On his death, he willed all his property to his second family alone. John Connolly, a son from his first marriage, sued Julia Woolrich for a share in his father's estate. The Quebec Superior Court declared the Cree customary marriage valid on the basis that the law of the Cree had prevailed in their territories until English law was declared to be received by the new sovereign.[40] The result in *Connolly* was that the son of the mixed Cree marriage was able to benefit from his father's estate alongside the legitimate children of the subsequent Christian marriage.

The decision in *Connolly* presumes that the best scenario for all concerned was achieved because all of William Connolly's offspring were able to share in the proceeds of his estate. The difficulty with this approach is that, but for the desire to appear to be fair in the distribution of the estate of a reputable and upstanding citizen (Connolly), Indigenous law (in this case, laws regarding marriage and divorce) would never have been a consideration for the courts. In other words, the English common law was not sufficiently developed in the 1860s to consider the inter-marriage between Indigenous and non-Indigenous people on its own terms.

Although *Connolly* is dated, it reflects an ethos that resonates with current pluralist approaches. Contemporary representations of this ethos can be found in the case of *Casimel v. Insurance Corporation of British Columbia,* in which the British Columbia Court of Appeal recognized the Carrier custom of adopting grandchildren; as a result, the grandparents in the case were treated as natural parents and entitled to part 7 benefits under the *Insurance (Motor Vehicle) Act*.[41] Although the case outcome was desirable for all parties concerned, little consideration was directed to the fact that the courts were embarking on a process that interpreted and applied Carrier laws regarding Carrier adoption in ways that suited the result desired by Western legal processes. In this scenario, Carrier law provided a way for the court to make a finding that was perceived as fair but that would not have been as readily available solely through legislation or the common law. In effect, the courts appropriated Carrier law and made it part of the English common law. Carrier legal processes and institutions and their treatment of adoption laws were otherwise irrelevant. Similarly, obligations arising from adoption in Carrier society were not a factor broached by the court.

Consider *Casimel* against the British Columbia Supreme Court case of *Prince v. Murdock*, launched by two young plaintiffs.[42] In *Prince*, the issue involved the distribution of the estate of Johnny Murdock. The plaintiffs, Marjorie Prince and her sister, Peggy Julian, claimed that Murdock had adopted them. At the time, Prince had been sixteen and had married shortly afterward. Despite evidence that verified both the adoption itself and the fact that Carrier laws permitted the adoption of adults, the court determined that insufficient evidence was present to confirm that Murdock had in fact adopted either sister. For Prince, this determination was made solely on the extent to which she had relied on Murdock for her daily care, sustenance, and survival. The court entertained no consideration for Carrier laws regarding adoption – instead, it concerned itself with whether Prince was able to fit the test for custom adoption as established by previous case law involving Indigenous custom adoption laws and incorporated into the English common law. It should be noted that at question was the interpretation of section 46 of the *Adoption Act* (BC), permitting the court to treat custom Aboriginal adoptions as though they were adoptions under the act, inclusive of succession rights for descendents as articulated in the act.[43] The result in *Prince* was that Johnny Murdock's estate was directed to the federal public trustee for the care of his elderly sister, who was otherwise provided for by the state.

A comparison of *Connolly*, *Casimel*, and *Prince* reveals a number of striking similarities. Each case represents a propensity for the dominant legal system to interpret Indigenous laws and legal processes for its sole benefit. The cases also disenfranchise Indigenous legal orders as a relevant and meaningful apparatus for the resolution of a complex dissonance resulting from the interaction between two distinct, separate, and independent systems. Moreover, recent legislative trends to incorporate Aboriginal laws as though they were laws passed by the state suggest that legal pluralist approaches expect Indigenous legal systems to conform to Western interpretations of democratic traditions. In this process, Indigenous laws and legal processes are fundamentally altered to suit the needs of Western legal orders. There is nothing pluralist about this approach – dominant legal orders expect to prevail. Instead, this approach can arguably be said to represent contemporary forms of colonization.[44]

Conclusion

As can be seen from the discussion above, the application of current legal pluralist approaches to the governance of Indigenous knowledge raises serious concerns. Given that contemporary understandings of legal pluralist approaches support Western interpretations of democratic traditions, it is unlikely that this limited approach will aid in negotiating the intersection between Indigenous and dominant legal orders, or provide the support needed by Indigenous peoples for the governance of their knowledge.

If dominant legal traditions do play a role in the emancipation of Indigenous peoples, and specifically Carrier people, it should not be one that authorizes them to delineate, interpret, and apply Indigenous understandings of their legal orders and ways of knowing. Clearly, to do so would move the realm of Indigenous knowledge development and exchange outside the Indigenous community and away from those who know.

If legal pluralism is to have any use as a construct in understanding the complex relationship between the divergent legal orders of contemporary society, legal anthropologists, sociologists, and theorists must move away from its contemporary presumptions to focus instead on its fundamental elements. In my view, those fundamental elements include co-existence, independence, and complementariness. From this perspective, true legal pluralism can be said to apply when two or more independent legal systems co-exist, operating side by side and interacting in ways that complement each other.

In this construction, co-existence is understood to embrace both independence and interdependence. Each legal system is understood to have legitimacy within its own right, denoting a measure of independence of each legal order. This is so because a recognition of another legal order's legitimacy also entails a recognition of the limits of one's own legal order. Although it is accepted that a legal order can never be fully independent and is always to some extent dependent upon the recognition of others, this does not mean that the concept of independence does not work. A point of example is the currently accepted understanding of legal pluralism regarding Indigenous legal orders, in which it is presumed that state law is the primary point of reference – leaving it the authority to determine the validity of non-state law and the normative order. In this approach, non-state law is wholly dependent on state law for its legitimacy and is therefore neither independent, interdependent, nor pluralist. Co-existence also entails interdependence, for though each legal system is understood to have legitimacy in its own right, not every law or normative order within a given legal order will be legitimate within another. Whether one legal order's particular concepts of law or normative order are relevant or applicable to another legal order is a matter of negotiation, and one that may evolve over time.

Finally, a fundamental element of legal pluralism is the notion of complementariness; here, each system is strengthened by the existence of the other through actions that contribute to a wider and deeper understanding of each other. As independent yet interdependent systems interact, they strengthen each other through an inherent respect for and understanding of each way of being and knowing. This approach challenges each legal order to set aside questions of legitimacy vis-à-vis itself, and instead to focus on understanding the underpinnings of the law and normative order expressed in the other.

As the construction of legal pluralism shifts towards its roots of independence, co-existence, and complementariness, it should be expected that Indigenous legal orders and processes will have greater opportunities to be validated and thus empowered to support structures that govern knowledge developed from within their own institutions and communities. In relation to medicine knowledge, there may now be a process that can be *trusted* to ensure that this specific form of knowledge is protected and preserved, and that its integrity is maintained over time.

Afterword

Perry's essay offers many insights that raise other questions. Had Perry lived, we would have continued to follow the development of his work, looking to gain further insight from his answers to the questions he has left us. This is no longer possible, for this chapter represents Perry Shawana's final scholarly work. We are still able to gain insight and inspiration from his life work, a legacy that lives on.

During his life, Perry worked with many hereditary chiefs, elders, youths, leaders, and communities on issues relating to governance (the Bah'lats), human and legal rights, land claims, and community development. Perry conducted his research and his work with love, passion, integrity, and respect. He was devoted to transforming systems utilizing Indigenous knowledge to reflect the ethos of community. His body of work is living testimony to his desire to rebuild Indigenous communities through reinvigorating cultural practices and traditions. Perry's legacy not only reflects who we were and who we are but also guides us into who we will become as strong Indigenous people. Perry's partner, Warner Adam, of the Lake Babine Nation, is committed to carrying the legacy Perry left into the future for the benefit of all Indigenous peoples.

Notes

1 To do so, he was conducting focus groups and interviews with hereditary chiefs, medicine knowledge holders, and community leaders.

2 Perry Shawana, "Thesis Proposal" (2005, on file with the author) at 1.

3 For a more detailed account of the ways in which Perry Shawana demonstrated this commitment in his life, see Carrier Sekani Family Services, "A Memorial to Perry Shawana," http://www.csfs.org/Files/Public/Index/perry.pdf.

4 Shawana, *supra* note 2.

5 Perry Shawana joined his mother, Jean Shawana (McLeod), and father, Ernest Shawana, in the spirit world, leaving, for a short time, his loving partner, Warner Adam, his brothers and sisters, Brian, Chris, David, Audrey, Beverly, and Carol Shawana, numerous other relatives and friends, and his faithful pug, Oji Adam.

6 I refer to "knowledge systems" in the plural to denote that discrete bodies of knowledge are maintained by Indigenous peoples around the world. Indigenous peoples have not generally distinguished between types of knowledge in the way that the Western tradition has, by embedding knowledge in separate disciplines (such as humanities, sciences, philosophy, and the like). Nonetheless, discrete bodies of Indigenous knowledge do exist that are akin to Western forms of disciplinary knowledge. For an excellent discussion of what constitutes Indigenous knowledge, see Marie Battiste and James (Sákéj) Youngblood Henderson, *Protecting Indigenous Knowledge and Heritage* (Saskatoon: Purich Publishing, 2001).

7 See contributions from John Borrows, "A Separate Peace: Strengthening Shared Justice" at 343-63, Val Napoleon, "Who Gets to Say What Happened? Reconciliation Issues for the Gitxsan" at 176-95, and Richard Overstall, "Reconciliation Devices: Using the Trust as an Interface between Aboriginal and State Legal Orders" at 196-212, all in Catherine Bell and David Kahane, eds., *Intercultural Dispute Resolution in Aboriginal Contexts* (Toronto: University of Toronto Press, 2004). Although most of these authors argue for separate and/or concurrent but independent Indigenous and Western justice systems for dispute resolution processes, the reasoning presented is very much applicable to the debate surrounding Indigenous knowledge.

8 See Gordon Christie, "Law, Theory and Aboriginal People" (Fall 2003) 2:1 Indigenous Law Journal 69 at 118-19, in which he argues that "Aboriginal people, on the other hand, have to begin by reconfirming the existence of, and implications emanating from, the cultural divide separating their ways of life from those built on certain Western precepts. In other words, they need to reaffirm the validity of their perception that the law is alien and oppressive and come to terms with the reasons for the validity of this perception. They then need to acknowledge the responsibilities attendant on this reconfirmation and re-invigorate their societies in alignment with traditional wisdom, but in ways which provide for the complexities inherent in living in the contemporary world."

9 I recognize that the reality in most Indigenous communities is the imposition of elected chief and council bodies under the *Indian Act,* with attendant powers authorized by the act. Nevertheless, it is also a reality that Indigenous peoples maintain legal orders that have come to be known as "hereditary" or "traditional" in that they embody governing structures that existed prior to contact with peoples from other parts of the world. One example of these governing structures is the Bah'lats, or potlatch, among the Carrier people. It is to these systems and legal orders that I refer when espousing an Indigenous polity. For further discussion on this topic, see Taiaiake Alfred, *Peace, Power, Righteousness: An Indigenous Manifesto* (Oxford: Oxford University Press, 1999); James (Sákéj) Youngblood Henderson, "Postcolonial Indigenous Legal Consciousness" (2002) 1 Indigenous Law Journal 1; and Patricia Monture-Angus, *Journeying Forward: Dreaming First Nations' Independence* (Halifax: Fernwood Press, 1999).

10 Stefan Matiation, "Biotechnology, Rights and Traditional Knowledge" in *A Brave New World: Where Biotechnology and Human Rights Intersect,* Biotechnology Strategy Reports (Ottawa: Government of Canada, 2005) at 4-12, http://biostrategy.gc.ca/HumanRights/Human RightsE/ch7_e.html (manuscript on file with the author).

11 *Ibid.*

12 Russel Barsh, "Defending Indigenous Science from Biopiracy: A Choice of Laws Approach" at 3, quoted in Matiation, *ibid.* at 7.
13 Much of the literature describing the medicinal uses of plants employed by Indigenous people has been written by ethno-biologists. See, for example, John Hawley and Jane Young, *The Medicines of Sophie Thomas* (Prince George, BC: University of Northern British Columbia Press, 2002), and Nancy Turner, *Plants of Haida Gwaii* (Winlaw, BC: Sono Nis Press, 2004). Other historical accounts include Mary-Ellen Kelm, *Colonizing Bodies: Aboriginal Healing in British Columbia 1900-50* (Vancouver, BC: UBC Press, 1998), and Maureen Lux, *Medicine That Walks: Disease, Medicine, and Canadian Plains Native People, 1880-1940* (Toronto: University of Toronto Press, 2001).
14 E-mail from Royal Roads University Centre for Non Timber Resources (14 January 2005, on file with the author). This call for participants states that "study participants will be asked to provide in depth descriptions of the types of preparations of devil's club they are using, when they usually harvest it and which part of the plant they use. They would be requested to provide ongoing samples of the preparations they are using so that these can be analysed."
15 Marie Battiste and James (Sákéj) Youngblood Henderson, "Indigenous Heritage and Eurocentric Intellectual and Cultural Property Rights" in Battiste and Henderson, *supra* note 6 at chap. 9. See also Paul Nadasdy, *Hunters and Bureaucrats: Power, Knowledge, and Aboriginal-State Relations in the Southwest Yukon* (Vancouver, BC: UBC Press, 2003).
16 Matiation, *supra* note 10 at 8.
17 See JoAnne Fiske and Betty Patrick, *'C'is dideen khat' When the Plumes Rise: The Way of the Lake Babine Nation* (Vancouver, BC: UBC Press, 2000) chap. 4. See also the works cited *supra* note 13.
18 See Alfred, *supra* note 9, and Borrows, Napoleon, and Overstall, *supra* note 7.
19 Carrier people maintain a traditional territory that spans more than seventy-six thousand square miles covering two primary watersheds (the Skeena and Fraser watersheds). Carrier people occupy fourteen primary communities, many of which have two or three settlements. Local agencies and political bodies estimate that there are more than twelve thousand Carrier people, the majority of whom are under forty. See *A Journey Home – Reclaiming Our Children*, DVD Production, Carrier Sekani Family Services and House of Talent (40 minutes), 2004.
20 There are a number of hereditary chiefs in Carrier society. Chieftainship is not dependent on individuals but rather reinforces Carrier connections to the land. Hereditary chiefs with "high" names assume specific territories, and such names survive individuals who may hold them throughout their lifetimes. The assuming of a name is therefore a significant act requiring the individual to know in detail the oral history and physical makeup of the territory connected to the name. For a fuller discussion of the assignment of hereditary chief titles, see Lizette Hall, *The Carrier, My People* (Prince George, BC: Papyrus Printing, 1992), and Fiske and Patrick, *supra* note 17.
21 *A Journey Home, supra* note 19.
22 Within Western legal traditions, many domestic and international initiatives are directed to the protection of proprietary interests in knowledge. However, one should note that it is widely accepted that international laws have considerably less force than nation-state domestic laws by virtue of the voluntary nature in which a nation-state may bind itself to comply with international conventions, treaties, and the like. It is also important to acknowledge that the enforceability of international forums and agreements is questionable in relation to nation-state actions. See Sharon Venne, *Our Elders Know Our Rights* (Penticton, BC: Theytus Books, 2002), and James Anaya, *Indigenous Peoples in International Law* (Toronto: Oxford University Press, 2000).
23 Vine Deloria Jr., *Red Earth and White Lies: Native Americans and the Myth of Scientific Fact* (New York: Scribner Publishing, 1995).
24 See Chief Justice Lamer's commentary in *Delgamuukw v. British Columbia*, [1997] 3 S.C.R. 1010 at para. 186. Lamer's remark – "Let us face it, we are all here to stay" – is a broad statement expressing the generally accepted sentiment that Indigenous and non-Indigenous peoples populate Canada and will continue to do so for years to come.

25 See Linda Tuhiwai Smith, *Decolonizing Methodologies: Research and Indigenous Peoples* (Dunedin, New Zealand: University of Otago Press, 1996), and Alfred, *supra* note 9.

26 See Borrows, in Bell and Kahane, *supra* note 7 at 343-63. Although he argues that Indigenous justice systems should be separate from intercultural dispute-resolution processes, Borrows clearly supports a series of separate systems for individual Indigenous peoples so as to ensure that dispute resolution processes do not become the "cutting edge of colonialism." In this sense, it follows that Indigenous people and others who know Indigenous systems would be preferred over those who reinterpret such systems from their own cultural perspective.

27 See Rosemary Coombe, "Sixth Annual Tribal Sovereignty Symposium: The Recognition of Indigenous Peoples' and Community Traditional Knowledge in International Law" (Winter 2001) 14 St. Thomas L. Rev. 275, and Gelvina Rodriguez Stevenson, "Trade Secrets: The Secret to Protecting Indigenous Ethnobiological (Medicinal) Knowledge" (2000) 32 N.Y.U.J. Int't L. & Pol. 1119. These authors and others have suggested that a number of domestic and international legal regimes could be useful in the desire to protect Indigenous knowledge. Coombe argues for a human rights approach to the issues, whereas Rodriguez Stevenson favours greater reliance on trade-secret laws. Yet others argue for sui generis domestic legislation: examples here include Daniel Gervais, "Spiritual but Not Intellectual? The Protection of Sacred Intangible Traditional Knowledge" (Summer 2003) 11 Cardozo J. Int'l & Comp. L. 467, and John Borrows, "Towards an Indigenous Cultural Property Regime" (2004, manuscript on file with the author).

28 For a discussion of pluralism in the context of health and medicine in Indigenous communities, see Kelm, *supra* note 13 at chap. 8.

29 See John Griffith, "What Is Legal Pluralism?" (1986) 24 Journal of Legal Pluralism and Unofficial Law 1 at 3-5, in which Griffith notes that law as an ideology of legal centralism is the law of the state, unified for all persons, exclusive of all other law, and administered by a single set of state institutions. He identifies two approaches to legal centralist conceptions: the first is a top-down approach dependent on the sovereign; the second is a bottom-up approach that derives its validity from several layers of norms that converge into one universal norm.

30 *Ibid.* at 3-4. See also Pierre Legrand, "The Return of the Repressed: Moving Comparative Legal Studies beyond Pleasure" (2000-1) 75 Tul. L. Rev. 1033 at 1036-37, in which Legrand argues that comparative legal studies that merely compare the sameness in the formulation of statutes or the outcome of decisions across jurisdictions offer little and are positively misleading, devoid of epistemological value – suggesting a need to embrace diversity and avoid uniformity. See also Sally Merry, "Anthropology, Law, and Transitional Processes" (1992) 21 Ann. Rev. Anthropology 357, and specifically at 358: she observes that legal pluralism is "generally defined as a situation in which two or more legal systems coexist in the same social field."

31 Griffith, *supra* note 29 at 5 and especially the reference to Jacques Vanderlinden, "Le pluralisme juridique: essai de synthèse" in John Gillissen, ed., *Le pluralism juridique* (Brussels: Université libre de Bruxelles, 1971) at 19-56.

32 Brian Tamanaha, "The Folly of 'Social Scientific' Concept of Legal Pluralism" (Summer 1993) 20:2 Journal of Law and Society 192. In the sense that all forms of social control are law and that law is synonymous with normative order, the legal includes the non-legal.

33 *Ibid.* at 205-8.

34 *Ibid.* at 209-11.

35 See Amanda Pask, "Cultural Appropriation and the Law: An Analysis of the Legal Regimes concerning Culture" (December 1993) 8 I.P.J. 57.

36 This point is effectively pursued in John Frow, "Public Domain and Collective Rights in Culture" (November 1998) 13 I.P.J. 39 at 51. Frow's point is grounded in an argument to support the recognition of Indigenous legal systems, as well as of the Indigenous perspectives regarding the private and public spheres of knowledge that are inherently embedded in those systems. This analysis is most notable for its recognition that Western legal traditions are not best equipped to address collective forms of property ownership and the

interplay between private duties and responsibilities of members of collectively held Indigenous knowledge. For a fuller analysis of this latter issue, see Peter Drahos, "Indigenous Knowledge and the Duties of Intellectual Property Owners" (August 1997) 11 I.P.J. 179 at 180, in which he argues that "economic forms of intellectual property rights should be relocated in a discourse which sees them treated as privileges that those who hold such privileges are thereby subject to duties. Indigenous property forms, on the other hand, should be linked to the protection of personality, both collective and individual."

37 Michael Halewood, "Indigenous and Local Knowledge in International Law: A Preface to Sui Generis Intellectual Property Protection" (1999) 44 McGill L.J. 953.

38 Pask, *supra* note 35.

39 For a dated discussion of Canadian cases in which Indigenous customary laws were considered, interpreted, and applied, see Norman Zlotkin, "Judicial Recognition of Aboriginal Customary Law in Canada: Selected Marriage and Adoption Cases" (1984) 4 C.N.L.R. 1. Tracing the evolution of Canadian cases that recognize the validity of Indigenous laws, Zlotkin reveals that the courts have developed a test to determine customary laws in Indigenous community, one based on English common law principles. In the case of child adoption, the test requires claimants to address consent, voluntary placement, rationale, and living memory of the customary practice. Zlotkin's analysis also shows that the courts have applied the test uniformly across Indigenous cultural divides, as if to suggest that all Indigenous legal orders follow the same method of determining when a child is formally adopted.

40 *Connolly v. Woolrich and Johnson et al.* (1867), 17 R.J.R.Q. 75, 11 L.C. Jur. 197; and Brian Slattery, *Canadian Native Law Cases* (Saskatoon: University of Saskatchewan, Native Law Centre, 1980) at 70.

41 *Casimel v. Insurance Corporation of British Columbia*, [1993] B.C.J. No. 183; Vancouver Registry CA014532, 14 September 1993; *Insurance (Motor Vehicle) Act*, R.S.B.C. 1996.

42 *Prince & Julian v. Her Majesty the Queen in Right of Canada and the Estate of Murdock* (7 July 2000), Prince George Registry 04390 (B.C.S.C.).

43 *Adoption Act*, R.S.B.C. 1996, c. 5, s. 46.

44 This is precisely the situation that Amanda Pask warns against. Pask, *supra* note 35.

Bibliography

Adoption Act, R.S.B.C. 1996, c. 5, s. 46.

Alfred, Taiaiake. *Peace, Power, Righteousness: An Indigenous Manifesto* (Oxford: Oxford University Press, 1999).

Anaya, James. *Indigenous Peoples in International Law* (Toronto: Oxford University Press, 2000).

Battiste, Marie, and James (Sákéj) Youngblood Henderson. *Protecting Indigenous Knowledge and Heritage* (Saskatoon: Purich Publishing, 2001).

Bell, Catherine, and David Kahane, eds. *Intercultural Dispute Resolution in Aboriginal Contexts* (Toronto: University of Toronto Press, 2004).

Borrows, John. "A Separate Peace: Strengthening Shared Justice" in Catherine Bell and David Kahane, eds., *Intercultural Dispute Resolution in Aboriginal Contexts* (Toronto: University of Toronto Press, 2004) 343.

–. "Towards an Indigenous Cultural Property Regime" (2004, manuscript on file with the author).

Casimel v. Insurance Corporation of British Columbia, [1993] B.C.J. No. 183; Vancouver Registry CA014532, 14 September 1993.

Christie, Gordon. "Law, Theory and Aboriginal People" (Fall 2003) 2:1 Indigenous Law Journal 69.

Connolly v. Woolrich and Johnson et al. (1867), 17 R.J.R.Q. 75, 11 L.C. Jur. 197.

Coombe, Rosemary. "Sixth Annual Tribal Sovereignty Symposium: The Recognition of Indigenous Peoples' and Community Traditional Knowledge in International Law" (Winter 2001) 14 St. Thomas L. Rev. 275.

Delgamuukw v. British Columbia, [1997] 3 S.C.R. 1010.

Deloria, Vine, Jr. *Red Earth and White Lies: Native Americans and the Myth of Scientific Fact* (New York: Scribner Publishing, 1995).

Drahos, Peter. "Indigenous Knowledge and the Duties of Intellectual Property Owners" (August 1997) 11 I.P.J. 179.

Fiske, JoAnne, and Betty Patrick. *'C'is dideen khat' When the Plumes Rise: The Way of the Lake Babine Nation* (Vancouver, BC: UBC Press, 2000).

Frow, John. "Public Domain and Collective Rights in Culture" (November 1998) 13 I.P.J. 39.

Gervais, Daniel. "Spiritual but Not Intellectual? The Protection of Sacred Intangible Traditional Knowledge" (Summer 2003) 11 Cardozo J. Int'l & Comp. L. 467.

Griffith, John. "What Is Legal Pluralism?" (1986) 24 Journal of Legal Pluralism and Unofficial Law 1.

Halewood, Michael. "Indigenous and Local Knowledge in International Law: A Preface to Sui Generis Intellectual Property Protection" (1999) 44 McGill L.J. 953.

Hall, Lizette. *The Carrier, My People* (Prince George, BC: Papyrus Printing, 1992).

Hawley, John, and Jane Young. *The Medicines of Sophie Thomas* (Prince George, BC: University of Northern British Columbia Press, 2002).

Henderson, James (Sákéj) Youngblood. "Postcolonial Indigenous Legal Consciousness" (2002) 1 Indigenous Law Journal 1.

Insurance (Motor Vehicle) Act, R.S.B.C. 1996.

A Journey Home: Reclaiming Our Children. DVD Production, Carrier Sekani Family Services and House of Talent Productions (40 minutes), 2004.

Kelm, Mary-Ellen. *Colonizing Bodies: Aboriginal Healing in British Columbia 1900-50* (Vancouver, BC: UBC Press, 1998).

Legrand, Pierre. "The Return of the Repressed: Moving Comparative Legal Studies beyond Pleasure" (2000-1) 75 Tul. L. Rev. 1033.

Lux, Maureen. *Medicine That Walks: Disease, Medicine, and Canadian Plains Native People, 1880-1940* (Toronto: University of Toronto Press, 2001).

Matiation, Stefan. "Biotechnology, Rights and Traditional Knowledge" in *A Brave New World: Where Biotechnology and Human Rights Intersect.* Biotechnology Strategy Reports (Ottawa: Government of Canada, 2005). http://biostrategy.gc.ca/HumanRights/HumanRightsE/ch7_e.html.

Merry, Sally. "Anthropology, Law, and Transitional Processes" (1992) 21 Ann. Rev. Anthropology 357.

Monture-Angus, Patricia. *Journeying Forward: Dreaming First Nations' Independence* (Halifax: Fernwood Press, 1999).

Nadasdy, Paul. *Hunters and Bureaucrats: Power, Knowledge, and Aboriginal-State Relations in the Southwest Yukon* (Vancouver: UBC Press, 2003).

Napolean, Val. "Who Gets to Say What Happened? Reconciliation Issues for the Gitxsan" in Catherine Bell and David Kahane, eds., *Intercultural Dispute Resolution in Aboriginal Contexts* (Toronto: University of Toronto Press, 2004) 176.

Overstall, Richard. "Reconciliation Devices: Using the Trust as an Interface between Aboriginal and State Legal Orders" in Catherine Bell and David Kahane, eds., *Intercultural Dispute Resolution in Aboriginal Contexts* (Toronto: University of Toronto Press, 2004) 196.

Pask, Amanda. "Cultural Appropriation and the Law: An Analysis of the Legal Regimes concerning Culture" (December 1993) 8 I.P.J. 57.

Prince & Julian v. Her Majesty the Queen in Right of Canada and the Estate of Murdock (7 July 2000), Prince George Registry 04390 (B.C.S.C.).

Rodriguez Stevenson, Gelvina. "Trade Secrets: The Secret to Protecting Indigenous Ethnobiological (Medicinal) Knowledge" (2000) 32 N.Y.U.J. Int't L. & Pol. 1119.

Slattery, Brian. *Canadian Native Law Cases* (Saskatoon: University of Saskatchewan, Native Law Centre, 1980).

Smith, Linda Tuhiwai. *Decolonizing Methodologies: Research and Indigenous Peoples* (Dunedin, New Zealand: University of Otago Press, 1996).

Tamanaha, Brian. "The Folly of 'Social Scientific' Concept of Legal Pluralism" (Summer 1993) 20:2 Journal of Law and Society 192.

Turner, Nancy. *Plants of Haida Gwaii* (Winlaw, BC: Sono Nis Press, 2004).
Venne, Sharon. *Our Elders Know Our Rights* (Penticton, BC: Theytus Books, 2002).
Zlotkin, Norman. "Judicial Recognition of Aboriginal Customary Law in Canada: Selected Marriage and Adoption Cases" (1984) 4 C.N.L.R. 1.

5
Territoriality, Personality, and the Promotion of Aboriginal Legal Traditions in Canada
Ghislain Otis

> Political institutions are neither naturally nor universally territorializable.
>
> – Bertrand Badie, *La fin des territoires*[1]

This short study is part of a more ambitious work on the role of territory in implementing Aboriginal self-government in Canada. The subject of this essay is very limited, addressing only whether the purely territorial model of Aboriginal government that has long been at the forefront in Canada is the most appropriate for enabling Aboriginals, if they so desire, to base the exercise of their normative powers on their legal traditions and to experiment, reinterpret, and mobilize these traditions in their pursuit of human, cultural, and economic development.

As a component of legal culture, legal *tradition* generally covers all law-related beliefs, doctrines, practices, and even techniques that "have current authority and legitimacy based on their real or alleged transmission from the past."[2] Thus, legal tradition is a living heritage that, to this day, organizes the consciences, thoughts, and practices of contemporary practitioners of this tradition. When differentiating between legal traditions, we tend to identify them by characteristics that confer a specific identity or quality. For example, the so-called non-Western[3] legal traditions are contrasted with "Western" traditions, which are themselves divided into different families, such as the Romano-Germanic tradition and the common law tradition.[4] Thus, the expression "Aboriginal legal traditions" is a double differentiation in that it conveys the idea of traditions that are both unique, in their common "aboriginality," and multiple, due to the internal diversity of the Aboriginal legal world.

The degree of specificity among legal traditions can be highly variable given the ongoing contact between legal cultures that influence and borrow – either reciprocally or not – from one another, sometimes to such an extent that it brings about true mixing. However, it should be noted from the start that, in this chapter, I am not proposing to study in any detailed manner the characteristics of Aboriginal legal traditions in general or any one of them in particular. Rather, to the specific issue of Aboriginal self-government as a potential means for mobilizing Aboriginal legal traditions, I am applying a more general reflection on territoriality and its limitations in the political organization of multicommunity or multinational states. Similarly, the discussion presented in the pages that follow will primarily address the fundamental characteristics of territoriality and personality as modes for demarcating power and Aboriginal legal orders. A detailed and technical analysis of the entire apparatus required for the implementation of a non-territorial or personal model for Aboriginal government, rather than a purely territorial one, is a considerable undertaking, which is better conducted elsewhere.

When considering the relationship between territory and Aboriginal power, we must keep in mind that the promotion of Indigenous legal traditions is but one of the elements to be addressed. In fact, we should not expect Aboriginals to be confined to any legal universe, however sanctified, that does not relate to their current aspirations and needs.

In the first part of the text, I will review the territorial and personal models for power structures and legal systems in the context of states that want to institutionalize the co-existence of nations or historical or founding ethnocultural groups. In the second part, I will examine the role that should be played by each of these models in promoting Canada's Aboriginal legal traditions.

Territoriality and Personality in Multicommunity or Multinational States

Territoriality

The anchoring of power in territory reflects a specific relationship of governance to space in modern Western constitutional theory and practice. The history of territoriality cannot be dissociated from that of the progressive emergence of the state:

> [T]erritory and its corollary, the border, are inventions of the State. The representation of a homogenous geographic space, delimited by a precise and linear border, over which the will of the Prince is exercised in a standard manner that is identical in every aspect, does not predate the end of the Middle Ages or the beginning of the modern era.[5]

Territorialist orthodoxy holds that the control of a geometrically delimited space is the *necessary* and *sufficient* condition of power and of a legal order. Territory as a *necessary* condition of legal order is based on two postu-lates: first, power and legal order exist only *by virtue of* territory; second, power and legal order exist only *in* the territory. According to the first pos-tulate, territory constitutes the essential source for establishing law. A hu-man community without its own territory cannot claim any distinct legal order. The other postulate holds, with some exceptions, that territory marks the spatial limit of a legal order. Beyond territory, there can be no legal order, and no formal participation in the territorialized community's legal culture can be expected by those who are located outside the geographic perimeter within which the legal order is confined.

Territory as a *sufficient* condition of legal order means that "simple loca-tion on, or attachment to territory by a subject of law; the accomplishment of an act; or the occurrence of a fact or a situation ... are likely to be decisive criteria for application of either a substantive or procedural rule."[6] In other words, territorial connection alone suffices to subject the population to the legal order. The criterion for individual and group participation in a legal culture and tradition legitimized by state law will be their connection to a given geographical area without regard for ethnocultural identities. The ter-ritorial logic is therefore one of normative standardization whereby the same duties, freedoms, and rights should, as a general rule, apply to all.

It can be seen that territory is the arena of a shared legal order and that its function is not only to provide the framework for control of the population and of a physical space. Its configuration also becomes the "structuring principle of a political community."[7] The demotic dimension of territory seems obvious here. In other words, the purely territorial approach con-structs a unified *demos,* which is understood as the human substratum of the legal order.[8] Territoriality institutes a single demos, a single political community defined by simple occupation of a common space. Thus, terri-tory has a unifying function: demos is one, power is one, legal order is one. The classical liberal representation of territory makes it a public space indif-ferent to ethnocultural difference, an idea that conveys freedom and equal-ity founded upon an identity that is "territorially constructed rather than culturally given."[9] Territoriality thus produces through a shared space a political togetherness that transcends community allegiances. The single territorial legal order is seen as the condition of a truly common citizen-ship. It is from this perspective that Jean-Étienne Portalis wrote that "men who depend upon the same sovereignty without being regulated by the same laws must be strangers to one another."[10]

Beyond its demotic value, territoriality allows the management of public affairs to be rationalized. It ensures centralization of power at the local or regional levels, thus potentially increasing administrative efficiency.[11] Con-centrated decision making simplifies political and administrative organization, which decreases the opportunity for conflict between laws and the legal uncertainty that results.

Personality

The "personality" of laws (or of the law) means that the law applicable to one individual, and thus individual participation in a legal order, is not determined solely as a function of territorial connection but on the basis of personal membership in a given ethnocultural or national group.[12] Whereas territoriality supposes that the exercise of political power is mediated by the land, personality grounds power and its exercise in the community itself. As a result, the principle of personality means that various ethnic or national groups who have a common territorial location may nevertheless be governed by their discrete legal rules; the law is thus "communalized" or "ethnicized." In modern states in which personality has currency, laws are never completely personal. In other words, personality is applied only for certain issues, whereas other matters fall under rules that are applied territorially and therefore become enforceable against all individuals found within a territorial unit regardless of their communal or national affiliation.[13]

The principle of personality in fact constitutes a multisecular manifestation of legal pluralism. It has been resorted to in very diverse political contexts, but in each case it has conveyed a potent concern for identity-based communal or national claims.[14] Personality has often been used in situations of contact or mixing of ethnically heterogeneous populations in order to foster an egalitarian relationship between national communities. Personal autonomy may even represent an original form of "personal federalism" when communal political entities have relationships among themselves and with the state that are similar to that usually associated with the federal model.[15]

Personalization of law marks a boundary that is both cultural and legal. It has, in the colonial or para-colonial[16] context, permitted segregation of colonizer and colonized by exempting, for example, European colonists from the Indigenous African law they held to be inferior and therefore reserved for Natives alone.[17] In terms of relationships between heterogeneous legal cultures and traditions, however, personality has often protected "the rights of the weakest" from acculturation:

> Recognition of personal status by the dominant society, which in part *departs from the general law,* has always been a means of structuring legal coexistence for sensitive issues. *It enabled some populations to maintain a legal distinction associated with their distinctive* identities and, at the same time, modified the overall legal system which found itself injected with a shot of pluralism.[18]

As will be seen in the second part of this essay, the need to protect and foster vulnerable or marginalized legal traditions may be one argument in favour of personality in the context of Aboriginal governance.

Personality acting simply as a criterion for applying legal rules can be differentiated from personality operating as a criterion for the attribution and demarcation of a normative jurisdiction. In the first case, a central law-making entity decides to submit various ethnic groups to personal laws that it decrees as a function of diverse legal cultures in existence on the territory.[19] Although there are several personal regimes, there is unity in the legal source of these regimes. In this case, the principle of personality is not a pluralistic power arrangement but rather a cultural or ethnic delineation of the scope of law. In other words, the laws applicable to each group are personal, but personality does not ground the political and normative autonomy of these groups.

In the other case, the principle of personality translates into true personal or "cultural autonomy"[20] for each national group, which then benefits, for many matters, from a governmental authority applicable exclusively to its members rather than to all people located within a given territory. Personal autonomy operates so that law and space are decoupled. Whereas territoriality carries uniformity, personality entrenches diversity and complexity. History provides several examples, ancient and modern, of various models of minority governance based on the principle of personality.[21]

Of course, the territorial reference is never totally eclipsed, since it is due only to the co-existence of distinct communities *within the same space and subject to the same overarching territorial sovereignty of the state* that the issue of the personal organization of power can be raised.[22] Nonetheless, we can speak of *complete personality* when the criterion of personality is the sole factor attributing jurisdiction to a group's institutions, without any spatial reference other than that inherent in the state. The law generated by the group is thus likely to apply to individual members of that group regardless of their place of residence within the state's territory. There will be *relative personality* when personal membership in a group, though constituting the necessary condition for the exercise of the group's jurisdiction and the application of its legal rules, is nevertheless combined with some specific territorial connection requirement.[23]

Territoriality and National or Communal Pluralism

Our conception of government, including Aboriginal self-government, is so embedded in territoriality that we sometimes find it difficult to think outside the "territorial box." Yet, as soon as several national or ethnocultural groups co-exist within the territory of a single state, the dynamic of normative standardization inherent in territoriality becomes a problem when

structuring institutional diversity, including the diversity of legal cultures
or traditions. Classical liberalism views territory as a culturally neutral concept. Citizenship of this territory has precedence over identity-based distinctions and communal solidarities. Yet, most often, experience refutes the
premise of a territorial order that is blind to differentialist projects and im-
pervious to identity-based machinations. Even in liberal democratic states,
territory is used to construct a "common social culture" that almost inevitably conveys the cultural traits of the numerically dominant national group.
Thus, members of this dominant group *de facto* find themselves privileged
with respect to their ability to access this common culture and benefit
therefrom.[24]

The demotic unit that territoriality tends to construct does not always fit
the concrete reality of heterogeneous societies. It is often at odds with the
plurality of groups motivated by an identity-based national consciousness,
thus creating "a need to understand the human bedrock of the state as an
institutionalized plurality, organized and controlled by the co-existence of
subnational groups."[25] As soon as the myth of neutral and universal territoriality is recognized as such, the composite population of a state may induce an intra-state territoriality to satisfy autonomist claims. In this case,
implementation of political autonomy for a sub-state group is based on
ethnocultural cartography, which – through internal fragmentation of the
state's territory – turns a national minority at the state level into a governing majority within a regional or local segment of the territory. The political boundary is therefore modulated to espouse the contours of the zones
inhabited by various national groups living within the state's territory.

This in fact reproduces the territorial technique of national construction
at the sub-state level, although this technique is tempered by the connection of sub-state national components to common supra-national state authorities. Just as the territory becomes internally fragmented, the demos is
no longer one but many within the state's order. The cartographic delimita-
tion of nations generates sub-state demotic units that are juxtaposed in
space and mutually exclusive rather than overlapping. To describe the highest
forms of intra-state territoriality that organize the political co-existence of
distinctive ethnocultural or national groups, political scientists use the term
"multinational federation":

> They are not all federations in the technical sense, but they all embody a
> model of the state in which national minorities are federated to the state
> through some form of territorial autonomy, and in which internal bounda-
> ries have been drawn, and powers distributed, in such a way as to ensure
> that each national group is able to maintain itself as a distinct and self-
> governing societal culture.[26]

It seems that the question of territorial pluralism cannot be ignored once one national group finds itself currently a majority in a space to which it may legitimately claim historic attachment. Disconnecting such a nation from the territory by resorting to purely personal autonomy would be problematic in most cases. In its modern Western aspect, the idea of personal or "cultural" autonomy for national sub-state communities is well known due, in particular, to the works of Otto Bauer[27] and Karl Renner on the so-called nationalities question of the old Austro-Hungarian empire.[28] Yet Renner, by proposing to do away with territory as a basis for national autonomy, has certainly underestimated its importance for the sustainability of national groups.

Purely personal autonomy does not reflect the often founding role of territoriality in the collective imagination and the sense of identity of national communities.[29] Furthermore, territory forms the basis for a set of economic, social, and cultural jurisdictions, all of which reinforce the ability of a national group to reproduce and perpetuate its culture and identity.[30] Notably, territory provides a forum for the dissemination of the national language and national symbols in the public sphere; it enables a majority group to maintain, in key areas of government action, a legal order that is consistent with its legal culture.

This is why national groups, concentrated on a territory where they have historically been a majority, do not generally demand personal autonomy, which would not satisfy them.[31] Promotion of such autonomy by the state authorities will appear justifiably suspect if it arises simply from a desire to dispute or defeat territorial claims in order to secure state interests. Those who advocate the deterritorialization of nations are in fact often motivated by strategic concerns that eclipse pluralist aims. By dissociating territory and nation, Renner wanted to avoid the dismantling of the Austro-Hungarian empire and facilitate the emergence of a socialism that transcended national divides within a secure state.[32] Similarly, in central and eastern European states that have recovered or recently acquired their sovereignty, personal autonomy for national minorities is often advanced to avert the threat of secession.[33] Yet there are no guarantees that denying claims for sub-state territorial autonomy will encourage the stability or even the integrity of these states over time.[34]

It must be concluded that territory will be a permanent issue in multinational or multicommunity governance and that, as will be explained in the second part of this chapter, the case of Aboriginal self-government in Canada is no exception here.

Beyond Territory: The Space for Personality
The enduring echo of Renner's works in today's scientific and political circles is due not only to the concern for the state's security or integrity. It can

also be explained by the many autonomist claims in increasingly complex and explosive demographic and political contexts. In fact, when populations are mixed, when some national groups are demographically marginal and geographically dispersed, conventional territorial arrangements will not provide a satisfactory solution to claims for autonomy and legal pluralism. Territorial processes tend to give rise to a cascading overlap of minorities; each majority arising from the spatial surgery will inevitably enclose elements of other national communities that are, in turn, likely to claim the benefits of political autonomy necessary for the protection of their own cultural identity. This reality of nested minorities demonstrates very well that territories cannot bow to "the tormented geography of peoples who overlap and may even be layered upon one another."[35]

For example, when various national groups are so intertwined in the same space that none constitutes a stable majority, the cartographic logic cannot satisfy, in a liberal and democratic fashion, the autonomist aspirations of these groups. Where democracy and human rights are not respected, the ethnic or cultural appropriation of territory – in other words, the idea that each national group must have its own territory – may lead to the worst scenarios of belligerent instrumentalization of territory. A commentator has used forceful words to describe this peril:

> An exclusively territorial approach to federalism is not innocent, because it propagates a culture of ethnic cleansing, of genocide, of transfer of populations, or in the least malignant case, forced integration.[36]

On the other hand, the principle of personality could allow national groups that are intermingled to be constituted as political units endowed with legal personality and given self-governance without spatial exclusivity in matters essential to their national development. These groups would nonetheless continue to cohabit the same territory under the aegis of common territorially applied laws. It is also generally admitted that the purely territorial formula is not appropriate for national groups that, for historical reasons, are distributed throughout the entire territory of the state and therefore cannot claim to be the majority occupants of a specific territory.[37] Pure territoriality is equally problematic for groups in which some members are geographically concentrated and a substantial segment of members are a minority outside the national community's territory of historical residence. For this intra-state diaspora, the territorial formula cannot be applied. A majority group's ability to pursue its territorial national project within the state will have the possible inverse effect of marginalizing the other nations present within the territory.

These enclaved and irremediably minoritized groups within a territory controlled by another national group may find in the principle of personality a formula that will temper the assimilationist pressures of the national majority that benefits from territorial autonomy. Applied to national diasporas or to minorities dispersed throughout a state, the principle of personality would in fact lead to a hybrid regime by virtue of which the institutions controlled by the territorial majority group would not have jurisdiction over minority members with respect to personalized matters. However, territorial jurisdiction will continue to exist over matters other than those that are personalized.

Personal autonomy may also be appropriate in other cases. For example, a national group that has for many years benefited from such autonomy may not want to challenge a modus vivendi that has strong historic legitimacy, although it may wish to adapt it to contemporary values.[38] Similarly, a national group that is in the majority in a given territory and has aspirations to territorial autonomy may, for pragmatic reasons, temporarily exercise purely personal jurisdiction over its members in areas such as culture, education, health, private law related to personal and family status, and social affairs. Personal autonomy as a transitional regime will have the benefit of making governmental autonomy progressively concrete in several sensitive areas while preventing personality from becoming a pretext for territorial dispossession.[39]

However, it must be granted that, at all times, the personality of laws in the context of communal or national pluralism has been a delicate and complex operation at the institutional level. Beyond issues relating to the division of powers and administrative organization, the main drawback of this system doubtless lies in the necessary connection of an individual to a community that is often defined in ethnocultural terms and the complexity arising from the inevitable legal interactions between individuals from different communities. One has only to look at the experience of states that have maintained customary personal status regimes for certain groups to measure the practical complexity of issues such as identifying criteria for individual membership in a group, conditions for relinquishment of membership, changes in or transmission of status, and determining the applicable law in the presence of legal relationships between individuals of differing national status.[40]

More fundamentally, however, there appears to be a need for caution in the ethnocultural configuration of the political community that personal autonomy entails. Nowadays, individual cultural freedom and mobility are highly valued, and culturally complex individual identities are increasingly common. The legal capture of group and individual ethnic identity rightly leads to fears that individuals might be trapped in an imposed, essentialized, and oppressive group difference. Any system that forces individuals to belong to a specific ethnocultural group for the purpose of circumscribing legal orders, and forces them to conform to an ethnically or culturally determined lifestyle, would in fact be committing liberticide. The right to difference cannot be perverted into an obligation to be different.

Consequently, the critique of personal autonomy advanced by certain liberal pluralists does have the merit of highlighting the need to avoid any solutions that constrain individuals to choose a national affiliation or in which the authorities take it upon themselves to assign national or ethno-cultural identity.[41] In this respect, the failings of the Lebanese model of confessional personal federalism, due to the inability of individuals to choose a non-religious personal status and be governed by non-religious personal laws, have been very well demonstrated.[42] As one author observes, "boundaries of membership ... can be quite hard if they are mutually exclusive and ascriptive rather than chosen,"[43] hence the importance of allowing individuals "to leave the objective determination of their culture of origin."[44] Sometimes there are also fears that personal autonomy will exacerbate ethnic differentiations to the detriment of friendly intercultural relations.[45]

The difficulty of reconciling individual freedom and the principle of personality cannot be denied, but it is not insurmountable if personal autonomy is operating in a context where national pluralism is effectively anchored in democracy and respect for human rights. This difficulty should not obscure the fact that the territorial principle may also have the effect of imposing cultural and identity-based constraints on individuals to the extent that this principle enables the dominant group to mobilize political institutions in the service of its culture and identity.

At this point, it is appropriate to examine how, in the context of Aboriginal self-government in Canada, the choice between territoriality and personality can affect the ability of Aboriginal peoples to access true political autonomy and promote their legal traditions.

Territoriality and Personality in Aboriginal Governance in Canada

From Ancestral Lands to Territory

Although it is not possible to present the archaeology of Aboriginal conceptions regarding the relationship between space and power, it should be emphasized that no one has yet demonstrated that the Western legal institution of territory is consistent with that of the pre-colonial political and legal world. We are becoming more and more familiar with regimes of land tenure in pre-colonial societies, and with the importance of the material and cultural connection with the land that was often a sacred space and the very foundation of communal life. Similarly, specialists are slowly shedding light on the internal modes of family and clan regulation that predate contact.[46] However, it is not certain that territory achieved all the political-legal functions in pre-Columbian societies that it does in the Western territorial order. In other words, the fact that land occupied a central position in the traditional world did not necessarily mean there was a comprehensive monopolistic concept of power applicable to all matters, to every person and thing within a rigorously laid-out geometric boundary that was unique and fixed in space.

Did the role of ancestral lands correspond perfectly to that of the political boundaries of the modern state such that territorial cartography invariably overruled, as a criterion for authority, family, clan, or tribal relationships? Did the control of individuals in all circumstances depend on control of the land? Similarly, did control of the land always, ipso facto, mean control in all matters of all individuals thereon without regard for family, clan, or tribal membership? One author has shown that, in the case of pre-colonial clan-based societies in sub-Saharan Africa, one must avoid confusing traditional *land* – or land as a mythical reference and marker of identity – with modern *territory* as the exclusive, necessary but sufficient basis for complete authority.[47] It would perhaps be ethnocentric to equate the traditional function of ancestral lands with the contemporary function of territory in the Western sense.

Regardless of how pre-colonial political cultures perceived space, the colonial state, by creating Indian reserves, proceeded to fuse land and territory in its strategy for administering Aboriginal communities.[48] In other words, the colonizer made "Indian" land rights (to be meticulously demarcated from this point on) coincide with control of relations between individuals and the land as well as with governmental authority over all individuals on the land. Thus, legislation established the land tenure applicable on reserves and created a local Indian administration entrusted to a "band council" with regulatory powers that strictly follow the Western principle of territoriality since they are enforceable upon all individuals located within the reserve and since they do not extend beyond it.[49]

This colonial model of the reserve has had a strong influence on the territorial discourse that often characterizes Aboriginal claims to political autonomy.

Territory: The Unavoidable Issue in the Quest for Aboriginal Self-Government

The historic demand for state recognition of Aboriginal title to traditional lands and Aboriginal political control of these lands constitutes the central determining factor in the contemporary relationship between the state and the First Peoples. This is why the demands of Aboriginal peoples for decolonization inevitably include a territorial dimension: because title to the land becomes a territorial issue as soon as it is accompanied by the desire for political control of the relations between individuals and the land, as well as relations between the people on the land. It is therefore understandable that a model of political autonomy that would in all cases disconnect the nation from the land and the territory, such as that imagined by Karl Renner for the central and eastern European minorities, would be stripped of all legitimacy in the context of the political emancipation of the Aboriginal peoples.[50]

Nor would it fit with the state's law as it has developed since the colonial assertion of sovereignty. This law tends to postulate a relationship of consubstantiality between land and territory by equating Aboriginal communal land rights with a degree of political control of the relationships between individuals and Aboriginal land. From the beginning of European colonization, especially since the *Royal Proclamation, 1763* recognized and protected the pre-existing rights of Aboriginals to their traditional lands, access to these lands and their control has been a central issue in the relations between Aboriginal peoples and the state.[51] Aboriginal title, first recognized and confirmed by the common law and then by section 35 of the *Constitution Act, 1982*,[52] has linked land and territory since this title carries exclusive collective control of lands traditionally occupied by an Aboriginal group.[53] Similarly, modern treaties signed since the 1970s have settled the question of land rights, thus laying the ground for the setting up of autonomous governments on the newly demarcated lands.

There is thus a superimposition of land and political power since the traditional relationship to the land simultaneously justifies land title and territoriality as a constitutional foundation for governmental authority. The land therefore accedes to the status of territory; the community holding title *ipso jure* acquires the quality of body politic. The Quebec formula, evoking the right of Aboriginal peoples to "self-government on lands of which they are the sole owners," expresses very well this superimposition of land and territory.[54] The policy of the federal government with respect to Aboriginal self-government also lies largely on the premise that a community with land rights to a given space should naturally also exercise political power there.[55]

Self-government for communities that are the majority occupants of a recognized, secure land base will therefore be achieved through significant territorial jurisdictions that will be the key to the protection and mobilization of community resources for communal development and for funding autonomy. These jurisdictions will extend in particular to all issues related to lands and resources and the environment. These jurisdictions will make it possible to deploy Aboriginal cultures and legal traditions. They will also be essential to the implementation of economic and fiscal policies favouring the production and distribution of an Aboriginal wealth that today is desperately lacking.

As for communities that do not yet possess their own lands formally recognized as such by state law, but claim to have been unjustly deprived of their traditional homeland, they generally consider access to territorial status as the condition for any self-government worthy of the name.

Therefore, there cannot be any question of applying a purely personal model for autonomy to all Aboriginal peoples. But it would also be incorrect to totally fuse land and territoriality by establishing an inescapable connection between Aboriginal control of the lands and control of individuals. This connection would in fact be doubly problematic due to the dispersion and overlap of populations. First, affirming the primacy of land and linear cartography over communal relations would defeat Aboriginal self-government where there is no Aboriginal control of the land. Second, by subjecting all individuals on Aboriginal lands to the laws of the Aboriginal community controlling these lands, without also territorializing political rights, one would create a truncated territoriality devoid of the democratic guarantees of the modern territory. In other words, equating land control and governmental authority in all cases will only perpetuate in contemporary Aboriginal governance the colonial spectre of the reserve as a small impenetrable enclave deemed ethnically homogeneous.

Beyond Territory: Aboriginals Dispersed in a Non-Native Environment
The historic model of the reserve under federal legislation gave colonial ethnic territoriality two goals. It involved, on the one hand, "territorializing" Aboriginals, and on the other hand, "aboriginalizing" the land. Territorialization of Aboriginals was to be achieved through the settlement of the community and its local administrative apparatus within the borders of the reserve, whereas aboriginalization of the land was to be accomplished by reserving its occupation for Aboriginals. However, the model failed on both fronts.

Territorialization of Aboriginals within the reserve has proven impossible given their traditional way of life, the insufficiency of reserve lands, and the mobility of individuals inherent in the contemporary social and economic context. Many Aboriginals use traditional lands well beyond the limits of the reserve. Community members, often the majority, leave the reserve, becoming scattered in neighbouring regions or urban centres in which the majority are non-Aboriginals.[56] Furthermore, certain Aboriginal communities are distributed throughout the state territory, either because they do not live on land that belongs to them or because they do not have exclusive lands and cannot obtain any in the immediate future, a phenomenon that cannot help but intensify with the gradual recognition of Métis Aboriginal rights.[57] In total, the majority of Aboriginals for whom the Canadian government recognizes a right to autonomy are not today found on land that could offer a suitable basis for territorial government.[58]

The traditional discourse postulating that Aboriginals have an ontological connection to the land that dates from time immemorial is one that has been fed by jurists who often define aboriginality in terms of a territorial determinism.[59] Such discourse is of little use in the face of the dispersion and intermixing of populations. It seems increasingly difficult to argue that Aboriginals who are cut off from their ancestral lands lose their aboriginality and their will to participate in the life of their people. Data on the migration of status Indians outside their community's reserve indicate that "the stream of migration from reserves to cities is smaller compared to the flow from cities to reserves."[60] This fact leads one to think that a significant proportion of the migration is temporary or cyclical such that the affected individuals maintain effective links with their community.

Furthermore, many Aboriginals not living on communal lands have from the outset objected to the purely territorial construct of a nation and its political autonomy; witness the strong claims to voting rights in band council elections under the *Indian Act* by Aboriginals in the diaspora. This claim expresses not only a sense of belonging but also a desire for inclusion in a political community based on personal bonds rather than on the limited canons of territoriality. By relying on the constitutional principle of non-discrimination to recognize the right of Indian band members living off reserve to vote in elections regulated by the *Indian Act*, the Supreme Court has sanctioned this portrayal of a band as a political community that transcends territory.[61]

Moreover, when Aboriginal rights are used as a basis for self-government claims, it must be remembered that such rights are not necessarily connected to a communal land. Aboriginal rights other than land rights are grounded on a community rather than a territorial bond.[62]

The need to move beyond the territorial reflex to consider the dispersion of Aboriginals into the non-Native environment is widely acknowledged in the literature and is also admitted by the federal government.[63] In fact, the principle of personality is increasingly used, albeit cautiously, in recent agreements or treaties related to Aboriginal self-government.[64] It remains to be seen whether these agreements will bring about effective personal autonomy and thus encourage the democratic expression of Aboriginal legal cultures while respecting individual rights.

It can already be observed that it will not be easy for some communities, bound tightly for generations to the legal and psychological confines of the reserve, to move to a more complex mode of personal governance that potentially includes the entire nation as a deterritorialized demos. These communities could prefer a progressive process that would allow them to move towards personal jurisdictions as a function of their degree of organizational and financial preparation, of the level of cooperation they can expect from the state, of the political and numerical significance of their diaspora, and of their social and economic development priorities. The transition to the exercise of significant personal jurisdiction will no doubt be facilitated by the creation of supra-communal institutions arising out of a political association of small local communities. The implementation of such "more inclusive, collective Aboriginal agents"[65] will create institutions able to efficiently exercise, in a coordinated manner, the responsibilities that are important with respect to a political community that naturally transcends the communities' usual territorial landmarks. Doubtless, the authorities arising from a federation of local communities could more easily reach an agreement with the state about how to cooperate in applying Aboriginal laws and how to deliver services to members of the nation who live outside Aboriginal territories.

Current attempts to introduce elements of personality into self-government agreements primarily target communities occupying formally demarcated lands. Yet, personal autonomy could be used as a transitory regime by peoples who, today, are not land-based, either because they do not possess any legally recognized land – as with the majority of Métis communities – or because they do not intend to settle, over the short or medium term, on the land that already belongs to them. For Aboriginals with a legitimate claim to historic rights to specific lands, personality would not be considered here as an alternative solution to territoriality, which would perpetuate the ancient dispossession of Aboriginals, but as an important step en route to the fastest and fairest settlement possible for the claim to land and resources.

This is why there should not be any question of subordinating access to self-government to the settlement of the land and territory issue. By making acquisition of a land base a prerequisite for self-government, state and Aboriginal authorities would fail to understand the legal nature of the inherent right to self-government. They could also cause considerable harm to the cultural vitality of communities already weakened by their dispersion into a non-Native environment. When the quest for political autonomy is based on the inherent right to self-government, it must be remembered that such a right is attached first to the community whose existence as a sociological, political, and legal entity does not depend on the possession of recognized ancestral lands. Territoriality is no more a condition for the very existence of the inherent right to self-government in Canada than the recognition of an "Indian country" is the prerequisite for "tribal sovereignty" in the United States. The Supreme Court of Alaska has ruled that tribes without recognized territory ("Indian country") are "sovereigns without territorial reach" capable of exercising personal jurisdiction with respect to their members.[66] Thus, Aboriginal political authority arising from the inherent right to self-government relies on community bonds rather than on a spatial connection.

In the negotiation of a new relationship between the state and Aboriginals, the land issue is the most sensitive since it involves an enduring redistribution of scarce resources as well as an identity-based reconfiguration of space, and also because it poses a problem with respect to the division of powers between the provinces and Aboriginal peoples over the land and natural resources. We know from experience that decades can pass before these new, vital equilibriums can be attained. While we await the historic day when all land claims are settled, the assimilationist pressures of the majority culture will continue to weaken communities that will therefore be all the less likely to benefit from territorial autonomy.

Furthermore, communities without state-recognized territory will often first need to rebuild or revitalize the communal fabric as well as the institutions required for national cohesion. Personal autonomy will favour such a gradual revitalization through communal jurisdiction over matters such as education, the family, health, social affairs, and culture. These communities will benefit from a transitory phase of purely personal autonomy because it will help them prepare for a modern territorial governance of which they have no experience.

Personal autonomy may also be considered as a lasting rather than transitory solution for dispersed communities, including those whose land claims will ultimately be settled. The demarcation of a formally recognized territory for a community that has been long off a land base will not put a complete end to this dispersion. If the land set apart by the land claim agreement does not coincide substantially with the usual living environment of individuals and families, it is not certain that the majority will migrate to the newly demarcated land base.[67] In such a case, the newly marked land will primarily represent a resource to be developed in the interest of the community rather than the political space for governing individuals and nurturing distinctive social institutions. At a minimum, it seems certain that the resolution of land claims will generate new diasporas whose integration into the life of the community will not be possible under a purely territorial system of self-government.

"Internal Minorities" in Aboriginal Territory

The colonial "Aboriginalization" of territory via the reserve did not prevent the constant presence, within the community, of individuals and families considered to be non-members.[68] In fact, several communities today have substantial minorities of non-members on their territory even though this *de facto* mix does not mean non-members have formal rights of political participation.[69] Political rights for the purposes of the *Indian Act* are "personal" insofar as they are restricted to those having status as band members.[70]

Not only are Aboriginal territories less culturally homogeneous than we think, they seem destined to experience increasing diversity. Mixed marriages will certainly continue to be a significant factor in the influx of non-members, but other elements related to the progressive settlement of land claims will add to the mix, making intermingling of populations a persistent factor in Aboriginal governance. The conclusion of modern treaties in many cases will lead to the demarcation of Aboriginal territories that are often substantially larger than former reserves. This new territorial division will mean that more and more non-members will see their residences attached to Aboriginal territories. Furthermore, the operation of new Aboriginal institutions and the economic activity likely to result from the settlement of claims will require labour largely comprised of non-members who will come to settle in Aboriginal environments.[71]

According to classical territorial doctrine, all individuals living on a territory are governed by the territorial law and benefit from it. The law is universally applied without respect to community membership. Territoriality extends to the political sphere since the democratic theory of the state closely links citizenship, political equality, and the right to vote. Thus, the equal participation of all citizens of the state in the exercise of sovereignty through legislative bodies constitutes an essential attribute of citizenship, which explains that, in a territorial federation, "every member of the polity is both a federal citizen and a citizen of the province in which he resides."[72] Therefore, the national majority group that enjoys territorial autonomy in a federation cannot but treat its interior minorities as full citizens. Territorial autonomy is thus in harmony with a common citizenship of all Canadians irrespective of ethnocultural identity. In Canada we find such citizenship recognized in section 3 of the *Canadian Charter of Rights and Freedoms,* which states that "[e]very citizen of Canada has the right to vote in an election of members of the House of Commons or of a legislative assembly and to be qualified for membership therein."

In the context of political autonomy not based solely on the inherent right to self-government, all citizens living in a region where Aboriginals constitute a majority can be part of a territorial political community. This is the case in Nunavut.[73] This is also the model proposed for self-government in Nunavik.[74]

Such a model will not be workable, however, if the geographic and demographic situation of the territory cannot ensure a stable Aboriginal majority, thus making the inherent right to self-government the preferred basis for Aboriginal autonomy. As mentioned above, the close correlation between Aboriginal land rights and normative jurisdiction necessarily leads to the territorialization of power for all matters relating to land and to the management or use of resources. In other words, exclusive community land ownership carries power for the Aboriginal group over the use of these lands by all individuals found there, whether or not they are members of the community holding collective title. In addition, Aboriginal rights, including the inherent right to self-government, are reserved only for members of the group holding that right so that individuals who do not belong to this group cannot participate in collective decisions inherent in the exercise of such right. It therefore follows that, for example, modern treaties based on Aboriginal title tend to perpetuate the historic model of the reserve that territorializes jurisdiction over the lands and resources while also personalizing the rights to participate in decisions because such rights are reserved only for members of the group holding land title.[75]

Although they will be subject to the Aboriginal laws relating to individual or communal use of the land and resources, including tax laws, Canadian citizens belonging to minority groups living within the territorial limits of an Aboriginal government would not enjoy the political rights that would allow them equal participation in the collective control of these issues. Such asymmetry between the territoriality of laws and the personality of political rights poses the problem of the democratic legitimacy of Aboriginal governance. As one author writes, "the ethnic citizenship prevalent in Aboriginal communities excludes many residents of other origins who nonetheless exercise essential social functions: education, health, social services, transportation, material infrastructures, decision planning, etc."[76]

There is little doubt that, when they exercise an inherent right to self-government or a treaty right derived from it, central Aboriginal institutions are the organic and functional equivalent of the federal and provincial legislative bodies because their jurisdiction is constitutionally guaranteed and not delegated by some hierarchically superior legislative authority.[77] It is also certain that Canadian citizens submitted to the authority of a constitutionally recognized legislative body will not normally expect to be treated as if they were strangers in their own country.[78]

Despite this, the Constitution does not extend the logic of federal citizenship to Aboriginal political communities, since section 3 of the Canadian *Charter* refers only to federal and provincial elections.[79] In addition, under section 25 of the *Charter,* exclusive Aboriginal enjoyment and exercise of Aboriginal rights, which includes the right to participate in related collective decisions, benefit from an explicit exception to equality rights guaranteed under the same *Charter.*[80] The Constitution therefore establishes, for the benefit of Aboriginals, what could be called "an asymmetrical co-citizenship"[81] giving them all the democratic rights enjoyed by other Canadian citizens within federal and provincial institutions but reserving for them an ethnocultural citizenship without equivalent for the provinces.

One of the purposes or rationales of the constitutional recognition of Aboriginal rights, including the inherent right to self-government, is the protection of historically disadvantaged ethnocultural communities. It may therefore be legitimate, when the Aboriginal territory is a small enclave within an overwhelmingly non-Aboriginal environment, to guarantee an Aboriginal people's control over governmental institutions by limiting the electoral body only to individuals who belong to that people. There is an understandable fear that granting non-members equal political rights with regard to Aboriginal rights issues may lead to dispossession or conflict. If we can therefore share the point of view of those who see a reasonable accommodation in reserving voting rights for members,[82] pushing this distortion of the ideal of a truly egalitarian and pluralist democracy any further than necessary must nonetheless be avoided.

It would be fully possible, in many cases, to preserve the Aboriginal people's control over the exercise of their unique historic rights while avoiding a territoriality that would infringe upon democratic principles. Although exclusive control of the land by the Aboriginal group has the effect of territorializing the legislative jurisdiction associated with it, the same could not be said of the other self-government prerogatives derived from Aboriginal or treaty rights. It could even be said that the principle of personality is, generally speaking, an intrinsic characteristic of Aboriginal and treaty rights that, by definition, extend only to Aboriginals who are members of the group holding these rights.[83] Thus, the exercise of an Aboriginal right not related to the exclusive control of the land and its communal use, but rather to social, family, or cultural issues, will concern only individuals belonging to the group holding this right. As a result, the normative authority of the group with respect to these issues can extend only to these individuals.

It follows that a self-government agreement intended to implement the inherent right should apply the principle of personality in areas other than those relating to control of the land. This would have the effect of removing non-members living on the community territory from Aboriginal authority with regard to a range of important issues.[84] This is just what some recent agreements have provided.[85] For personalized matters, non-members belonging to an Aboriginal diaspora could fall under the personal jurisdiction of their community, whereas non-Aboriginals would be regulated by state laws. The non-members who are not subject to Aboriginal laws cannot lay claim, in the name of the democratic principle, to political rights that allow them to participate in the adoption of these laws. For personalized matters, their democratic rights should be exercised within the representative state or Aboriginal institutions that have jurisdiction over them.

For its part, the Aboriginal majority will be assured, as a result of the principle of personality, of long-term control not only over the management of land and resources but also over the exercise of essential prerogatives related to social, family, and cultural issues. In this context, the principle of personality greatly attenuates the deficit in democratic legitimacy experienced by Aboriginal governmental institutions and encourages the coexistence of heterogeneous populations on Aboriginal territories. It will, in effect, decrease the alienation of non-members who, although they do not have exactly the same political rights as those who belong to the ethnocultural majority, will be exempt from Aboriginal power for a range of issues that are extremely important to them. It will therefore be easier for them to envisage a compromise and accept a form of political participation that does not include voting rights with regard to issues relating to Aboriginal territorial jurisdiction.[86]

Furthermore, since the Aboriginal majority will not have to share power with non-members with respect to all the issues essential to its development and culture, it will feel less threatened by their presence and may be less inclined to secure its control of the territory and institutions by restricting non-member residency. In this way, freedom of movement of all citizens and economic development of Aboriginal communities may be fostered by the principle of personality.[87] Resistance within the majority society to the emergence of governments that are "ethnic" or "based on nation" could decrease, thereby strengthening the movement for the political emancipation of Aboriginal peoples and the revitalization of their legal cultures.

Conclusion

Moving beyond territory without discarding it: this is the direction to be taken in Canada in order to create the constitutional space required to promote Aboriginal legal orders and the traditions that structure them. For the majority of Aboriginal peoples, the land and its resources will constitute the foundation for governmental jurisdiction. It will mean control of the land and of the relationships between individuals and the land.

However, it would be a mistake to hold that control of territory and control of individuals are indissolubly linked. For centuries, the principle of the personality of laws has played a role in allowing the peaceful co-existence of heterogeneous legal cultures in a single territory. The overlapping of non-Native and Aboriginal populations is now a permanent feature of Canada's demographic evolution. Strict obedience to the dictates of territoriality could create an impasse that would harm Aboriginal self-government and the ability of an increasing number of Aboriginals to participate in the contemporary development of their legal traditions.

Thus, the ability of Aboriginal communities with a territorial base to mobilize, maintain, and promote their own legal cultures and traditions could be threatened if it were impossible for them to integrate, through personal jurisdiction, individuals belonging to these communities but located off the land base. The case of hunting and fishing activities on traditional land outside the community's exclusive land base illustrates particularly well the essential correlation between Aboriginal legal traditions and the principle of personality. These activities conducted by community members are at the heart of traditional legal systems related to the land and resources. They must necessarily fall under the personal jurisdiction of the community holding Aboriginal hunting and fishing rights.

Moreover, due to the very nature of "personalizable" matters – such as personal status, family, cultural issues, justice, education, and social affairs

– the principle of personality will probably mobilize the values that are the most central to the sense of identity of a community. This factor could encourage the affirmation of cultural difference within the Aboriginal legal order, thus permitting the community to mobilize its legal heritage in order to trace its own course between traditionalism and modernism. This aspect of the principle of personality will have great significance for communities that do not yet have their own territory and that cannot realistically expect to have an exclusive territory over the short term. Transitional personal autonomy could be the key to strengthening community cohesion and re-vitalizing the legal traditions related to personal status, as well as to social and cultural institutions. For some of these communities, settlement of the land claim might not be sufficient to put an end to their dispersion in non-Native environments; in this case, personal jurisdiction will become a per-manent solution.

Furthermore, the cultural legitimacy and intelligibility of a legal tradition are important conditions for it to be effective. The principle of personality, which is based on voluntary membership of Aboriginal individuals in the personalized legal order, will tend to consolidate the cultural validity of the legal tradition. Whether Aboriginal legal traditions are legitimate for non-members living on Aboriginal territory will also be at issue. Egalitarian and democratic co-citizenship within the state creates, in principle, a correla-tion between the exercise of public power and the political rights of all citizens. The territoriality of governmental power to control all citizens is matched by the territoriality of democratic rights, and therefore all citizens of the state living on its territory should have equal democratic rights.

Yet our constitutional system makes it possible to depart from democratic territoriality and introduce a personality of political rights for the exercise of Aboriginal powers arising from Aboriginal or treaty rights. This is to say that, inasmuch as Aboriginal power is based on the logic of Aboriginal rights, this power can be exercised only by members of the Aboriginal group hold-ing these rights. Here the Constitution departs fundamentally from the prin-ciple of territoriality for the benefit of personal Aboriginal political status. But precisely because Aboriginal rights carry a logic of personality, the Aboriginal power that they entail can be enforceable only against the group holding Aboriginal rights other than Aboriginal title to land. As a result, the principle of personality should be applied in such a way as to exclude non-members living in Aboriginal territory from the application of Aboriginal laws related to a range of personalizable matters, without affecting Aboriginal control of the land. Here, the principle of personality will reinforce the democratic legitimacy of Aboriginal power, allow Aboriginals to be stake-holders in their legal tradition for personal matters, and protect them from any challenge as to the cultural validity of this tradition by non-members. This use of the principle of personality, in favour of non-members, will facilitate the harmonious co-existence of populations without compromising the control of Aboriginal peoples over the exercise of their historic rights.

The central conclusion of this study is therefore that it has become necessary to develop hybrid institutional solutions combining territoriality and personality in contemporary Aboriginal governance based on the political and legal model of Aboriginal rights. For a group of matters intimately related to control of the land and the relationships between individuals and the land, which includes many issues associated with common use of space, the principle of territoriality imposes itself as soon as a community has lands that can be used as a substratum for jurisdiction. For another group of matters, Aboriginal jurisdiction could be personal, that is, limited only to members even if they do not reside on Aboriginal territory. Such institutions, reflecting the contemporary reality of Aboriginal peoples, would make it possible to move beyond the colonial reserve.

Notes

1 Bertrand Badie, *La fin des territoires: essai sur le désordre international et sur l'utilité sociale du respect* (Paris: Fayard, 1995) at 46. [Unless otherwise noted, all translations were prepared for this chapter.]

2 André Jean Arnaud *et al.*, eds., *Dictionnaire encyclopédique de théorie et de sociologie du droit*, 2nd ed. (Paris/Brussels: Librairie générale de droit et de jurisprudence/E. Story-Scientia, 1993) at 619.

3 In particular, see Wanda Capeller and Takanori Kitamura, eds., *Une introduction aux cultures juridiques non occidentales* (Brussels: Bruylant, 1998).

4 See, for example, René David and Camille Jauffret-Spinosi, *Les grands systèmes de droits contemporains*, 11th ed. (Paris: Dalloz, 2002) pts. 1 and 3.

5 Norbert Rouland, Stéphane Pierré-Caps, and Jacques Poumarède, *Droits des minorités et des peuples autochtones* (Paris: Presses universitaires de France, 1996) at 74. See also Badie, *supra* note 1 at 17-51.

6 Denis Alland and Stéphane Rials, eds., *Dictionnaire de la culture juridique* (Paris: Lamy-Presses universitaires de France, 2003) *s.v.* "territoire" at 1475.

7 Badie, *supra* note 1 at 12.

8 For an analysis of the demotic dimension of constitutional law, see Vlad Constantinescu and Stéphane Pierré-Caps, *Droit constitutionnel* (Paris: Presses universitaires de France, 2004) at 291-97.

9 Badie, *supra* note 1 at 48.

10 As quoted in Antoine Khair, "Les communautés religieuses au Liban, personnes morales de droit public" in CEDROMA, *Droit et religion* (Brussels: Bruylant, 2003) 457 at 467.

11 Ronald John Johnston *et al.*, eds., *The Dictionary of Human Geography*, 4th ed. (Malden: Blackwell Publishers, 2000) *s.v.* "territoriality" at 823-24.

12 Rémi Rouquette, *Dictionnaire du droit administratif* (Paris: Le Moniteur, 2002) *s.vv.* "territorialité" and "personnalité" at 585 and 794.

13 In particular, see the use of personality in the laws of the following states: Lebanon, France (New Caledonia), the United States, Belgium, Estonia, and Hungary.

14 For example, personal laws persisted in Frankish monarchies for centuries after the fall of the Roman Empire; this has been attributed to the fact that, for the Frankish kings, "an attachment to the practice of an ethnic law was a strong marker of identity." Rouland, Pierré-Caps, and Poumarède, *supra* note 5 at 59.

15 Stéphane Pierré-Caps, *La multination: l'avenir des minorités en Europe centrale et orientale* (Paris: Éditions Odile Jacos, 1995) at 255-82 [Pierré-Caps, *Multination*]; Antoine Nasri Messarra, *La gouvernance d'un système consensuel: Le Liban après les amendements constitutionnels de 1990*

(Beirut: Librairie Orientale, 2003) at 67-108; Antoine Nasri Messarra, "Principe de territorialité et principe de personnalité en fédéralisme comparé: le cas du Liban et perspectives actuelles pour la gestion du pluralisme" in Jean-François Gaudreault-DesBiens and Fabien Gélinas, eds., *Le fédéralisme dans tous ses états, gouvernance, identité et méthodologie (The States and Moods of Federalism: Governance, Identity and Methodology)* (Brussels/Cowansville: Bruylant/ Yvon Blais, 2005) 227 at 254-56 [Messarra, "Principe"].

16 Jacques Lafon, "Les capitulations ottomanes: un droit para-colonial?" (1998) 28 Droits 155.

17 See Rouland, Pierré-Caps, and Poumarède, *supra* note 5 at 509-11. Under the regime of Capitulations, Western foreigners were immune from the territorial law and the courts of the state in which they lived. They enjoyed personal laws that subjected them to the laws of their country of origin: Lafon, *supra* note 16. This system was quite incompatible with equality between states and was often perceived as a way for Western powers to exempt their nationals from laws and jurisdictions they viewed as primitive.

18 Alland and Rials, *supra* note 6 at 4 *s.v.* "acculturation juridique" (by Norbert Rouland).

19 Thus, during the early Middle Ages, the Frankish and German kings established in their respective territories of ancient Roman Gaul adopted different laws for each of the ethnic groups under their authority. See, specifically, Jean Bart, *Histoire du droit*, 2nd ed. (Paris: Dalloz, 2002) at 7-8. Today, personal laws enacted by a central state authority for diverse cultural or religious groups are still found in several countries; see Ayelet Shachar, *Multicultural Jurisdictions: Cultural Differences and Women's Rights* (Cambridge: Cambridge University Press, 2001) at 78-85.

20 Because autonomous organs founded on the principle of personality will often have jurisdiction over matters considered essential to the maintenance and promotion of a distinctive culture within a community, some authors speak of "cultural autonomy," which they contrast with "territorial autonomy." See, for example, Rainer Bauböck, "Autonomie territoriale ou culturelle pour les minorités nationales?" in Alain Dieckhoff, ed., *La constellation des appartenances: nationalisme, libéralisme et pluralisme* (Paris: Presses de Sciences Po, 2004) at 317 [Bauböck, "Autonomie"]. This chapter was also published in English: Rainer Bauböck, "Territorial or Cultural Autonomy for National Minorities?" in Alain Dieckhoff, ed., *The Politics of Belonging: Nationalism, Liberalism, and Pluralism* (Lanham, MD: Lexington Books, 2004) 221; Will Kymlicka, "La justice et la sécurité dans la prise en compte du nationalisme minoritaire" in Alain Dieckhoff, ed., *La constellation des appartenances: nationalisme, libéralisme et pluralisme* (Paris: Presses de Sciences Po, 2004) 181 [Kymlicka, "Justice et sécurité"]. Also published as "Justice and Security in the Accommodation of Minority Nationalism" in Dieckhoff, *Politics of Belonging*.

21 For a brief but complete overview of precedents in this respect, from the Ottoman Empire to recent legislation in Central and Western Europe, see John McGarry and Margaret Moore, "Karl Renner, Power Sharing and Non-territorial Autonomy" in Ephraim Nimni, ed., *National Cultural Autonomy and Its Contemporary Critics* (London: Routledge, 2005) 75 at 79-80.

22 As Pierré-Caps observes, "the principle of personality cannot operate without the territorial principle. The two principles even refer dialectically to one another. The personal principle individualizes nations at the same time as it makes them exist legally." Pierré-Caps, "Le principe de l'autonomie personnelle: une solution d'avenir?" in Dieckhoff, *supra* note 20 at 383 [Pierré-Caps, "Solution d'avenir"]. Also published as "The Principle of Personal Autonomy: A Solution of the Future?" in Dieckhoff, *Politics of Belonging*.

23 See, for example, the personal jurisdiction of the Belgian linguistic communities in the Brussels region; see Mary Farrell and Luk van Langenhove, "Towards Cultural Autonomy in Belgium" in Nimni, *supra* note 21 at 222.

24 See, among others, Will Kymlicka, "Le nouveau débat sur les droits des minorities" in Isabelle Schulte-Tenckhoff, ed., *Altérité et droit, contributions à l'étude du rapport entre droit et culture* (Brussels: Bruylant, 2002) 91 at 100-10; for the English-language version of this chapter, consult "The New Debate on Minority Rights" in Wayne Norman and Ronald Beiner, eds., *Canadian Political Philosophy: Contemporary Reflections* (Oxford: Oxford University Press, 2000); Jocelyn Maclure, "Entre le culturel et le civique: les voies (accidentées) de l'accommodement raisonnable" (2005) 23 Cités 57 at 58-61.

25 Constantinescu and Pierré-Caps, *supra* note 8 at 301.
26 Kymlicka, "Justice et sécurité," *supra* note 20 at 186.
27 See, specifically, Otto Bauer, *La question des nationalités et la social-démocratie*. Trans. by Nicole Brune-Perrin and Johannès Brune. Études et documentations Internationales [International studies and documents] (Paris: Arcantère Éditions, 1987) vol. 2. Also published as *The Question of Nationalities and Social Democracy*. Trans. by Joseph O'Donnell. Ed. by Ephraim Nemni (Minneapolis: University of Minnesota Press, 2000) vol. 2.
28 Karl Renner, *La nation, mythe et réalité*. Trans. by Stéphane Pierré-Caps and Claude Tixador (Nancy: Presses Universitaires de Nancy, 1998); Synopticus, *Staat und Nation* [State and nation] (Vienna, 1899) vol. 3; Rudolph Spinger, *Der Kampf der österreichischen Nationen um den Staat* [The Struggle of Austrian nationalities for the state] (Leipzig-Vienna, 1902); see also Yves Plasseraud, "How to Solve Cultural Identity Problems. Choose Your Own Nation," *Le monde diplomatique*, May 2000, http://www.globalpolicy.org/nations/citizen/region.htm; Georges Haupt, Michaël Löwy, and Claudie Weill, *Les marxistes et la question nationale 1848-1914*, 2nd ed. (Paris: L'Harmattan, 1997) at 111ff.
29 McGarry and Moore, *supra* note 21 at 83; Geoffrey Brahm Levey, "National Cultural Autonomy and Liberal Nationalism" in Nimni, *supra* note 21 at 154.
30 McGarry and Moore, *supra* note 21 at 82-84.
31 Kymlicka, "Justice et sécurité," *supra* note 20 at 213-14; Levey, *supra* note 29 at 155-56; Rainer Bauböck, "Political Autonomy or Cultural Minority Rights? A Conceptual Critique of Renner's Model" in Nimni, *supra* note 21 at 102-5 [Bauböck, "Conceptual Critique"].
32 Pierré-Caps, "Solution d'avenir," *supra* note 22 at 374 and 385.
33 Kymlicka, "Justice et sécurité," *supra* note 20 at 213-14; Will Kymlicka, "Renner and the Accommodation of Sub-state Nationalism" in Nimni, *supra* note 21 at 143-46 [Kymlicka, "Renner"]; McGarry and Moore, *supra* note 21 at 80-82.
34 Kymlicka, "Justice and sécurité," *supra* note 20 at 212-18.
35 Badie, *supra* note 1 at 255.
36 Messara, "Principe," *supra* note 15 at 260. This author also writes, at 256-57, that in a plural society, the "general law," in the Jacobin sense, is equivalent to the application of the law of the strongest to the detriment of minority groups because all minority claims to specificity are categorized as threats to the "general law."
37 Pierré-Caps, "Solution d'avenir," *supra* note 22 at 372; McGarry and Moore, *supra* note 21 at 80 and 82; Bauböck, "Autonomie," *supra* note 20 at 329. For a case study of the Romani, who consider themselves a non-territorial nation, see Ilona Klimova-Alexander, "Prospects for Romani National Cultural Autonomy" in Nimni, *supra* note 21 at 124.
38 This seems to be the case in Lebanese confessional communities that enjoy a form of personal autonomy; see Messara, "Principe," *supra* note 15.
39 One author also expressed the opinion that personal autonomy, in a context in which the rule of law and democracy have yet to be consolidated, may allow a transition towards a territorial autonomy that brings stability; see Bauböck, "Autonomie," *supra* note 20 at 361-65.
40 French overseas departments provide fertile ground for personal status issues generated by the principle of personality. See, among others, Olivier Guillaumont, "La constitution et le statut civil de droit local à Mayotte: état des réformes entreprises et des questions en suspens après la loi du 11 juillet 2001 relative à Mayotte" (2003) 11 Civitas Europa 43; Guy Agniel, "Le statut civil coutumier" in Jean-Yves Faberon and Guy Agniel, eds., *La souveraineté partagée en Nouvelle-Calédonie et en droit comparé* (Paris: La documentation française, 2000) 128; Régis Lafargue, *La coutume judiciaire en Nouvelle-Calédonie: aux sources d'un droit coutumier judiciaire* (Aix-en-Provence: Presses universitaires d'Aix-Marseille, 2003) at 54-90.
41 Bauböck, "Autonomie," *supra* note 20 at 338-42; Bauböck, "Conceptual Critique," *supra* note 31 at 101-2; Levey, *supra* note 29 at 157-60; Geneviève Nootens, "Nations, States and the Sovereign Territorial Ideal" in Nimni, *supra* note 21 at 57.
42 See Léna Gannagé, "Religion et droits fondamentaux dans le droit libanais de la famille" in *Droit et religion, supra* note 10 at 517; Jean Salem, "Un ordonnancement constitutionnel

sous hypothèque, religion et constitutionnalisme au Liban" in *Droit et religion, ibid.* at 469; Pierre Gannegé, "Le principe d'égalité et le pluralisme des statuts personnels dans les États multicommunautaires" in *L'avenir du droit: Mélanges en hommage à François Terré* (Paris: Dalloz/Puf, 1999) 431. For a recent condemnation of the lot of women in the various Lebanese religious communities, see Adbelkrim Debbih, "Dans la tourmente libanaise, les femmes perdent au change" (2005) 12:2 Alternatives 2.

43　Bauböck, "Autonomie," *supra* note 20 at 365.

44　Pierré-Caps, "Solution d'avenir," *supra* note 22 at 377.

45　Bauböck, "Autonomie," *supra* note 20 at 342-45. This author mentions this subject at 365: "the problem of CA (cultural autonomy) lies in the fact that it reinforces the boundaries of national communities. Policies cannot, for the most part, overlap. If national identities become distinct communities, they must have a clearly delineated identity."

46　See, specifically, Jean-Paul Lacasse, *Les Innus et le territoire, Innu Tipenitamun* (Sillery: Septentrion, 2004) at 27-45; James Y. Henderson, "Mikmaw Tenure in Atlantic Canada" (1995) 18 Dal. L.J. 216; Jacques Leroux *et al., Au pays des peaux de chagrin: occupation et exploitation territoriales à Kitcisakik (Grand-Lac-Victoria) au XXe siècle* (Quebec City: Presses de l'Université Laval, 2004).

47　Badie, *supra* note 1 at 75-77.

48　However, the exclusive constitutional jurisdiction of the Parliament of Canada to legislate for "Indians" is a classic example of personal jurisdiction. Parliament has from the outset used this power to define conditions for inclusion in the Indian Registry and to establish some elements of a personal Indian status regarding the capacity of persons and succession. This is the principle of personality acting as a simple criterion for the application of legal rules and not as a criterion for attribution of normative jurisdiction.

49　*Indian Act,* R.S.C. 1985, c. I-5.

50　See also Paul Patton, "National Autonomy and Indigenous Sovereignty" in Nimni, *supra* note 21 at 118-19.

51　R.S.C. 1985, App. II, No. 1.

52　*Calder v. British Columbia,* [1973] S.C.R. 313; R.S.C. 1985, App. II, No. 44. The first paragraph of s. 35 provides, "The existing aboriginal and treaty rights of the aboriginal peoples of Canada are hereby recognized and affirmed."

53　*Delgamuukw v. British Columbia,* [1997] 3 S.C.R. 1010; *R. v. Marshall; R. v. Bernard,* 2005 SCC 43.

54　See principle no. 6 of "The 15 principles" in Quebec, Secrétariat aux affaires autochtones, *The Basis of the Québec Government's Policy on Aboriginal Peoples* (Quebec City: Publications du Québec, 1988) at 4.

55　Canada, *Aboriginal Self-Government: Federal Policy Guide* (Ottawa: Public Works and Government Services Canada, 1995) at 21-26 [Canada, *Federal Policy Guide*].

56　For example, according to the 2001 Statistics Canada census, approximately 28 percent of the 976,305 individuals who reported an Aboriginal identity lived in urban centres. The Aboriginal population in urban centres would therefore have doubled and even, in some cases, tripled, specifically due to demographic factors such as mobility. See Andrew J. Siggner and Rosalinda Costa, *Aboriginal Conditions in Census Metropolitan Areas, 1981-2001,* Trends and Conditions in Census Metropolitan Areas (Ottawa: Industry Canada, 2005). In addition, a 2004 Department of Indian Affairs and Northern Development (DIAND) publication estimated that, in 2005, approximately 42.3 percent of the registered population would live off reserve. See Canada, DIAND, *Registered Indian Mobility and Migration: An Analysis of 1996 Census Data* (Ottawa: Public Works and Government Services Canada, 2004) at 5 [Canada, *Mobility and Migration*], http://www.ainc-inac.gc.ca/pr/ra/rimm/rimm_e.pdf.

57　The Maliseet First Nation and the Hunter's Point Algonquin Band are two Quebec examples of First Nations that live on land that does not belong to them. According to the Department of Indian Affairs and Northern Development, dozens of Indian bands do not have reserve lands under the *Indian Act, supra* note 49. For example, according to the *Band Classification Manual,* the following bands are in this situation: Micmac Nation Gespeg, Wolf Lake, Animbiigoo Zaagi'igan Anishinaabek, Caldwell, McDowell Lake, Missanabie

Cree, Sandpoint, Smith's Landing First Nation, New Westminster, Tsay Keh Dene, Deline, and West Point First Nation. Canada, DIAND, *Band Classification Manual,* May 2005 at 4 *et seq.,* http://www.ainc-inac.gc.ca/pr/pub/fnnrg/2005/bandc_e.pdf. See also Canada, DIAND, *First Nation Profiles,* 2005, http://sdiprod2.inac.gc.ca/FNProfiles/. Only the Métis communities in Alberta have their own communal lands on which they exercise a form of local government; see *Metis Settlement Act,* L.R.A. [R.S.A.] 2000, c. M-14. See also Canada, Royal Commission on Aboriginal Peoples, *Report of the Royal Commission on Aboriginal Peoples: Perspectives and Realities,* vol. 4 (Ottawa: Canada Communication Group, 1996) at 275-82 [RCAP, *Report*]. There is no question of considering those Aboriginals who live in non-Native environments and who come from various territorial nations as a sort of territory-less "composite Aboriginal nation." Proposals for non-territorial Aboriginal governance based on a community of interest rather than on a nation can be seen in RCAP, *Report: Restructuring the Relationship,* vol. 2 at 172-75 and 300-8.

58 Robert Groves, "Territoriality and Aboriginal Self-Determination: Options for Pluralism in Canada" in Rene Kuppe and Richard Potz, eds., *Indigenous Self-Determination and Legal Pluralism,* Law and Anthropology: International Yearbook for Legal Anthropology, vol. 8 (The Hague: Martinus Nijhoff, 1996) at 124-25.

59 Recall that according to the working definition of Aboriginal peoples proposed by UN Special Rapporteur José R. Martinez Cobo, territory would be a determining characteristic of Aboriginal difference, since traditional lands are "the basis of their continued existence as peoples." See Sub-commission on Prevention of Discrimination and Protection of Minorities, *Study of the Problem of Discrimination against Indigenous Populations,* United Nations Publications, UN ESCOR, 1986, E/CN.4/Sub.2/1986/7/Add. 4 at para. 379. Furthermore, the UN Meeting of Experts wrote that "Indigenous territory and the resources it contains are essential to the physical, cultural and spiritual existence of indigenous peoples and to the construction and effective exercise of indigenous autonomy and self-government." See Sub-commission on Prevention of Discrimination and Protection of Minorities, *Report of the Meeting of Experts to Review the Experience of Countries in the Operation of Schemes of Internal Self-Government for Indigenous Peoples,* UN ESCOR, 1991, E/CN.4/1992/42 at para. 5. Canadian experts adopt the same point of view, which is well illustrated by the position of Professor Patrick Macklem in his *Indigenous Difference and the Constitution of Canada* (Toronto: University of Toronto Press, 2001) at 98-106.

60 Canada, *Mobility and Migration, supra* note 56 at 18.

61 *Corbière v. Canada,* [1999] 2 S.C.R. 203. This deterritorialization of the band for the purpose of participation in governance which itself remains territorial should also be valid for bands that choose their leaders according to band custom; see Ghislain Otis, "Élection, gouvernance traditionnelle et droits fondamentaux chez les peuples autochtones du Canada" (2004) 49 McGill L.J. 393 at 409-16.

62 The Supreme Court specifically recognized that several Aboriginal rights do not necessarily include the territorial dimension; see *Delgamuukw v. British Columbia, supra* note 53 at paras. 138 and 178; *Mitchell v. M.N.R.,* [2001] 1 S.C.R. 911 at para. 56.

63 Groves, *supra* note 58; RCAP, *Report, supra* note 57 at 4:168-72 and 4:287-90; John Weinstein, *Aboriginal Self-Determination off a Land Base,* Background Paper 8 (Kingston: Institute of Intergovernmental Relations, 1986); Patton, *supra* note 50 at 120; McGarry and Moore, *supra* note 21 at 82; Canada, *Federal Policy Guide, supra* note 55 at 23-24.

64 *Nisga'a Final Agreement,* signed on 27 April 1999 and published jointly by the Government of Canada, the Government of British Columbia, and the Nisga'a Nation. *Land Claims Agreement between the Inuit of Labrador and Her Majesty the Queen in Right of Newfoundland and Labrador and Her Majesty the Queen in Right of Canada,* 2005. *Agreement-in-Principle of a General Nature between the First Nations of Mamuitun and Nutashkuan and the Government of Quebec and the Government of Canada,* signed on 31 March 2004. *Anishnaabe Government Agreement,* signed on 7 December 2004 (the agreement must be approved and ratified by the First Nations and by Canada). *Land Claims and Self-Government Agreement among the Tlicho and the Government of the Northwest Territories and the Government of Canada,* ratified on 25 August 2003. *The Kwanlin Dun First Nation Self-Government Agreement* between the Kwanlin Dun First Nation and Her Majesty the Queen in Right of Canada and the Government of

the Yukon. Published with the permission of the Department of Indian Affairs and Northern Development, Ottawa, 2004. The *Kluane First Nation Self-Government Agreement* among the Kluane First Nation and Her Majesty the Queen in Right of Canada and the Government of the Yukon, published with the authorization of the Minister of Indian and Northern Affairs Canada, Ottawa, 2003. *Ta'an Kwach'an Council Self-Government Agreement,* dated 13 January 2002 between the Ta'an Kwach'an Council and Her Majesty the Queen in Right of Canada and the Government of the Yukon. Published with the permission of the Department of Indian Affairs and Northern Development, Ottawa, 2001. *The Little Salmon/ Carmacks First Nation Self-Government Agreement,* signed on 21 July 1997 by the Little Salmon/ Carmacks First Nation and Her Majesty the Queen in Right of Canada and the Government of the Yukon, 1997. *Selkirk First Nation Self-Government Agreement,* signed on 21 July 1997 by the Selkirk First Nation and Her Majesty the Queen in Right of Canada and the Government of the Yukon, published with the authorization of the Minister of Indian and Northern Affairs Canada, Ottawa, 1998. *The Tr'ondëk Hwëch'in Self-Government Agreement,* signed on 16 July 1998 by the Tr'ondëk Hwëch'in, formerly known as the Dawson First Nation, and Her Majesty the Queen in Right of Canada and the Government of the Yukon. *Westbank First Nation Self-Government Agreement* between Her Majesty the Queen in Right of Canada and the Westbank First Nation, 2003. *Meadow Lake First Nations Tripartite Agreement-in-Principle,* signed on 22 January 2001 between the Meadow Lake First Nations and Her Majesty the Queen in Right of Canada and Her Majesty the Queen in Right of Saskatchewan. *Gwich'in and Inuvialuit Self-Government Agreement-in-Principle for the Beaufort-Delta Region,* signed on 16 April 2003.

65 Jean Leclair, "L'aménagement institutionnel de la diversité" in Pierre Noreau and José Woehrling, eds., *Appartenances, institutions et citoyenneté* (Montreal: Wilson and Lafleur, 2005) 127 at 128; RCAP, *Report, supra* note 57 at 4:198-99.

66 See *Baker v. John,* 982 P. 2d 738 at 759 (Alaska 1999). Thus, although the Supreme Court of the United States ruled in *Alaska v. Native Village of Venetie Tribal Government,* 522 U.S. 520 at 526 (1998) that a majority of them have not, since 1971, had a land base – called "Indian country" – recognized by federal law, the Alaskan tribal communities enjoy personal jurisdiction over their members for a potentially considerable range of matters; see Geoffrey D. Strommer and Stephen D. Osborne, "Indian Country, and the Nature and Scope of Tribal Self-Government in Alaska" (2005) 22 Alaska L. Rev. 1 at 7-18.

67 We should also mention that the increase in existing communal territories following the settlement of a land claim will not necessarily induce the diaspora to make a massive return home and will therefore not prevent further dispersion of the group.

68 In certain exceptional situations, the majority of residents will not be members of the band; see the case of the Westbank First Nation in British Columbia, where the population can be estimated at more than 160,000 people, although only 4,220 of them declared an Aboriginal identity in the 2001 census conducted by Statistics Canada.

69 According to data collected by Statistics Canada during the 2001 census, several Aboriginal communities in Quebec include a non-Aboriginal minority of greater than 15 percent. This is the case with the Odanak (28.2 percent), Wôlinak (31.5 percent), Wendake (24.6 percent), Essipit (26.4 percent), and Kuujjuaq (18.8 percent) communities. However, the data for several communities are not available.

70 See the *Indian Act, supra* note 49, ss. 2 and 75.

71 For example, in the wake of the *James Bay and Northern Quebec Agreement* [Northeastern Quebec Agreement], Kuujjuaq has become a significant regional administrative centre in which 19.3 percent of the population are non-Inuit, according to data collected during the 2001 census by Statistics Canada. It is believed that more than 20 percent of the labour in Nunavik is not Aboriginal. See Jean-Jacques Simard, *La réduction, l'autochtone inventé et les amérindiens d'aujourd'hui* (Sillery: Septentrion, 2003) at 226.

72 Bauböck, "Autonomie," *supra* note 20 at 333.

73 In this case, however, certain collective rights related to the land and resources recognized by the *Nunavut Agreement,* and therefore certain powers related to these matters, retain an exclusively ethnocultural basis.

74 See Commission du Nunavik, *Amiqqaaluta/Partageons: tracer la voie vers un gouvernement pour le Nunavik* (N.p., 2001) at 10-11. Also published as *Amiqqaaluta: Let Us Share Mapping the Road: Toward a Government for Nunavik* (N.p., 2001).

75 Thus, the *Nisga'a Final Agreement* provides territorial jurisdiction over land issues (ss. 44-58 of c. 11). See also the *Tlicho Agreement*, s. 8.4.1d; *Kluane First Nation Self-Government Agreement*, s. 13.3 (agreements covered by the *Yukon First Nations Self-Government Act, 1994* c. 35 are based on the same model) as well as the *Land Claims Agreement between the Inuit of Labrador and Her Majesty the Queen in Right of Newfoundland and Labrador and Her Majesty the Queen in Right of Canada*, pt. 17.9. However, the *Nisga'a Final Agreement* also provides a limited right of participation for non-Nisga'a residents who are affected by these issues (ss. 19 *et seq.* of c. 11); see also the *Tlicho Agreement*, s. 7.1.2 (d), (e), and (f), and the *Land Claims Agreement between the Inuit of Labrador*, s. 17.9.7. Finally, the agreements reached in the Yukon all provide for ethnic government.

76 Simard, *supra* note 71 at 224. See also Leclair, *supra* note 65 at 138-39.

77 See Ghislain Otis, "La gouvernance autochtone avec ou sans la Charte canadienne?" in Ghislain Otis, ed., *Droit, territoire et gouvernance des peuples autochtones* (Quebec City: Presses de l'Université Laval, 2004) 127 at 146-49. Also published as "Aboriginal Governance with or without the Canadian Charter?" in Gordon Christie, ed., *Aboriginality and Governance: A Multidisciplinary Perspective* (Penticton, BC: Theytus Books, 2006) 217. In *Campbell v. British Columbia*, [2000] 4 C.N.L.R. 1, the Court erred in comparing the Nisga'a Government to municipal institutions on this point; see paras. 160-61.

78 Relying on the Canadian *Charter*, the non-Aboriginals living in the territory of BC's Westbank First Nation challenged a self-government project that did not grant them the same political rights as those granted to the members of the Westbank First Nation. See *Hardy v. Westbank First Nation*, [2003] B.C.J. No. 2540 (B.C.S.C.).

79 *Campbell*, *supra* note 77 at para. 162; *Haig v. Canada*, [1993] 2 S.C.R. 995 at 1031.

80 Otis, *supra* note 77 at 158-59; *Campbell*, *supra* note 77 at para. 166.

81 Charles Taylor, "Les raisons du *self-government* autochtone" in Tom Flanagan, *Premières nations? seconds regards* (Sillery: Septentrion, 2002) 247 at 254.

82 Taylor, *ibid.* at 252-53.

83 In *R. v. Van der Peet*, the Supreme Court stated that Aboriginal rights benefit *"aboriginal people because they are aboriginal"*: *R. v. Van der Peet*, [1996] 2 S.C.R. 507 at 535 (underlined in the original). Similarly, see *R. v. Marshall*, [1999] 3 S.C.R. 533 at para. 17; *R. v. Simon*, [1985] 2 S.C.R. 387 at 407; *R. v. Powley*, [2003] 2 S.C.R. 207 at para. 34.

84 A possibility envisaged by the Canadian government in its policy document on Aboriginal self-government: Canada, *Federal Policy Guide*, *supra* note 55 at 13.

85 With respect to personal jurisdiction over communal territory, see notably *Nisga'a Final Agreement*, *Tlicho Agreement*, *Westbank First Nation Self-Government Agreement*, *Anishnaabe Government Agreement*.

86 See the recommendation of the Royal Commission on Aboriginal Peoples: RCAP, *Report*, *supra* note 57 at 4:324. Thus the *Nisga'a Final Agreement* provides a right of consultation for non-Nisga'a at s. 19 *et seq.* of c. 11.

87 A proponent of territoriality, Bauböck has overlooked this advantage of personal autonomy in the Aboriginal context, which led him to hold as legitimate and valid close control of freedom of movement on Aboriginal territories; see Bauböck, "Autonomie," *supra* note 20.

Bibliography

Legislation

Constitution Act, 1982, being Schedule B to the *Canada Act 1982* (U.K.), 1982, c. 11.
Indian Act, R.S.C. 1985, c. I-5.
Metis Settlement Act, L.R.A. 2000, c. M-14.
Royal Proclamation, 1763, R.S.C. 1985, App. II.

Jurisprudence

Alaska v. Native Village of Venetie Tribal Government, 522 U.S. 520 (1998).

Baker v. John, 982 P. 2d 738 (Alaska 1999).
Calder v. British Columbia, [1973] S.C.R. 313.
Campbell v. British Columbia, [2000] 4 C.N.L.R. 1 (B.C.S.C.).
Corbière v. Canada, [1999] 2 S.C.R. 203.
Delgamuukw v. British Columbia, [1997] 3 S.C.R. 1010.
Haig v. Canada, [1993] 2 S.C.R. 995.
Hardy v. Westbank First Nation, [2003] B.C.J. No. 2540 (B.C.S.C.).
Mitchell v. M.N.R., [2001] 1 S.C.R. 911.
R. v. Marshall, [1999] 3 S.C.R. 533.
R. v. Marshall; R. v. Bernard, 2005 SCC 43.
R. v. Powley, [2003] 2 S.C.R. 207.
R. v. Simon, [1985] 2 S.C.R. 387.
R. v. Van der Peet, [1996] 2 S.C.R. 507.

Books and Chapters
Agniel, Guy. "Le statut civil coutumier" in Jean-Yves Faberon and Guy Agniel, eds., *La souveraineté partagée en Nouvelle-Calédonie et en droit comparé* (Paris: La documentation française, 2000) 128.
Alland, Denis, and Stéphane Rials, eds. *Dictionnaire de la culture juridique* [Dictionary of legal culture] (Paris: Lamy-Presses universitaires de France, 2003).
Arnaud, André Jean *et al.,* eds. *Dictionnaire encyclopédique de théorie et de sociologie du droit* [Encyclopedic dictionary of legal theory and sociology], 2nd ed. (Paris/Brussels: Librairie générale de droit et de jurisprudence/E. Story-Scientia, 1993).
Badie, Bertrand. *La fin des territoires: essai sur le désordre international et sur l'utilité sociale du respect* [The end of territories: Essay on international disorder and on the social utility of respect] (Paris: Fayard, 1995).
Bart, Jean. *Histoire du droit* [History of law], 2nd ed. (Paris: Dalloz, 2002).
Bauböck, Rainer. "Autonomie territoriale ou culturelle pour les minorités nationales?" in Alain Dieckhoff, ed., *La constellation des appartenances: nationalisme, libéralisme et pluralisme* (Paris: Presses de Sciences Po, 2004) 317. Also published as "Territorial or Cultural Autonomy for National Minorities?" in Alain Dieckhoff, ed., *The Politics of Belonging: Nationalism, Liberalism, and Pluralism* (Lanham, MD: Lexington Books, 2004) 221.
–. "Political Autonomy or Cultural Minority Rights? A Conceptual Critique of Renner's Model" in Ephraim Nimni, ed., *National Cultural Autonomy and Its Contemporary Critics* (London: Routledge, 2005) 97.
Bauer, Otto. *La question des nationalités et la social-démocratie.* Trans. by Nicole Brune-Perrin and Johannès Brune. Études et documentations Internationales [International studies and documents] (Paris: Arcantère Éditions, 1987) vol. 2. Also published as *The Question of Nationalities and Social Democracy.* Trans. by Joseph O'Donnell. Ed. by Ephraim Nemni (Minneapolis: University of Minnesota Press, 2000) vol. 2.
Canada. *Aboriginal Self-Government: Federal Policy Guide* (Ottawa: Public Works and Government Services Canada, 1995).
–. Department of Indian Affairs and Northern Development. *Band Classification Manual.* May 2005, http://www.ainc-inac.gc.ca/pr/pub/fnnrg/2005/bandc_e.pdf.
–. Department of Indian Affairs and Northern Development. *First Nation Profiles.* 2005, http://sdiprod2.inac.gc.ca/FNProfiles/.
–. Department of Indian Affairs and Northern Development. *Registered Indian Mobility and Migration: An Analysis of 1996 Census Data* (Ottawa: Public Works and Government Services Canada, 2004), http://www.ainc-inac.gc.ca/pr/ra/rimm/rimm_e.pdf.
–. Royal Commission on Aboriginal Peoples. *The Report of the Royal Commission on Aboriginal Peoples: Restructuring the Relationship,* vol. 2, and *Perspectives and Realities,* vol. 4 (Ottawa: Canada Communication Group, 1996).
–. Statistics Canada. *2001 Census Aboriginal Population Profile,* http://www12.statcan.ca/english/profil01ab/PlaceSearchForm1.cfm.
Capeller, Wanda, and Kitamura Takanori, eds. *Une introduction aux cultures juridiques non occidentals* [An introduction to non-Western legal cultures] (Brussels: Bruylant, 1998).

Commission du Nunavik. *Amiqqaaluta/Partageons: tracer la voie vers un gouvernement pour le Nunavik* (N.p., 2001).

Constantinescu, Vlad, and Stéphane Pierré-Caps. *Droit constitutionnel* [Constitutional law] (Paris: Presses universitaires de France, 2004).

David, René, and Camille Jauffret-Spinosi. *Les grands systèmes de droits contemporains (The Great Contemporary Legal Systems),* 11th ed. (Paris: Dalloz, 2002).

Farrell, Mary, and Luk van Langenhove. "Towards Cultural Autonomy in Belgium" in Ephraim Nimni, ed., *National Cultural Autonomy and Its Contemporary Critics* (London: Routledge, 2005) 222.

Gannagé, Léna. "Religion et droits fondamentaux dans le droit libanais de la famille" [Religion and fundamental rights in Lebanese family law] in CEDROMA, *Droit et religion* [Law and religion] (Brussels: Bruylant, 2003) 517.

Gannegé, Pierre. "Le principe d'égalité et le pluralisme des statuts personnels dans les États multicommunautaires" [The principle of equality and the pluralism of personal status in multicommunity states] in *L'avenir du droit: Mélanges en hommage à François Terré* [The future of law: Miscellany in honour of François Terré] (Paris: Dalloz/PUF, 1999) 431.

Groves, Robert. "Territoriality and Aboriginal Self-Determination: Options for Pluralism in Canada" in Rene Kuppe and Richard Potz, eds., *Indigenous Self-Determination and Legal Pluralism.* Law and Anthropology: International Yearbook for Legal Anthropology, vol. 8 (The Hague: Martinus Nijhoff, 1996) 123.

Haupt, Georges, Michaël Löwy, and Claudie Weill. *Les marxistes et la question nationale 1848-1914* [Marxists and the national issue of 1848-1914], 2nd ed. (Paris: L'Harmattan, 1997).

Hoebel, Edward Adamson. *Law of Primitive Man: A Study in Comparative Legal Dynamics* (Cambridge: Harvard University Press, 1954).

Johnston, Ronald John *et al.*, eds. *The Dictionary of Human Geography,* 4th ed. (Malden: Blackwell Publishers, 2000).

Khair, Antoine. "Les communautés religieuses au Liban, personnes morales de droit public" [Religious communities in Lebanon, legal persons established in the public interest] in CEDROMA, *Droit et religion* [Law and religion] (Brussels: Bruylant, 2003) 457.

Klimova-Alexander, Ilona. "Prospects for Romani National Cultural Autonomy" in Ephraim Nimni, ed., *National Cultural Autonomy and Its Contemporary Critics* (London: Routledge, 2005) 124.

Kymlicka, Will. "La justice et la sécurité dans la prise en compte du nationalisme minoritaire" in Alain Dieckhoff, ed., *La constellation des appartenances: nationalisme, libéralisme et pluralisme* (Paris: Presses de Sciences Po, 2004) 181. Also published as "Justice and Security in the Accommodation of Minority Nationalism" in Alain Dieckhoff, ed., *The Politics of Belonging: Nationalism, Liberalism, and Pluralism* (Lanham, MD: Lexington Books, 2004) 127.

–. "Le nouveau débat sur les droits des minorities" [The new debate on minority rights] in Isabelle Schulte-Tenckhoff, ed., *Altérité et droit, contributions à l'étude du rapport entre droit et culture* [Alterity and law: Contributing to the study of the relationship between law and culture] (Brussels: Bruylant, 2002) 91.

–. "Renner and the Accommodation of Sub-state Nationalism" in Ephraim-Nimni, ed., *National Cultural Autonomy and Its Contemporary Critics* (London: Routledge, 2005) 137.

Lacasse, Jean-Paul. *Les Innus et le territoire, Innu Tipenitamun* [The Innu and the territory, Innu Tipenitamun] (Sillery: Septentrion, 2004).

Lafargue, Régis. *Lacoutume judiciaire en Nouvelle-Calédonie: aux sources d'un droit coutumier judiciaire* [Judicial custom in New Caledonia: Sources of judicial customary law] (Aix-en-Provence: Presses universitaires d'Aix-Marseille, 2003).

Leclair, Jean. "L'aménagement institutionnel de la diversité" [Institutional development of diversity] in Pierre Noreau and José Woehrling, eds., *Appartenances, institutions et citoyenneté* [Belonging, institutions and citizenship] (Montreal: Wilson and Lafleur, 2005) 127.

Leroux, Jacques *et al. Au pays des peaux de chagrin: occupation et exploitation territoriales à Kitcisakik (Grand-Lac-Victoria) au XXe siècle* [To the country of skin of sorrow: Territorial occupation and development at Kitcisakik (Grand Lac Victoria) in the twentieth century] (Quebec City: Presses de l'Université Laval, 2004).

Levey, Geoffrey Brahm. "National Cultural Autonomy and Liberal Nationalism" in Ephraim Nimni, ed., *National Cultural Autonomy and Its Contemporary Critics* (London: Routledge, 2005) 150.

Macklem, Patrick. *Indigenous Difference and the Constitution of Canada* (Toronto: University of Toronto Press, 2001).

McGarry, John, and Margaret Moore. "Karl Renner, Power Sharing and Non-territorial Autonomy" in Ephraim Nimni, ed., *National Cultural Autonomy and Its Contemporary Critics* (London: Routledge, 2005) 74.

Messarra, Antoine Nasri. *La gouvernance d'un système consensuel: Le Liban après les amendements constitutionnels de 1990* [Consensual governance: Lebanon after the constitutional amendments of 1990] (Beirut: Librairie Orientale, 2003).

–. "Principe de territorialité et principe de personnalité en fédéralisme comparé: le cas du Liban et perspectives actuelles pour la gestion du pluralisme" [Principle of territoriality and principle of personality in comparative federalism: Lebanon and current pluralism management perspectives] in Jean-François Gaudreault-DesBiens and Fabien Gélinas, eds., *Le fédéralisme dans tous ses états, gouvernance, identité et méthodologie (The States and Moods of Federalism: Governance, Identity and Methodology)* (Brussels/Cowansville: Bruylant/Yvon Blais, 2005) 227.

Nootens, Geneviève. "Nations, States and the Sovereign Territorial Ideal" in Ephraim Nimni, ed., *National Cultural Autonomy and Its Contemporary Critics* (London: Routledge, 2005) 51.

Otis, Ghislain. "La gouvernance autochtone avec ou sans la Charte canadienne?" in Ghislain Otis, ed., *Droit, territoire et gouvernance des peuples autochtones* [Law, territory and governance of Aboriginal peoples] (Quebec City: Presses de l'Université Laval, 2004) 127. Also published as "Aboriginal Governance with or without the Canadian Charter?" in Gordon Christie, ed., *Aboriginality and Governance: A Multidisciplinary Perspective* (Penticton, BC: Theytus Books, 2006) 265.

Patton, Paul. "National Autonomy and Indigenous Sovereignty" in Ephraim Nimni, ed., *National Cultural Autonomy and Its Contemporary Critics* (London: Routledge, 2005) 112.

Pierré-Caps, Stéphane. *La multination: l'avenir des minorités en Europe centrale et orientale* [Multination: The future of minorities in Central and Eastern Europe (Paris: Éditions Odile Jacos, 1995).

–. "Le principe de l'autonomie personnelle: une solution d'avenir?" [The principle of personal autonomy: A solution of the future?] in Alain Dieckhoff, ed., *La constellation des appartenances: nationalisme, libéralisme et pluralisme* (Paris: Presses de Sciences Po, 2004) 371. Also published as "The Principle of Personal Autonomy: A Solution of the Future?" in Alain Dieckhoff, ed., *The Politics of Belonging: Nationalism, Liberalism, and Pluralism* (Lanham, MD: Lexington Books, 2004) 259.

Quebec. Aboriginal Affairs Secretariat. *The Basis of the Québec Government's Policy on Aboriginal Peoples* (Quebec City: Publications du Québec, 1988).

Renner, Karl. *La nation, mythe et réalité (The Nation: Myth and Reality)*. Trans. by Stéphane Pierré-Caps and Claude Tixador (Nancy: Presses Universitaires de Nancy, 1998).

Rouland, Norbert, Stéphane Pierré-Caps, and Jacques Poumarède. *Droits des minorités et des peuples autochtones* [Rights of minorities and Aboriginal peoples] (Paris: Presses universitaires de France, 1996).

Rouquette, Rémi. *Dictionnaire du droit administratif* [Dictionary of administrative law] (Paris: Le Moniteur, 2002).

Salem, Jean. "Un ordonnancement constitutionnel sous hypothèque, religion et constitutionnalisme au Liban" [A constitutional order under threat, religion and constitutionalism in Lebanon] in CEDROMA, *Droit et religion* [Law and religion] (Brussels: Bruylant, 2003) 469.

Scharar, Ayelet. *Multicultural Jurisdictions: Cultural Differences and Women's Rights* (Cambridge: Cambridge University Press, 2001).

Siggner, Andrew J., and Rosalinda Costa. *Aboriginal Conditions in Census Metropolitan Areas, 1981–2001*. Trends and Conditions in Census Metropolitan Areas (Ottawa: Industry Canada, 2005), http://www.statcan.ca/bsolc/english/bsolc?catno=89-613-MWE2005008.pdf.

Simard, Jean-Jacques. *La réduction, l'autochtone inventé et les amérindiens d'aujourd'hui (The Reduction of North American Natives)* (Sillery: Septentrion, 2003).

Spinger, Rudolph. *Der Kampf der österrieichischen Nationen um den Staat* [The struggle of Austrian nationalities for the state] (Leipzig-Vienna, 1902).

Synopticus. *Staat und Nation*, vol. 3 [State and nation] (Vienna, 1899).

Taylor, Charles. "Les raisons du *self-government* autochtone" in Tom Flanagan, *Premières nations? seconds regards (First Nations? Second Thoughts)* (Sillery: Septentrion, 2002) 247.

Weinstein, John. *Aboriginal Self-Determination off a Land Base*. Background Paper 8 (Kingston: Institute of Intergovernmental Relations, 1986).

Articles

Debbih, Adbelkrim. "Dans la tourmente libanaise, les femmes perdent au change" [In the Lebanese turmoil, women lose] (2005) 12:2 Alternatives 2.

Guillaumont, Olivier. "La constitution et le statut civil de droit local à Mayotte: état des réformes entreprises et des questions en suspens après la loi du 11 juillet 2001 relative à Mayotte" (2003) 11 Civitas Europa 43.

Henderson, James Y. "Mikmaw Tenure in Atlantic Canada" (1995) 18 Dal. L.J. 216.

Lafon, Jacques. "Les capitulations ottomans: un droit para-colonial?" [Ottoman capitulations: A paracolonial right?] (1998) 28 Droits 155.

Macklem, Patrick. "First Nations Self-Government and the Borders of the Canadian Legal Imagination" (1991) 36 McGill L.J. 382.

Maclure, Jocelyn. "Entre le culturel et le civique: les voies (accidentées) de l'accommodement raisonnable" [Between culture and civics: (Rugged) paths to a reasonable arrangement] (2005) 23 Cités 57.

Otis, Ghislain. "Élection, gouvernance traditionnelle et droits fondamentaux chez les peuples autochtones du Canada" [Election, traditional governance and basic rights for the Aboriginal peoples of Canada] (2004) 49 McGill L.J. 393. Also published as "Elections, Traditional Aboriginal Governance and the Charter" in Gordon Christie, ed., *Aboriginality and Governance: A Multidisciplinary Perspective* (Penticton, BC: Theytus Books, 2006) 217.

Plasseraud, Yves. "How to Solve Cultural Identity Problems. Choose Your Own Nation" *Le monde diplomatique* [Diplomatic world] (May 2000), http://www.globalpolicy.org/nations/citizen/region.htm.

Strommer, Geoffrey D., and Stephen D. Osborne. "Indian Country, and the Nature and Scope of Tribal Self-Government in Alaska" (2005) 22 Alaska L. Rev. 1.

International Texts

Sub-commission on Prevention of Discrimination and Protection of Minorities. *Report of the Meeting of Experts to Review the Experience of Countries in the Operation of Schemes of Internal Self-Government for Indigenous Peoples*. UN ESCOR, 1991, E/CN.4/1992/42.

–. *Study of the Problem of Discrimination against Indigenous Populations*. Report by Special Rapporteur Mr. José R. Martinez Cobo, 5 vols. United Nations Publications. UN ESCOR, 1986, E/CN.4/Sub.2/1986/7 and Add. 1-4.

Self-Government and Comprehensive Land Claim Agreements

Agreement-in-Principle of a General Nature between the First Nations of Mamuitun and Nutashkuan and the Government of Quebec and the Government of Canada, dated 31 March 2004.

Anishnaabe Government Agreement, dated 7 December 2004 (the First Nations and Canada must approve and ratify the Agreement).

Gwich'in and Inuvialuit Self-Government Agreement-in-Principle for the Beaufort-Delta Region, dated 16 April 2003.

The Kluane First Nation Self-Government Agreement among Kluane First Nation and Her Majesty the Queen in Right of Canada and the Government of the Yukon. Published with the permission of the Department of Indian Affairs and Northern Development, Ottawa, 2003.

The Kwanlin Dun First Nation Self-Government Agreement between the Kwanlin Dun First Nation and Her Majesty the Queen in Right of Canada and the Government of the Yukon. Published with the permission of the Department of Indian Affairs and Northern Development, Ottawa, 2004.

Land Claims Agreement between the Inuit of Labrador and Her Majesty the Queen in Right of Newfoundland and Labrador and Her Majesty the Queen in Right of Canada, 2005.

Land Claims and Self-Government Agreement among the Tlicho and the Government of the Northwest Territories and the Government of Canada, ratified on 25 August 2003.

The Little Salmon/Carmacks First Nation Self-Government Agreement, dated 21 July 1997 between the Little Salmon/Carmacks First Nation and Her Majesty the Queen in Right of Canada and the Government of the Yukon, 1997.

Meadow Lake First Nations Tripartite Agreement-in-Principle, signed on 22 January 2001 between the Meadow Lake First Nations and Her Majesty the Queen in Right of Canada and Her Majesty the Queen in Right of Saskatchewan.

Nisga'a Final Agreement, dated 27 April 1999 and published jointly by the Government of Canada, the Government of British Columbia, and the Nisga'a Nation.

Selkirk First Nation Self-Government Agreement, dated 21 July 1997 between the Selkirk First Nation and Her Majesty the Queen in Right of Canada and the Government of the Yukon. Published with the permission of the Minister of Indian and Northern Affairs Canada, Ottawa, 1998.

Ta'an Kwach'an Council Self-Government Agreement, dated 13 January 2002 between the Ta'an Kwach'an Council and Her Majesty the Queen in Right of Canada and the Government of the Yukon. Published with the permission of the Department of Indian Affairs and Northern Development, Ottawa, 2001.

Tripartite Agreement-in-Principle, dated 22 January 2001 between the Meadow Lake First Nations and Her Majesty the Queen in Right of Canada and Her Majesty the Queen in Right of Saskatchewan.

The Tr'ondëk Hwëch'in Self-Government Agreement, dated 16 July 1998 between the Tr'ondëk Hwëch'in, formerly known as the Dawson First Nation, and Her Majesty the Queen in Right of Canada and the Government of the Yukon.

Westbank First Nation Self-Government Agreement between Her Majesty the Queen in Right of Canada and the Westbank First Nation, 2003.

Contributors

Andrée Lajoie retired as research professor at the Centre de Recherche en Droit Public of Faculty of Law of the University of Montreal. Her research bears on constitutional law, especially on federalism, constitutional theory, and aboriginality and governance. A member of Academy I of the Royal Society of Canada, she has published numerous articles and books, including *Quand les minotirés font la loi* (2002), *Théories et émergence du droit: pluralisme, surdétermination et effectivité* (1998), and *Jugements de valeurs* (1997). She is also director of *Le droit aussi*, a series of books on the theory of law.

Minnawaanagogiizhigook (Dawnis Kennedy) is Anishinabe-kwe of the Waabizheshi clan. Her home community is Bigaawinazhkoziibing, which is also known as Roseau River Anishinabe First Nation. With support from the Trudeau Foundation, she is currently pursuing a doctoral degree at the University of Toronto Faculty of Law. Minnawaanagogiizhigook has travelled from coast to coast, benefiting from the generous support of many communities and people. Still, the greatest gift and honour she has received in this world is being given the opportunity to know who she is as Anishinabe-kwe: an opportunity safeguarded by the determination of her family, her community, and the Anishinabe people.

Ghislain Otis is a lawyer and member of the Barreau du Québec since 1984. He holds a PhD in Law from the University of Cambridge and specializes in constitutional and Aboriginal law. He has been law professor at Université Laval since 1989. He is also a research associate with the Centre interuniversitaire d'études et de recherches autochtones (CIÉRA) at Université Laval and the Centre de recherche en droit public (CRDP) at Université de Montréal. Professor Otis has published numerous scientific articles on the rights of Aboriginal peoples.

Paulette Regan completed her doctoral studies in the Indigenous Governance Program at the University of Victoria in 2006. In 2006-7 she participated in an academic interchange between the Department of Justice Canada (BC Region) and the UBC History Department. In 2007-8, she will take up a post-doctoral fellowship in the History Department at UBC. She is a consulting director with Peacemakers Trust, a Canadian non-profit organization for research, education, and training in conflict transformation, peacebuilding, and reconciliation.

Ted Palys is a professor in the School of Criminology at Simon Fraser University. He researches and writes in the area of Aboriginal justice and changing relations between Indigenous and non-Indigenous peoples in Canada and internationally. He was honoured to supervise Wenona Victor's MA thesis and has been introduced to the Stó:lō through her. Professor Palys also teaches and writes regarding research methods in the social sciences. His book concerning social science research methods and the sociology of science – *Research Decisions: Qualitative and Quantitative Perspectives* – is used as a text in universities and colleges across the country, with a fourth edition scheduled for release in 2007.

Perry Shawana was Anishinabe from the Serpent River First Nation. He was associate professor and chair of the First Nations Studies Program at the University of Northern British Columbia (UNBC) in Prince George, BC. On leave from UNBC, Perry was a student in the combined LLM/PhD program at the University of Victoria. Perry crossed over to the spirit world on 1 June 2005. As a barrister and solicitor, Perry specialized in Aboriginal issues in the law, served as a tribunal panel member for the Children's Commission, and was a member of the Access to Justice Committee for the Law Society of British Columbia. For over twenty years, Perry was actively involved in self-determination initiatives in Indigenous communities, including serving as co-principal investigator on two large national (Canada) research studies examining Indigenous child care.

Wenona Victor, a member of Stó:lō Nation, has served for seven years as the manager of the Stó:lō Nation Justice program. Wenona completed her Master's degree from Simon Fraser University in 2001; her thesis, titled "Searching for the Bone Needle: The Stó:lo Nation's Continuing Quest for Justice," focused predominately on documenting the Stó:lō's traditional concepts of justice. She recently returned to Simon Fraser University to commence her doctorate in criminology and plans to broaden her research in the field of traditional Stó:lō justice as it relates to self-determination, family law, including child welfare practices, and implications for the Stó:lō, with particular attention to Stó:lō women and high-risk Aboriginal youth.

Index

AANO Committee. *See* House of Commons Standing Committee on Aboriginal Affairs and Northern Development (AANO)

Aboriginal Healing Foundation, 43, 46, 54, 69n16

Aboriginal justice. *See* legal traditions, Indigenous

Aboriginal Justice Directorate, 14

Aboriginal Justice Strategy, 14, 34, 53, 71n45

Aboriginal legal traditions. *See* legal traditions, Indigenous

Aboriginal rights: and common law, 81, 82, 90, 92, 94, 95, 97, 98-100, 110n113; and Crown sovereignty, 82-83, 86, 90-91, 92, 93-94, 95-96, 100; debate regarding, 80, 106n18; extinguishment of, 15, 82, 106n21, 108n80; inherent, 12, 150, 152-53, 154; and land, 147-48, 149, 150, 154, 156; and reconciliation, 50; sourced in Aboriginal law, 97-98; as *sui generis*, 83-84, 85-86, 90, 91, 97, 99-100, 101, 107nn36, 38; and Supreme Court, 3, 5, 6, 7, 9, 10, 50, 161n62. *See also* section 35 (of *Constitution Act, 1982*)

Aboriginal self-government. *See* self-government, Aboriginal

absorption model, 91, 94-96, 97, 100, 101-2, 109nn90, 92

Acorn, Annalise, 48-49, 61

adoption, Carrier, 126-27

ADR program. *See* alternative dispute-resolution (ADR) model

AFN. *See* Assembly of First Nations (AFN)

Alaska v. Native Village of Venetie Tribal Government, 162n66

Alfred, Taiaiake, 48, 68n4, 103

alternative dispute-resolution (ADR) model: claims filed, 46; flaws of, 44-45, 47, 52-55, 56, 60, 70n22; government perspective on, 58, 59, 60; media coverage of, 58-59; pilot projects, 46, 60, 68n2; purpose of, 44, 47, 48; tort based, 44, 46, 48, 52, 57, 71n40; voluntary, 47; Western nature of, 51-52, 67

Anishinabe, 77, 103-4, 111n126, 114

Archibald, Joanne, 21, 37n25

Assembly of First Nations (AFN), 47, 52-53, 54, 57, 58, 59, 60

assimilation, 13, 34, 41, 45, 102, 151

asymmetrical co-citizenship, 153

Bah'lats. *See* potlatch

Barkan, Elazar, 48, 49

Barsh, Russel, 118

Battiste, Marie, 50, 71n33

Baubök, Rainer, 158n20, 159n39, 160n45, 163n87

Bauer, Otto, 142

Baxter, 53-54

Bernard, Joshua, 96. *See also R. v. Marshall; R. v. Bernard*

Binnie, Ian, 90-94, 95, 96, 105n9, 108nn75, 80, 109nn82, 86

Borrows, John, 50, 69n11, 132n26

Bradford, William, 49

Calder v. Attorney General of British Columbia, 81, 106n21

Canadian Bar Association (CBA), 53, 54, 58, 59

Canadian Charter of Rights and Freedoms, 81n33, 82, 106n32, 152, 153, 163n78

Carrier people, 131n19

Casimel v. Insurance Corporation of British Columbia, 126-27

chiefs, 40, 41, 42, 62, 63, 64, 65, 67, 119-20, 122, 131n20
Child and Family Services (Stó:lō), 16, 24
circles, 4, 17-18, 26-29, 30, 31-32, 36n9, 44, 53
CJS. *See* criminal justice system (CJS)
clans, Carrier, 119-20
colonial law, 78-79, 92, 109n90
colonialism: compassionate, 109n94; and healing, 37n29; and Indian residential schools, 5, 41, 43-44, 45, 56, 63, 66; and Indigenous knowledge, 121; internalized, 37n30; and land, 146, 148, 151; in language, 19; and normative forms, 7, 9-11; and personalization of law, 139, 158n17; and pluralism, 8, 128. *See also* decolonization
Connolly v. Woolrich, 126, 127
Corntassel, Jeff, 103
criminal justice system (CJS), 23-24, 25, 26, 27, 29, 33, 34-35, 37n33
customary laws, 10, 94, 126, 133n39

Daniels, Matilda, 62, 63, 65, 67
decolonization, 11; and Hazelton Apology Feast, 3, 5, 6, 7, 42; and Indigenous knowledge, 3-4, 6, 121; and normative forms, 9; and Qwi:qwelstóm, 23, 33; territorial dimension of, 146-47
Delgamuukw, 70n30, 90, 93, 105nn7, 8, 131n24
Department of Indian Affairs and Northern Development (DIAND), 4, 16, 46
deterritorialization, 142, 149, 161n61
devil's club, 118, 131n14
Dickson, Brian, 81, 84, 98
dispute resolution, 5, 6, 19, 21, 132n26. *See also* alternative dispute-resolution (ADR) model
Draft Declaration on the Rights of Indigenous Peoples, 12-13
Drahos, Peter, 133n36

eagle down, 63
elders: on Aboriginal justice, 20-21; as advisors, 17; and circles, 28-29; as experts, 22, 32; and Hazelton Apology Feast, 41-42, 62, 63, 64; and Qwi:qwelstóm, 4, 16, 18, 26, 27, 30, 32, 37n35
extra-state pluralism. *See* pluralism, legal, strong

Fisheries Act, 84

Gardner, Ethel (Stelómethet), 15

Gathering Strength: Canada's Aboriginal Action Plan, 46
Greschner, Donna, 14, 36n9
Griffith, John, 8, 124, 132n29
Gus-Wen-Tah (treaty), 109n86

Halewood, Michael, 126
Hazelton alternative dispute-resolution pilot project, 41, 67, 68n2
Hazelton Apology Feast, 5, 10, 40; and elders, 41-42, 62, 63, 64; hosts of, 41, 62, 63, 64, 65, 66-67; protocols of, 61-62, 63; purpose of, 43, 63; teachings of, 64, 65, 67
Heiltsuk, 88-89
Henderson, James (Sákéj) Youngblood, 50, 71n33
House of Commons Standing Committee on Aboriginal Affairs and Northern Development (AANO), 45, 53, 54-57, 58, 59-60, 61, 65
House of Elders (Lalems Ye Siyolexwe), 15
House of Justice (Stó:lō), 4, 7, 8-9, 10, 15, 21, 23
House of Leaders (Lalems Ye Stó:lō Sí:yá:m), 15
Howard, Keith, 65

Iacobucci, Frank, 60-61
Independent Assessment Process, 42-43
Indian Act, 23, 130n9, 149, 151, 160n57
Indian and Northern Affairs Canada. *See* Department of Indian Affairs and Northern Development (DIAND)
"Indian country," 150, 162n66
Indian residential schools, 5; apology for, 46, 55, 57, 59, 62, 65, 67; compensation for, 42-43, 46-47, 50-51, 53-54, 58, 59, 61; legacy of, 40-41, 45, 50, 53, 56, 57, 58, 66, 69n14; literature on, 45, 69n13; Political Agreement (May 2005), 60-61; purpose of, 43, 45-46; and Royal Commission on Aboriginal Peoples, 46
Indian Residential Schools Resolution Canada (IRSRC), 46, 58, 59-60, 68n2
Indian Residential Schools Settlement Agreement, 42-43, 50-51, 61
Indians and the Law, 13
Indigenous knowledge: debate regarding, 116, 121; definition, 117, 118, 130n6; demand for, 118-19; and dominant legal traditions, 120-21, 122; governance of, 115, 116-17, 119-20, 121, 122, 123, 125-26; preserving/maintaining, 121, 122, 123; private/public, 115, 120, 122, 123,

125, 132n36; protecting, 121, 122, 123, 125, 132n27; and secrecy, 122-23; static, 117; and Western concepts, 116, 117, 120, 121, 130n6. *See also* pluralism, legal, and Indigenous knowledge

intellectual property law, 10, 116, 117, 120-21, 125, 131n22

internal sovereignty, 23, 37n31

interveners Delgamuukw, 87

intra-state pluralism. *See* pluralism, legal, weak

IRSRC. *See* Indian Residential Schools Resolution Canada (IRSRC)

Joseph, Robert, 54-55, 65, 67

La Forest, Gérard, 81, 82, 98

LaCapra, Dominick, 57, 65-66

Lamer, Antonio, 84, 85, 86-89, 90, 91, 92, 93, 95, 97-98, 100, 107nn52, 55

Laskin, Bora, 81

LeBel, Louis, 97, 99-100, 110nn105, 116

Lederach, John Paul, 62, 64

legal traditions, Canadian: and adverse relations with Indigenous legal traditions, 78, 79, 80, 84, 89-90, 91, 95, 96, 97, 100, 102; and colonialism, 3; definition, 136; impact on Indigenous people, 6, 7, 9, 13, 79, 81; respect for Indigenous legal traditions, 77, 78, 79-80, 106n14, 115; and universality, 105n11. *See also* criminal justice system (CJS)

legal traditions, Indigenous: acknowledgment of, 44, 77-78, 94-95, 109n92; assimilation of, 95, 96; and colonial law, 78-79; definition, 3, 13, 21, 35, 44, 77, 104n2, 136; denial of, 78, 80, 102; evolutive, 3, 5, 41, 87-88; frozen, 5, 10, 87-88, 108n60; government reaction to, 13-14, 34, 78; and international law, 78, 79; nature of, 77, 80, 89, 96, 101, 103-4, 117, 123, 130n9; and reconciliation, 49; revival of, 3, 12, 13, 21-22, 35, 51, 155; *sui generis*, 50; transmission of, 3, 77, 103; and treaties, 78. *See also* Indigenous knowledge, governance of

L'Heureux-Dubé, Claire, 84

Little Bear, Leroy, 83

Llewellyn, Jennifer, 53, 69n14

Lyon, Noel, 82

Mabo v. Queensland [No. 2], 85, 87, 107n52

Macdonald, Rod, 3

Maori, 16, 17, 18

Marshall, Stephen Frederick, 96. *See also R. v. Marshall; R. v. Bernard*

Matiation, Stefan, 117

McLachlin, Beverley, 84, 86, 90, 91, 94, 97-99, 109n90, 110nn95, 105, 111n121

McLellan, Anne, 58, 59-60

medicine knowledge, 6, 8, 115, 116, 117, 118-19, 129, 131n13

Merrick, Flora, 56-57

Métis, 148, 150, 161n57

migration, Indigenous, 149, 150, 151, 156, 160n56, 162n67

Mitchell, Michael, 90-91. *See also R. v. Mitchell*

Mohawk Institute, 53

Monture-Angus, Patricia, 35, 36n9

Napoleon, Val, 48, 49, 62

Nelson, Charles, 103

non-members. *See* territory, non-members

Nunavut Agreement, 162n73

Pask, Amanda, 126

personal federalism, 6, 7, 9, 11, 139, 145

personality, legal, 6; and activities off the land base, 156; complete, 140; cultural autonomy, 140, 142, 154, 158n20, 160n45; definition, 139; in Frankish monarchies, 157n14, 158n19; limitations of, 144-45, 148, 154; and national groups, 143-44; as protection, 140, 143-44, 156; relative, 140; strengths of, 154-57; and transition, 149-50, 151, 156, 159n39

pluralism, legal, 7; definition, 8, 123-24, 128-29; in dominant legal regimes, 125-26, 127-28; and Indigenous knowledge, 115, 116-17, 119, 123-24; and personality, legal, 139, 140, 142, 144, 145; strong, 8, 11, 124-25; and territoriality, 141-42, 143; weak, 6, 8, 124

Portalis, Jean-Étienne, 138

potlatch, 40, 62, 63, 114, 119-20, 130n9. *See also* Hazelton Apology Feast

Prince v. Murdock, 127

Qwi:qwelstóm, 14; challenges facing, 32-34; and circles, 4, 17-18, 26-29; discussions regarding, 22-23; and education, 32; elders council of, 21; and family, 30-31; and Family Group Conferencing, 16, 17; and first-time offenders, 23, 25; funding, 33; and language, 19-20, 37n32; name, meaning of, 20; principles, 18, 20, 21, 26-27; referrals, 4, 24-25, 29; and responsibility, 18-19, 22, 25; and self-determination, 4, 18, 36n12; and Stó:lō culture, 4, 21, 32-33; "Stó:lō Nation Alternative Justice Programme," 19 *Qwi:qwelstóm ye Smómíyelhtel,* 21, 25, 26-27, 31, 37n27

R. *v. Bernard. See R. v. Marshall; R. v. Bernard*
R. v. Gladstone, 88-89, 93
R. v. Gladue, 13
R. v. Guerin, 83
R. v. Marshall; R. v. Bernard, 81, 96-100, 110nn105, 106, 109, 112, 113
R. v. Mitchell, 81, 90-96, 97, 100, 105n9, 108nn75, 80, 109nn90, 91
R. v. Moses, 17
R. v. Sioui, 107n41
R. v. Sparrow, 81-84, 86, 87, 88, 90, 92, 107nn33, 38, 108n80
R. v. Van der Peet, 81, 84-90, 91, 93, 94, 95, 97, 110n95, 163n83
RCAP. *See* Royal Commission on Aboriginal Peoples (RCAP)
reconciliation: and Canadian government, 46, 49-50; and decolonization, 6; disagreement regarding, 47-48, 51-52; and Hazelton Apology Feast, 42, 43, 62, 64-65, 66-67; and Indian residential schools, 5, 7, 52, 71n43; Indigenous vision of, 49, 54-55, 61, 66; literature on, 70n25; and section 35 of *Constitution Act, 1982,* 102, 110n96, 111n121; and Supreme Court case law, 80, 93, 95-96, 109n87; and tokenism, 48-49
Renner, Karl, 142-43, 147
reserves, Indian, 146, 148, 149, 151, 152, 153, 157, 160nn56, 57
Residential Schools Legacy: Is Reconciliation Possible? (conference), 47, 48, 52
Romani, 159n37
Royal Commission on Aboriginal Peoples (RCAP), 46, 103, 161n57, 163n86
Royal Proclamation of 1763, 82-83, 147

SATRC. *See* South African Truth and Reconciliation Commission (SATRC)
section 35 (of *Constitution Act, 1982*): and Aboriginal rights, 5, 12, 50, 71n33, 80-81, 83-84, 85, 92; and absorption model, 94, 95, 97, 101-2, 109n92; and fisheries, 84; and land, 147; and *R. v. Marshall; R. v. Bernard,* 96, 97-100, 101; and *R. v. Mitchell,* 90-96; and *R. v. Sparrow,* 82, 83-84, 100-1, 108n60; and *R. v. Van der Peet,* 84-90, 101, 110n95; as source of rights, 93, 97, 105n9, 109n92; and sovereign

incompatibility, 109n90; test for, 85, 86-88, 89, 93, 94, 101, 107nn52, 55, 108n57; and treaties, 80, 91
self-determination, Aboriginal, 4, 12-13, 18, 34, 49, 51, 83, 118, 119
self-government, Aboriginal, 137, 140, 142, 147-48, 149, 150, 152-53, 154, 155
"Settler problem," 44
simgigyat. *See* chiefs
Simon, Roger, 66, 69n8
S'ólh Téméxw, 14-15, 20
South African Truth and Reconciliation Commission (SATRC), 52, 71n43
Sparrow, Ronald Edward, 81. *See also R. v. Sparrow*
Stewart, Jane, 46
Stó:lō justice program. *See* Qwi:qwelstóm
Stó:lō Nation, 14-15
Stó:lō Society (SS), 15, 16
Stó:lō Tribal Council (STC), 15, 16
Stuart, Barry, 17, 36n19
Supreme Court. *See R. v. Marshall; R. v. Bernard; R. v. Mitchell; R. v. Sparrow; R. v. Van der Peet*

talking piece/talking stick, 31, 32, 62
Tamanaha, Brian, 124-25
Task Force on Aboriginal Languages and Cultures, 50
territorial determinism, 149
territoriality, 6, 7; and demos, 138, 141; and emergence of the state, 137-38; limitations of, 137, 140-41, 143, 145, 149, 151, 155; and multinational federation, 141; as neutral, 141; and normative standardization, 138, 140-41, 156; strengths of, 142, 144, 157; and Supreme Court, 149
territory: and Aboriginal difference, 161n59; communities lacking, 148-49, 150, 151, 156, 160n57; and consubstantiality with land, 147, 148; and cultural autonomy, 140; and non-members, 151-55, 156, 162nn68, 69, 71; and personality, legal, 140, 144; power anchored in, 137-38, 146; and pre-colonial societies, 145-46; unifying function, 138, 152
treaties: created by Indigenous law, 78; and Euro-derived law, 105n11; force of, 131n22; *Gus-Wen-Tah,* 109n86; Mi'kmaq, Maliseet, and Passamaquoddy, 97; modern, 147, 149, 152, 153; and personality, legal, 154, 156; and *R. v. Sioui,* 107n41; and section 35 (of *Constitution Act, 1982*), 80, 91; and surrender of interests, 95

Truth and Reconciliation Commission (TRC), 41, 42, 43, 44, 50-51, 59, 67
truth-telling, 41, 42, 43-44, 45, 52, 56, 57, 61, 63, 65, 66

United Church of Canada, 40, 41, 62, 63, 65

Van der Peet, Dorothy Marie, 84. *See also R. v. Van der Peet*
Van der Peet test. *See* section 35 (of *Constitution Act, 1982*), test for
Vanderlinden, J., 11n7
Victor, Amy, 12, 19

Victor, Wenona, 16-18, 20-21, 22, 36nn10, 19, 37n25
violence in Aboriginal communities, 23, 26

Walters, Mark D., 86, 109n87
Webber, Jeremy, 111n120
Weber, Max, 8
Worcester v. Georgia, 93

Xyolhemeylh. *See* Child and Family Services (Stó:lô)

Yamamoto, Eric, 49

Printed and bound in Canada by Friesens

Set in Stone by Artegraphica Design Co. Ltd.

Copy editor: Deborah Kerr

Indexer: Deborah Kerr